IN THE
VALLEY
OF THE
SACRED
MOUNTAIN

An Introduction to
Prehistoric Upper Coquetdale
100 Years after David Dippie Dixon

Paul Frodsham

*The hills and moorlands around are studded with camps, hut-circles, standing-stones,
and sepulchral cairns - rude memorials of a pre-historic race that in early times occupied
the rising grounds on the banks of the Coquet.*

(D D Dixon, 1903)

Photo: Simon Fraser.

First published in the United Kingdom in 2006 by Northern Heritage Publishing.

Northern Heritage
Units 7&8 New Kennels, Blagdon Estate, Seaton Burn,
Newcastle upon Tyne NE13 6DB
Telephone: 01670 789 940
www.northern-heritage.co.uk

Text copyright:
© 2006 Paul Frodsham

Photographic Acknowledgements:
Unless otherwise credited, all illustrations are
© Paul Frodsham and/or Northumberland National Park Authority

Design and layout:
© 2006 Ian Scott Design

Printed and bound by Compass Press Limited.

British Library Cataloguing in Publishing Data
A catalogue record for this book is available from the British Library.

ISBN 0-9544777-5-8

Cover images
Front. Main image: Simonside from near Rothbury. *Photo: Simon Faser*
Inset images. Left to right: Excavations at Low Trewhitt in 1909, Rock art at Lordenshaws, Excavations at Harehaugh in 2005.
Back: David Dippie Dixon.

Contents

Weathered rock exposure, Simonside.
Photo: Simon Fraser.

Foreword and Acknowledgements

2003 marked two very important anniversaries in the history of Northumberland. 1603 saw the Union of the English and Scottish Crowns under King James I, in many ways setting the scene for the development of the tranquil county of Northumberland after some three centuries of more or less continuous cross-border violence. Exactly a thousand years earlier, 603 is the generally agreed date for the founding of the great Anglian kingdom of Northumbria, arising out of the union of Bernicia and Deira under King Aethelfrith. In contrast to these momentous events, the publication of David Dippie Dixon's *Upper Coquetdale*, in 1903, may justifiably be regarded as of little consequence. Nevertheless, it was this that I decided to concentrate on commemorating during 2003.

I first encountered the work of David Dippie Dixon during an introductory tour of Upper Coquetdale in the company of my colleague Andrew Miller, soon after I arrived in Northumberland in autumn 1992. Andrew is a multi-talented individual whose expertise ranges from traditional music and poetry to leading the Northumberland Mountain Rescue Team, as well as working full time for the Northumberland National Park Authority. He was born and bred in the Coquet Valley, and there is little about the place of which he is unaware. I recall sitting in his living room while he disappeared upstairs to retrieve his original copy of *Upper Coquetdale*, which was clearly stored away in some special safe place. As I began to look through it, I realised that it was indeed something very special. I soon invested in a copy of my own, bought for what I considered to be a bargain £50 from Hamish Dunn's splendid second-hand bookshop on Wooler High Street.

This original soon found itself a home on the shelf in my library reserved for my most precious books. A few weeks later I was discussing books in my library with a friend, and took *Upper Coquetdale* from the shelf, explaining how marvellous I thought it was. At the same time I took out the book which, quite by chance, was lying next to it on the shelf: a copy of T. Cato Worsfold's *The French Stonehenge*, about the great Neolithic tombs and standing stones of Carnac in Brittany. I had purchased this book from a second-hand bookshop in Llandudno, North Wales, several years previously. Imagine my surprise when I noticed the hand-written inscription inside it: 'to David D. Dixon, from W. S. Cope, in recollection of many pleasant chats on kindred subjects at Rothbury. 1902.' I have no knowledge of W. S. Cope, or of how this volume found its way from Dixon's personal library to Llandudno, and I had never even heard of Dixon when I'd first placed this book on my shelf. This was one of those bizarre little coincidences that can make life seem even more surreal than it really is!

Andrew Miller and I decided to write a book between us to commemorate the centenary of the publication of *Upper Coquetdale*. I would concentrate on the prehistoric and medieval archaeology, and he would write about historical events, local characters and the natural environment. In the event, sadly, Andrew did not have time in his absurdly busy schedule to complete his part of the deal, and with considerable regret he withdrew from the project. But, in spite of numerous other commitments, I could not give up! Instead, I decided to concentrate on the prehistory (that is, the pre-Roman archaeology), which is the only thing I really know anything about. Hence the present volume. Although Andrew was not closely involved in its production, it would never have happened without his initial enthusiasm for a joint production, and I remain most grateful to him for his support, and, of course, for initially introducing me to the joys of Dixon's *Upper Coquetdale*. Having decided to plough my own lonely furrow, I was delighted to have the opportunity to address both the Newcastle upon Tyne Society of Antiquaries and the Rothbury and Coquetdale History Society during the latter half of 2003. Both lectures gave me the opportunity to present and discuss my developing ideas which would eventually form the framework for this book. The Rothbury lecture was delivered in December 2003, to commemorate the exact centenary of the date given by Dixon in his Preface to *Upper Coquetdale* (which he signs off 'D.D.D. Rothbury. December 1903'). I must have given well over a hundred public lectures at various venues throughout Northumberland over the past decade, but have never felt more honoured (or nervous!) than I did standing in front of an audience in David Dippie Dixon's own adopted town lecturing about his beloved Upper Coquetdale. It was a pity he couldn't have been there to share the wine and mince pies, but several people observed that they thought he was there in spirit. If so, then I hope he approved of what I had to say. Whether or not he would have approved of the title of this volume I cannot be sure. When I first began explaining my contention that Simonside must have functioned as a sacred mountain in prehistoric times, I expected a degree of scepticism amongst colleagues and local people. Some colleagues have indeed been a little sceptical, but many local people have explained to me that they regard Simonside as somehow 'special' even today, and have little doubt that their prehistoric ancestors would have thought likewise. References to Simonside abound throughout this volume, hence the title *In the Valley of the Sacred Mountain*.

I would like to thank everyone I have met at various events in Upper Coquetdale over the years for stimulating discussion about many aspects of local archaeology. Special thanks go to the members of the Rothbury and Coquetdale History Society for making me feel so welcome in the valley. I will never forget the events of one particular Tuesday night in the mid 1990s at the Rose & Thistle, Alwinton. Having given my first lecture to the Rothbury society, I was asked whether I would do a repeat as many people were unable to attend for various reasons. I agreed to do a repeat, but suggested doing it somewhere else in the valley. The Rose & Thistle was the chosen venue. I duly arrived at 7.45 for an 8pm start, to find hardly a parking place left in the village. My colleague Russell Tate met me in the street with a relieved look on his face: unbeknown to me, the event had been advertised locally with a start time of 7.30, and about 100 people had been crammed into the back room of the pub for half an hour wondering where I was! The landlady told me that more alcohol had been sold in that time than any other Tuesday half-hour that she could remember. I suspect that it was on the strength of this fact, rather than anything to do with the lecture, that I was asked whether I would like to give a lecture every Tuesday night for the rest of the year! Events like this can be entertaining and educational, but they are also of great importance to people like me. It is the recognition of our work by local people that makes the daily slog worthwhile, and the chance to discuss projects at local events is very much appreciated.

Our current understanding of the prehistory of Upper Coquetdale is based on the work of many different people over a couple of centuries. I have been fortunate to have been involved in many recent projects, but must admit to having undertaken little primary research of my own. Although naming names always runs the risk of inadvertently overlooking someone important, I would like to take this opportunity to thank the following, all of whom have contributed in some way to recent projects relating to the prehistory of Upper Coquetdale (many of which are featured in this book): Harry Beamish, Stan Beckensall, Colin Burgess, Richard Carlton, Peter Carne, Beryl Charlton, Richard Cross, Tim Gates, the late George Jobey,

Iain Hedley, Kim Hobson, Robert Manners, Roger Miket, Andrew Miller, Jamie Quatermaine, Peter Topping, Clive Waddington, Adam Welfare and James Whitford.

A very big thank-you must go to Keith Hartnell, Chris Hartnell and Ian Scott for enthusiastically embracing the idea of this publication and transforming my tatty manuscript and jumbled-up slides into an attractive volume. I would also like to thank Elanor Johnson, Andrew Hillier, Rob Young, Keith Hartnell, Stan Beckensall, Penny Gough, Mary Gough, Sarah Wilson and Gill Thompson for their comments on a draft version of the text, as a direct result of which several improvements were made prior to publication. Thanks are also due to all the farmers and landowners, too numerous to list here, who have permitted and in many cases encouraged archaeological work on their land. Local farmers are well aware that they are merely temporary custodians of their land, continuing the traditions of land management stretching back over thousands of years, the evidence for which is preserved within today's historic environment. Grateful thanks are also due to Lindsay Allason-Jones at the Newcastle upon Tyne Museum of Antiquities, and Clare Baxter, Lisa Little and Gemma Bates at Alnwick Castle Museum, for permission to examine and photograph many of the artefacts pictured on the following pages. In addition, for help with various aspects of the research and production of this volume, I am grateful to Tish Armstrong, Gordon Barclay, Tom Chadwin, Hugh Dixon, Keith Elliot, Simon Fraser, Tim Gates, Iain Hedley, Ian Hobson, Tony Hopkins, Lindsay Jones, Rose Krause, Roger Miket, Stewart Needham, David Owen, Jim Proudfoot and Frank Graham. In spite of all this help, some errors, omissions and dubious interpretations will inevitably lurk within the published text: responsibility for these must, as ever, be mine and mine alone.

Despite some changes during the twentieth century (such as a degree of afforestation, agricultural improvement, gravel quarrying, and the development of the Otterburn Training Area) most of today's Upper Coquetdale landscape has changed little from that with which David Dippie Dixon was familiar. He would, I'm sure, have supported the efforts of the National Park Authority, the Ministry of Defence, and others, to ensure the conservation of this exquisite landscape over recent decades. No doubt he would have marvelled at some scientific developments and consequent improvements in our knowledge about the past, and would have supported the efforts of various people over the past 100 years to discover more about the archaeology of Upper Coquetdale. I hope he would have approved of this book, which is offered as a personal tribute to his wonderful work. I cannot hope to approach his eloquence, or his depth and breadth of local knowledge, but I hope that the following pages will encourage local people, and visitors, to discover some of Coquetdale's fascinating prehistoric heritage for themselves. I hope it will also stimulate some readers to visit their local library, or an antiquarian bookshop, in search of an original or facsimile copy of *Upper Coquetdale.* It may even stimulate a few to take up the study of local prehistory for themselves (see Chapter 6), something of which David Dippie Dixon would most certainly have approved.

PF. July 2006

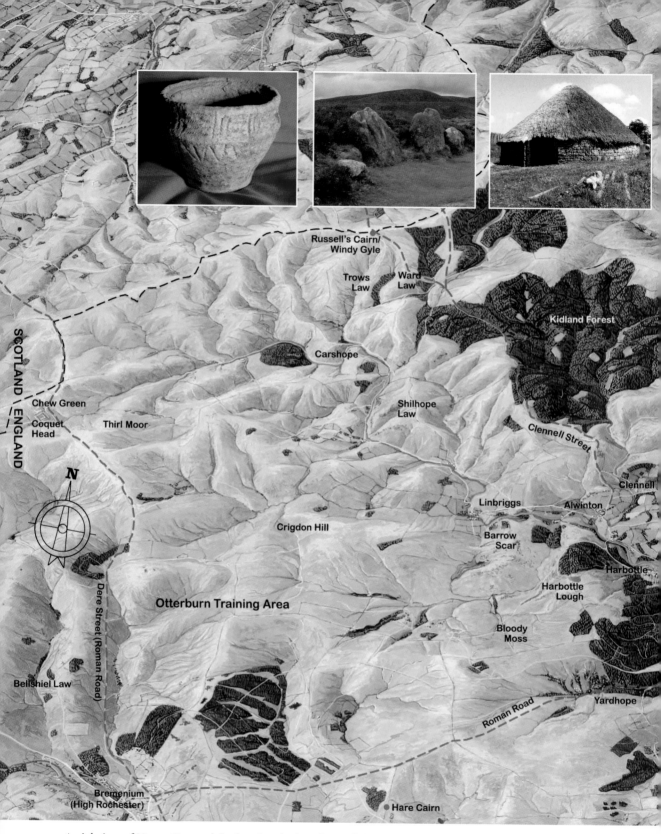

Aerial view of Upper Coquetdale showing the locations of places referred to in this book.(Approx. 1cm:1km).

Ingram

Wether Hill

High Knowes

Devil's Causeway (Roman Road)

Castlehill

Alnham

Whittingham

Low Learchild

Roman Road

Thrunton

Scrainwood

Harden Quarry

Elilaw

Biddlestone

Burradon

Roman Road

Low Trewhitt

Cartington

Sharpeton

Debden

Debden Whitefield

Holystone

Warton

Cragside

ipville

The Five Barrows

Low Farnham

Thropton

Rothbury

Caistron

The Five Kings

Hepple

Tosson

he eacon

Harehaugh

Lordenshaws

Witchy Neuk

Simonside

David Dippie Dixon.
Reproduced from Newbigin 1930.

Chapter 1

David Dippie Dixon and Prehistory in Upper Coquetdale

Time, that tireless sieve, has diminished David Dippie Dixon, shading and diminishing his image, scattering the elements of his life-story, and reducing him to little more than a curious name on the title pages of two local history books seen by relatively few readers. It is a familiar process, of course, but especially lamentable where the victim has been a personality, an original, a peculiarly worthy landmark in his community. I am glad to have this opportunity of rescuing from oblivion something of the man and his work, incomplete though the result may be.

David Dippie Dixon

The above words are from Roland Bibby's introduction to the first facsimile edition of *Upper Coquetdale*, published in 1974 and now, in itself, a rarity in local second hand bookshops. I use them here because Bibby's eloquently expressed objective is similar to my original aim in commencing this book: to bring David Dippie Dixon's *Upper Coquetdale* to the attention of a wider audience in its centenary year. A second main aim is to provide a modern overview of Upper Coquetdale's fascinating prehistory. A third, which is as much about future as it is about the past, is to provide a stimulus for local people to begin building on Dixon's work by undertaking new archaeological projects in the region.

This introductory chapter has benefited greatly from access to David Dippie Dixon's unpublished *Private Family History*. This was brought to my attention by David's great-nephew, Hugh Dixon, who kindly lent me his personal photocopy of the entire manuscript. The title page of this is inscribed as follows:

A Private Family History
compiled by one of its members.
David Dippie Dixon.
Rothbury.
Northumberland.

Commenced at Rothbury Oct 1909.
Completed at Cragside May 1st 1912.

'and what is writ is writ -
would it were worthier'

The original, in David's immaculate handwriting in a ruled, school-type exercise book, is held by his descendents in Australia. It contains an addendum written by David's grandson, David

1.1 An early twentieth-century photograph of David Dippie Dixon with his grandson, John Maxwell Dixon. *Image kindly provided by Roger Miket.*

1.2 John Turnbull Dixon. *Image kindly provided by Hugh Dixon.*

Maxwell Dixon (fig. 1.1), which brings the family history up to 1975: hopefully someone will continue to keep it up to date. The volume includes details of family members extending back to the mid-eighteenth century, and many characters, places and events are brought vividly to life though Dixon's splendid prose. While much of the detail does not concern us directly here, the work does include some fascinating information relating to Dixon's life and publications. It will, therefore, be referred to several times in the following pages. Although primarily of interest to members of the Dixon family (and families linked by marriage: the Hindhaughs and Maxwells of Rothbury, the Turnbulls of Wooler and Glanton, and the Carrs of Humbleton) it would also be of much general interest throughout Coquetdale were it ever to be published.

David Dippie Dixon was born on 1st September 1842. His father was a draper in the picturesque village of Whittingham, on the River Aln, about 10km north of Rothbury. His middle name, by which he is generally referred to by local people, is a family name, having been his great grandfather's surname. In his family history, he notes that 'family tradition has always been that the Dippies originally came over to England from Dieppe', and that his direct ancestors had probably 'fled from France during the Huguenot persecutions of the seventeenth century' and had settled in Edinburgh. The Dippies were present in north Northumberland by the late eighteenth century. David's mother, Jane, was from a family well established in Wooler by the early eighteenth century - the Turnbulls. Tragically, she did not survive the birth (on 25th October 1844) of her second son, John Turnbull Dixon (fig. 1.2), who was given her family name. As we will see throughout this book, John was a very talented artist (fig. 1.3) whose illustrations are used to fine effect in his brother's publications.

All of David's formal education was at Whittingham village school, which he left at the age of thirteen to join the family business. In 1862, he moved to Rothbury to set up a new shop on the High Street, known as 'William Dixon & Sons' (later 'Dixon Brothers'), which he ran with his brother (figs. 1.4, 1.5). He travelled widely throughout Upper Coquetdale on business, developing an intimate knowledge of the valley and its people. He became very knowledgeable in local history, archaeology, natural history, music and folklore, and was active in the Church. His *Private Family History* lists the various offices that he held (including positions of authority relating to the Rothbury Brass Band, the Rothbury Mechanics Institute, and the Rothbury Street Lighting Committee) and societies of which he was a member: this list takes up two pages. By all accounts, he was keen to share his knowledge and enthusiasm with everyone. In a memoir published in *Archaeologia Aeliana* in 1930, Edward Newbigin noted that 'Mr Dixon…had

an insatiable desire for knowledge' and that he 'learned all he could and gave out as he learned'. Newbigin also recorded that 'Mr Dixon was a man of kindly disposition with a gift of humour and a happy knack of eliciting the confidence and friendship of others'.

Something of the background to Dixon's literary work is provided in his *Private Family History*, in which he notes that:

> *From my boyhood I was much inclined to literary pursuits; when about twelve years of age I sent my first paragraph to 'the Alnwick Journal' giving an account of a Whittingham School Picnic to Thrunton and Callaly Crags, and for many years after coming to Rothbury acted as local correspondent to 'the Newcastle Daily Journal' of which newspaper my friend Mr Robert Redpath was manager. Eventually I began to write articles describing places of historic interest in Upper Coquetdale and Alndale for the columns of 'the Newcastle Courant' which was also under the management of Mr Redpath. For these articles I was very well paid, and the monies came in most useful for my wife's private purse.*

In his *Private Family History,* he includes a lengthy section about his own publications, noting that 'It may appear to be somewhat egotistical on my part that I here record some of my various writings, but my dear family who will probably read these lines know my nature better than to think so.' He then lists sixteen articles about historic Coquetdale published in the *Newcastle Courant,* seven papers read before the Newcastle Society of Antiquaries in the Old Castle, Newcastle upon Tyne, fifteen country meetings at which he acted as guide and expositor, and thirteen other papers in various publications. (Several more publications

1.4 Coquetdale House on Rothbury High Street, where Dixon and Sons (later Dixon Brothers) was located.

appeared subsequent to the compilation of this list.) The list ends with reference to his two great books, *Whittingham Vale* and *Upper Coquetdale*, both published in Newcastle by Robert Redpath, about which he provides the following background information.

1895. 'Whittingham Vale' illustrated with pen and ink sketches by my brother John Turnbull Dixon (this is my favourite piece of work).
347 pages
Copies printed: 200 copies Quarto deluxe at 10/6
*   1100 copies Octavo at 3/6*
Total production cost: £240.8.10
Now out of print. Master vols secondhand 21/. Octavo 7/6.

1.5 An advertisement for Dixon Brothers.

Clearly the second-hand market was already proving lucrative for those who had invested in an original copy, and were prepared to part with it! A second edition of Whittingham Vale was published in 1899, including a list of corrections and amendments. A facsimile of the first edition, published by Frank Graham of Newcastle in 1979, is now itself hard to find for less than £50, although copies can usually be found in local antiquarian bookshops.

1903. 'Upper Coquetdale' illustrated by John Turnbull Dixon.
498 pages and xi index pages. The manuscript consisted of 1600 pages of master German paper, closely written, which occupied my leisure hours (only) for twelve months. The matter was the result of twenty years observation and making notes.
Copies printed: 200 Quarto deluxe copies at 21/.
*   1226 octavo copies at 5/.*
Total production cost: £333.14.5.

Both of these books repaid our labour, in each case the number of copies sold before a volume was issued paid the expenses.

Although *Whittingham Vale* is a beautiful book, exactly why Dixon should have considered it his 'favourite piece of work' in preference to *Upper Coquetdale,* which I consider to be a superior work for a variety of reasons, is unclear. To someone like me, who works on a modern word processor, chopping and changing bits of text right up until the publication deadline (and often demanding further changes even when a book is typeset and ready for printing!) it is impossible to imagine the powers of self-discipline and concentration that must have lain behind the production of Dixon's manuscripts. His books may have been labours of love, but they must also have been very hard work. I hope he gained great pleasure and satisfaction from them both.

1.6 Looking across the lake at Cragside towards the house in which Dixon lived from 1911 until his death in 1929.

Dixon also notes in his *Private Family History* that 'the firm of Dixon Brothers got into financial difficulties in the May of 1911, when we were obliged to place our affairs in the hands of our auditors, most of whom treated us in the most kindly and considerate manner.' After this, he was offered a cottage in the grounds of Cragside (fig. 1.6), rent free for twelve months, by his 'good kind friend' Lord Armstrong. He and his wife moved to Cragside, and for a while he walked daily down to the shop in Rothbury (fig. 1.7). Eventually, when Dixon Brothers folded, he was offered the post of librarian at Cragside, enabling him to retain the cottage of which he was very fond. He remained here, engaged in the study of his beloved Upper Coquetdale, for the rest of his life.

David Dippie Dixon died in 1929, apparently never fully recovering from a nasty fall while out on his own inspecting wild flowers. He is buried in the 'new' cemetery at Rothbury. His gravestone is shared with his brother, John Turnbull Dixon, and both of their wives (fig. 1.8). The wives, Mary and Jane Hindhaugh, were sisters, the Hindhaughs having been a large and influential family in Coquetdale since at least the mid-seventeenth century. Both couples had

1.7 Looking down over Rothbury from the Alnwick road in about 1900. David Dippie Dixon would have enjoyed this view on his daily walk to work from Cragside.
Photo by Henry Armstrong. Reproduced from an original print in the possession of Tish Armstrong.

one son, although John's tragically died at birth. David's son emigrated to Australia, where, as we have already noted, his direct descendants still live today.

It is interesting to note the 'FSA' (Fellow of the Society of Antiquaries of London) after David's name on the gravestone. I do not know whether he requested this himself, or whether someone else made the decision. However, he was apparently very proud of his election to this prestigious society; no

1.8 The Dixon gravestone in Rothbury Cemetery. The inscription reads 'In memoriam: JANE, THE BELOVED WIFE OF JOHN TURNBULL DIXON, DIED JANUARY 29 1907 AGED 68 YEARS. MARY SISTER OF THE ABOVE AND BELOVED WIFE OF DAVID DIPPIE DIXON, DIED AT CRAGSIDE FARM MARCH 26 1918 AGED 71 YEARS. THE ABOVE JOHN TURNBULL DIXON, DIED AT WHITTINGHAM MAY 28 1926 IN HIS 82ND YEAR. ALSO OF DAVID DIPPIE DIXON. F.S.A., DIED AT CRAGSIDE FARM OCT. 28 1929 AGED 87 YEARS.'

mean achievement for a village draper's son who received no formal education after the age of 13 (fig. 1.9). There are not many newspaper cuttings pasted into his *Private Family History,* but the inclusion of this one, from the *Rothbury Parish Magazine* of April 1908, suggests that the recognition of his work by the Society of Antiquaries did indeed mean a great deal to him:

We offer our most sincere congratulations to Mr. D. D. Dixon, who, at a meeting held last month in the Society's Rooms, Burlington House, London, was elected a Fellow of the Society of Antiquaries. This much coveted distinction was conferred on Mr. Dixon in recognition of the fact that by his many years of research into the antiquities and folk-lore of Upper Coquetdale and of the Parish of Rothbury he has been enabled to compile the history of a wide and important district, and moreover that in doing so - in his works on 'Whittingham Vale' and 'Upper Coquetdale' - he has exhibited great literary power and the ability to make a difficult subject of extreme interest to general readers. It is also a recognition of the many delightful popular lectures that Mr. Dixon has given on this subject, and of the more technical papers that he has read from time to time to various Antiquarian Societies, also of the assistance that he has given to the many learned societies that have visited Rothbury, and that have recorded that they found in him 'a guide, philosopher and friend'.

1.9 David Dippie Dixon's great nephew, Hugh Dixon, thinks this photograph may have been taken while David was 'en route' to the Society of Antiquaries in 1908.
Image kindly provided by Hugh Dixon.

Upper Coquetdale: the place and the book.

I hope that most copies of this book will find homes on local bookshelves, and local people will need no introduction to the exhilarating landscapes of Upper Coquetdale. Those that don't know the area should pay it a visit without delay. It is one of Northumberland's most magnificent valleys (fig. 1.10), from its lonely source high on the Border Ridge at Coquethead, through the high hills of what is now the Ministry of Defence's Otterburn Training Area, to the dramatic profile of Simonside and the more gentle but still beautiful landscape around Rothbury. I can well remember my first trip up the Coquet to the isolated Roman camps at Chew Green. I was immediately struck by the contrasting wide-open spaces of the emerald green hills and the clear, fresh silver-blue of the fast-flowing Coquet. In many ways it reminded me of parts of western Ireland, which I had fallen in love with earlier that same summer. But Coquetdale was right here, on my own doorstep!

Although not a native, I have grown to love the Cheviot Hills with a passion that I do not fully comprehend, though I know it is somehow rooted in a combination of sublime landscapes and outrageously rich archaeological heritage. Both of these are present in Upper Coquetdale, but this region also has a flavour all of

1.10 A selection of views of the Upper Coquetdale landscape from the Northumberland National Park Authority's slide library.

Opposite page
Top: **Looking towards Cheviot from Windy Gyle.**
Bottom left: **Rowhope and Windy Gyle.**
Bottom right: **Ward Law/Rowhope.**

Above
Top: **The Coquet at Shillmoor.**
Centre: **View from Hepple Whitefield towards Holystone.**
Bottom: **The Grasslees Valley from Billsmoor Park.**

1.11a Two beautiful sketches of the higher reaches of Upper Coquetdale by John Turnbull Dixon. *Reproduced from* Upper Coquetdale.

1.11b A view near the source of the Coquet taken by Henry Armstrong in about 1900. Given the striking similarity between the two, it is tempting to suggest that John Turnbull Dixon may have based his drawing *(above)* on a copy of this photograph.
Reproduced from an original print in the possession of Tish Armstrong.

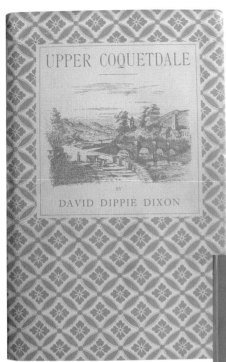

1.12 The inscription in the author's personal 'de luxe' copy of *Upper Coquetdale (left)*, together with the signed title page *(below)*.

its own, thanks in no small part to David Dippie Dixon.

Upper Coquetdale, Northumberland. Its history, traditions, folklore and scenery is a beautiful book. Its attractiveness owes much to John Turnbull Dixon's excellent drawings (fig. 1.11). Indeed, David makes it clear in his introduction that the book should be regarded not only as his own work, but as the 'leisure-hour employment of

1.13 The two facsimile editions of Upper Coquetdale, 1974 *(left)* and 1987 *(far left)*.

two village tradesmen'. Original copies, in their gold-embossed green covers, can usually be found in local antiquarian bookshops, but often now cost well in excess of £100. Rather more rare are copies of the 'de-luxe edition', with characteristic red-leather spine, of which only 200 individually numbered copies were produced. I am most fortunate to own one of these (number 187), one of my most treasured possessions. I found it in a second-hand bookshop in Cornwall, about as far away from Rothbury as it is possible to get without a passport! It is a presentation copy (fig. 1.12), given by the Dixon family to 'Dr and Mrs David Macnair on their Wedding Day - 28th March 1911'. For readers who may wish to obtain a more affordable copy of *Upper Coquetdale*, there are two facsimile editions available, although even these are now likely to cost in excess of £50 on the second-hand market. The first was published by the well-known Newcastle antiquarian publisher Frank Graham, in 1974; the second, itself limited to 1000 numbered copies, by Sandhill Press, Warkworth, in 1987 (fig. 1.13). It is

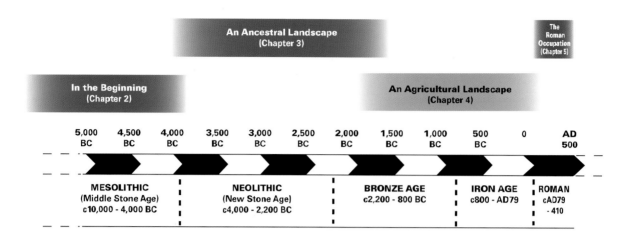

5,000 BC	4,500 BC	4,000 BC	3,500 BC	3,000 BC	2,500 BC	2,000 BC	1,500 BC	1,000 BC	500 BC	0	AD 500

An Ancestral Landscape (Chapter 3)

The Roman Occupation (Chapter 5)

In the Beginning (Chapter 2)

An Agricultural Landscape (Chapter 4)

MESOLITHIC (Middle Stone Age) c10,000 - 4,000 BC

NEOLITHIC (New Stone Age) c4,000 - 2,200 BC

BRONZE AGE c2,200 - 800 BC

IRON AGE c800 - AD79

ROMAN cAD79 - 410

1.14 Time chart showing the conventional prehistoric 'ages' and the chronological framework adopted in this book.

perhaps now time for a third facsimile to cater for the demands of the modern market.

I have occasionally heard Dixon criticised for having 'copied the work of others'. This criticism presumably arises from the extended quotations from earlier publications which Dixon incorporates within his books. However, these are all properly referenced and due credit is always given to the original authors. I believe that one of the great values of *Upper Coquetdale* is the way in which it combines consideration of earlier work with accounts of Dixon's own research and opinions. In this volume I have tried to emulate Dixon's approach, by providing interesting accounts of earlier work alongside some personal observations and speculation.

Prehistoric time and modern archaeology

Dixon's *Upper Coquetdale* is about a great deal more than prehistoric archaeology, but, as I have explained in the foreword, it is prehistory that concerns us here. Conventionally, prehistory (literally 'before history', meaning the time before written evidence exists to complement archaeological evidence) is regarded as the archaeology of pre-Roman times. In upland Northumberland, however, there is only negligible written evidence relating to Roman times, so the Roman occupation is included in this book, although we will not be considering the Roman army in any detail. A case could also be made for including post-Roman times, for which relevant written evidence is just as negligible, but we must draw the line somewhere.

Dixon's chapters on what he terms 'The British Period' provide a valuable overview of local prehistory at the turn of the twentieth century, but vast strides have been taken in our understanding of the prehistoric past since then. In comparison to many other parts of Britain there has been a sad lack of survey and excavation in Upper Coquetdale over recent decades, but work elsewhere now enables us to consider Coquetdale within an emerging regional framework, and thus make more sense of the valley's prehistory than was possible in Dixon's day. Today, prehistory is conventionally divided into the Stone Age, the Bronze Age and the Iron Age, with the Stone Age further subdivided into the Palaeolithic (old stone age), Mesolithic (middle stone age) and Neolithic (new stone age). These conventional timescales are shown graphically in fig. 1.14. This 'Three-Age System', as it is called, is not an ideal way of dividing up prehistory, as it suggests periods of stability interspersed with periods of transition when actually there were many important developments which bore little relation to the development of stone, bronze or iron technologies. In seeking to stress this point, I often point out in public lectures that 'nobody ever went to sleep in the Neolithic and woke up in the Bronze Age, and no Bronze Age mother ever gave birth to an Iron Age baby'. No Bronze Age person had ever heard of 'the Bronze Age', and no-one ever described themselves as an 'Iron Age man' or 'Stone Age woman': these are identities that we impose on ancient people that bear no relation to the way these people thought about themselves. In reality, most transitions were gradual, even where, in the context of archaeological timescales, they may appear dramatic. Changes that used to be explained as the result of 'invasions' by people with new technologies are now generally accepted as the result of the adoption of new technologies and new ways of life by existing populations, although this is not to deny the possibility that a few incomers may have arrived from time to time.

Given these problems with chronology, I considered structuring this book thematically rather than chronologically, with chapters on, for example, settlement, hunting and agriculture, or religion through time. Such an approach, however, has its own problems, as prehistoric people would not have distinguished between these different subjects as we do today. Settlement, hunting, agriculture and religious belief would have been inextricably linked together within the complex web of everyday life, and to write effectively of one without reference to other elements of contemporary life would be difficult. In the end, I decided on a compromise, and have provided thematic subsections within broadly chronological chapters. I have tried not to be overly obsessive about presenting everything in neat chronological order, but at the same time have tried to emphasise the importance of relative and absolute chronology to our understanding of prehistory. I have not imposed a uniform structure on the different chapters, as the nature of the archaeology discussed in each is different and is best approached in correspondingly different ways, placing appropriate emphasis on the available evidence.

Any division of prehistory into separate periods tends to deny change and exaggerate continuity *within* those periods, while exaggerating change and under-emphasising continuity between them. No such division is perfect, but the Three-Age system is so firmly ingrained into the minds of archaeologists that it is difficult to do away with. It is almost impossible to write of prehistory without referring to objects such as 'Neolithic axes' or 'Iron Age pottery', or sites like 'Mesolithic settlements' or 'Bronze Age burial cairns'. In this book, I have retained these conventional labels, but have adopted a new four-fold division of prehistory which I think is probably more appropriate for Coquetdale than the standard Three-Age model. The next chapter (In the Beginning) deals with the geological background and the Mesolithic, when we know, from the discovery of their stone tools, that people were living in the valley. Chapter 3 (An Ancestral Landscape) covers the Neolithic and early Bronze Age, a time when the archaeological record is dominated by structures erected for ritual and burial. Chapter 4 (An Agricultural Landscape) covers the later Bronze Age and the pre-Roman Iron Age, during which evidence for settlement and farming becomes steadily more extensive. Chapter 5 deals with the coming of the Romans and the end of prehistory. Chapter 6 considers a potentially very exciting future for prehistory in Upper Coquetdale.

Understandably, given the lack of information at the time, Dixon did not attempt to discuss the detailed chronology of prehistoric Upper Coquetdale. Indeed, some of his published work could be criticised for appearing to merge discussions of later prehistoric sites with earlier flint tools, and for lumping everything together within his so-called 'British Period'. This tendency can be seen in the reference to 'a pre-historic race' (singular) in the quotation on this volume's title page. To dwell on any such criticisms would, however, be unfair, as Dixon had no way of dating sites or objects in terms of calendar years. Today, thanks to a variety of modern

1.15 Military training inevitably leads to restrictions on public access on the Otterburn Training Area, but the use of the land by the military during the twentieth century has resulted in less damage to archaeological remains through agriculture and forestry than in some adjacent areas. The surviving archaeological landscapes of the OTA are consequently of very great importance.

scientific techniques, we are fortunate to be able to discuss prehistory within a generally accepted chronological framework, although it is worth noting here that such a linear chronology would almost certainly have appeared alien to people in prehistory. We will suggest in the following chapters that prehistoric people probabably understood time primarily as cyclical, based on the seasons, and would certainly not have worried unduly, as archaeologists do today, about classifying all aspects of the past by reference to a single, neat, linear timescale.

Perhaps the most extraordinary technique available to modern archaeologists, of which antiquaries like Dixon could never have dreamt, is radiocarbon dating. This is a complex science in its own right, and generates much controversy amongst archaeologists. It enables the dating of organic objects with reasonable accuracy, so any archaeological deposit containing organic material, sometimes in only very small quantities, can be dated. The technique was invented in the 1950s, and relies on the fact that all living things on earth contain carbon, a small proportion of which (known as carbon-14) is radioactive. This carbon-14 decays at a known rate once an organism is dead, so that careful measurement of the quantity of it in a sample (which can be of wood, bone, shell, or virtually any organic material) will generally date the death of the organism from which that sample originated. Complicating factors conspire to ensure that radiocarbon dates cannot be expressed simply as calendar years. They can, however, be 'calibrated' to give decent estimates of dates in real years BC or AD. Calibration is in itself a complex exercise, based essentially on relating radiocarbon determinations to known calendar dates obtained from tree-ring studies. Unfortunately, due to the lack of recent fieldwork, only three radiocarbon dates have been obtained from archaeological sites throughout Upper Coquetdale. However, radiocarbon chronologies based on fieldwork elsewhere in Northumberland provide a general framework which should be applicable here.

Developments in the field of geophysics, such as ground penetrating radar, can sometimes enable us to 'see' archaeological deposits without having to dig them up, but hardly any such work has yet taken place in our region. In any case, the results of such surveys can often be confusing and usually cannot be fully understood without recourse to excavation. While the general principles of a modern archaeological excavation would be familiar to Dixon, the wealth of complex scientific methods used to analyse finds and samples recovered during an excavation most certainly would not. For example, soil analysis can tell us much about activities which took place on a site thousands of years ago, while microscopic examination and chemical analysis of finds can tell us how artefacts were made and what they were used for.

While little excavation has taken place in Upper Coquetdale in modern times, a considerable amount of archaeological survey has been undertaken. Many previously unknown sites have been discovered, and the relative distribution of sites in the landscape is now much better understood. Archaeological survey takes place on a number of different scales, from the recording of the individual 'humps and bumps' on a particular site to the analysis of extensive landscapes using aerial photography. Reference will be made to several archaeological survey projects in this book, perhaps the most important of which was the aerial survey of the Ministry of Defence's Otterburn Training Area (OTA) undertaken by Tim Gates in the 1990s. Tim is a brilliant air photographer, who has been flying over north-east England with his camera for a quarter of a century. He must have discovered thousands of sites, some as earthworks in remote upland settings, some as 'cropmarks' (resulting from differential crop growth over buried remains) in lowland fields. His survey of Otterburn was undertaken in order to inform an archaeological management plan for the Training Area (fig. 1.15), intended to minimise damage to sites through military training, agricultural practice or forestry work. As a result of this survey, we now know that the archaeological landscape at Otterburn is of exceptional quality and importance, and the management plan should ensure that the most important remains are preserved for the future. Range Conservation Officer and retired OTA commandant, Richard Cross, who was instrumental in setting up and implementing the project, once memorably described the MoD's funding of the archaeological survey as 'like paying the bloody Luftwaffe to bomb London!' As more money was spent, more sites were discovered, and restrictions recommended for increasingly large expanses of the Training Area! Nevertheless, the archaeological management plan remains in place and Richard and his colleagues are to be congratulated for such an enlightened approach, for which future generations will without doubt be grateful. Several of Tim Gates' magnificent air photographs (including some taken as part of the OTA survey) are reproduced within this book.

Another important technique of archaeological survey worthy of specific mention in this introduction is that of fieldwalking. This involves the recovery of flint tools and other objects from the surface of ploughed fields, and can tell us a great deal about the nature and distribution of activity in the landscape thousands of years ago. David Dippie Dixon records several such discoveries in *Upper Coquetdale,* and these will be considered in Chapters 2 and 3 of this book. Chapter 6 considers the enormous potential for further such work, in which local people should be able to participate after no more than a single brief session of training.

One of the most fascinating developments in archaeological fieldwork during the twentieth

1.16 Exposed section of peat in Caudhole Sike. The white flag is placed at the point from which stumps and cones of Scots pine were recovered.

1.17 Andrew Miller's 7000 year old pine cone from Caudhole Moss.

century has been in palaeoenvironmental studies, enabling us to reconstruct the environment through time and identify changes in agricultural practice. Given his interest in the natural environment, this area of research would have been of special interest to David Dippie Dixon. There are many techniques of palaeoenvironmental reconstruction, but by far the most widely used is pollen analysis. Although rather more complex in practice, the principle of pollen analysis is simple: a core of peat (or other soil in which pollen grains are preserved) is taken, and pollen grains preserved at various depths are counted. The makeup of the surrounding vegetation at the time that that particular deposit was originally laid down can then be estimated through the relative presence of pollen grains from different species. If radiocarbon dates can be obtained for a number of levels within the core, then changes in vegetation can be dated and related to local archaeological sites.

Considering the potential for palaeoenvironmental research in Upper Coquetdale, and the value of such work to geography, ecology and archaeology, it is perhaps surprising that so little has taken place to date. The only such work that I am aware of is the analysis of two peat cores by students Andy Moores and Adrian Manning, under the supervision of Dave Passmore at the University of Newcastle's Department of Geography. These are from Caudhole Moss, south-east of Simonside, and Bloody Moss, 3km south-west of Harbottle on the Otterburn Training Area. As someone who trained in geography prior to taking up archaeology, I have some first-hand experience of the work involved in the production of a pollen diagram. It is excruciatingly tedious, involving many hours staring down the lens of a microscope. I am physically incapable of doing it, as I develop eye-strain and a throbbing headache after only a few minutes. Those who do undertake such mundane work, and interpret their results for the benefit of the rest of us, are deserving of much praise. Their results are fundamental to the study of prehistory, as is the work of many other archaeological scientists whose laboratories represent alien worlds to those of us more familiar with archaeological sites out in the landscape.

The Caudhole Moss site was first brought to my attention by Andrew Miller, who had recovered what appeared to be worked pieces of Scots pine from the side of Caudhole Sike, a natural erosion gully, at a depth of some 4 metres below the present ground surface (fig. 1.16). Andrew had also recovered a perfectly preserved pine cone (fig. 1.17) from the same level, something which he still uses as a very effective prop on guided walks when talking about landscape change. When first presented with the apparently worked stakes from Caudhole Sike I was a bit stumped as to what to do with them, so I bought some time by sending a sample away for radiocarbon dating. While this sample was being analysed I became convinced, following discussion with various experts, that these apparently worked pieces of ancient timber were actually the result of natural erosion, and consequently they lost some of their interest. However, this interest became rekindled when the results came back from the radiocarbon laboratory. The timber (and consequently the pine cone) were about 7,000 years old. I remember taking His Grace, the Duke of Northumberland, who had expressed an interest in seeing some of the archaeological remains at nearby Lordenshaws, to see this site, and his surprise at learning that the perfectly preserved wood sticking out of the side of the gully had been there for seven millennia. (I recall discussing the fact that the wood looked 'just like something one would buy from a DIY shop', which left me wondering how often His Grace popped down to B&Q on a Sunday morning - though I didn't ask!). Given that this timber does survive so well, it was clear to me that Caudhole Moss must offer great potential for serious palaeoenvironmental study. Eventually, a sample core a little over 10 metres deep was taken, and the earliest levels, dating from c5860 - 4325 BC were analysed in some detail and are discussed in Chapter 2 of this volume. The later levels of the Caudhole Moss core will undoubtedly have much to tell us about the local environment during later prehistoric and early historic times, but at the time of writing these still await detailed analysis.

The second core taken in recent years is from Bloody Moss. All the correct procedures were followed in obtaining this core, but one or two people at OTA subsequently expressed some surprise that an auger had been driven down into a site within a 'danger' area, along with relief that it hadn't disturbed any unexploded bombs or missiles, some of which may apparently lie buried in this general area. Under these circumstances the chances of ever obtaining a further core from here are understandably slim, but the precious 6.44 metre core of mud which currently resides in a fridge in the Geography Department at Newcastle University already holds the key to our understanding of the changing environment of this area. Provisional analysis has proved that this core is of very good quality, and although it doesn't stretch back as far as that from Caudhole, it does provide a record stretching back to about 3,700BC. The provisional results from the Bloody Moss core will be referred to at various points throughout this volume.

In addition to all the new forms of evidence about the past, developments in archaeological theory have given us new ways of interpreting this evidence. Since David Dippie Dixon was writing a hundred years ago, numerous different theoretical perspectives have been applied to the study of British prehistory, some of which have proved rather more stimulating than others. Ideas have been borrowed from other academic disciplines including geography, mathematics, sociology, history, philosophy and (perhaps most usefully) anthropology, all of which offer differing approaches to the study of the past. In fact, the study of the development of archaeological theory is taught in many universities as a subject in its own right, but that need not concern us here. In this volume I will borrow ideas from various theoretical approaches, but will seek to present them in clear 'non-theoretical' language.

The purpose of this volume

In writing this book, my intention was never to try to discuss every prehistoric site or find from Upper Coquetdale: to do so in a meaningful way would at least double the size of the volume. A list of all known sites and finds was included within volume XV of *A History of Northumberland*, published in 1940, and, despite subsequent discoveries, this still lists most of the relevant sites and finds in the region. Unfortunately, the discussion within that volume, although providing a fascinating summary of knowledge at the time, does include some factual inaccuracies and dubious interpretations so cannot really be recommended as an introduction to the subject. Anyone who wants up to date information about archaeological sites or finds from a particular area of Upper Coquetdale should consult the computerised Northumberland Sites and Monuments Record (SMR), details of which can be obtained from the County Archaeologist's office at County Hall, Morpeth. (Alternatively, for those with access to the internet, information from the SMR can be studied on-line at www.keystothepast.info).

What I have attempted to do in this volume is to provide an overview of everyday life for the 500 or so generations of people who lived in Upper Coquetdale between the arrival of Mesolithic hunters, some 10,000 years ago, and the end of the Roman period shortly after AD400. This is no straightforward task. People in the past were all individuals, who loved and lost just as we do today. At any given time, in any one community, there would be lazy, greedy and boring people living alongside more hardworking, generous and entertaining colleagues. People would no doubt have had different attitudes towards the conventional beliefs of the day, just as people today believe to differing degrees of orthodoxy in the teachings of the Christian Church. There is clearly a need to generalise in a book like this, but in doing so I do not seek to deny the role of the individual. Every individual person who lived in prehistoric Upper Coquetdale, whether a Mesolithic hunter or a Romano-British farmer, was as important in their world as you or I are in ours today. Individuals conformed to a degree with the demands of their own society, but each had their own personality and interests.

Using raw archaeological data to suggest how prehistoric people may have thought about their world is fraught with danger, but this does not mean that we shouldn't try to do it. To me, much of the value of archaeology comes from thinking about what it *might* have been like to have been alive in the distant past, even though I accept that I will never know for sure (fig.1.18). In this book, I have tried to temper my enthusiasm to speculate at great length about certain 'favourite' subjects in the attempt to provide a balanced account. However, I have included a large amount of speculation about some things, which I hope will tempt readers to think for themselves about the lives of real people in the distant past. To have written only of what we know for certain about prehistoric Upper Coquetdale would have been tedious. In many ways, discussions of what we do not (and often can not) know can be more interesting than accounts of what we think we know for certain! Such discussions inevitably rely on a large degree of informed speculation, and I hope I have distinguished clearly between fact and speculation throughout this account.

1.18 Looking over the ramparts of West Hills hillfort, near Rothbury, towards Simonside. Prehistoric people would have enjoyed similar views to those we cherish today, but would no doubt have thought about them in very different ways.
Photo: Simon Fraser.

The following chapters present and discuss data from a variety of sources. Amongst these sources, the work of David Dippie Dixon remains of paramount importance to anyone studying the history or archaeology of this stunningly beautiful and spiritually uplifting place. That is why this chapter has considered him in such detail, and why his name occurs so frequently on the pages which follow.

Exposures and scree of 380 million year old andesite, the
rock that forms most of the high hills of Upper Coquetdale.
Photo: Simon Fraser.

Chapter 2

In The Beginning
The geological background (from 400 million years ago)
and the Mesolithic (c10,000 - 4,000BC)

The making of the land

We will never know exactly when the first people wandered into the region we now refer to as Upper Coquetdale. Archaeological evidence in the form of ancient stone tools, preserved in caves, proves that bands of hunters were present in north Wales over 200,000 years ago. These Palaeolithic (old stone age) people were probably Neanderthals, who died out not long after anatomically modern 'homo sapiens sapiens' appeared on the scene about 50,000 years ago. They lived by hunting and scavenging, and probably hunted woolly mammoths, bears, bison, elephant and rhinoceros, along with smaller species such as deer and horse. People presumably passed through Northumberland at the same time, and during other warm 'interglacial' periods of the Ice Age, but any evidence for their presence has been scoured away by subsequent glacial erosion. The present day landscape owes much to the Ice Age of the past couple of million years, but the geological development of Coquetdale extends back over hundreds of millions of years.

The Coquet makes its own journey through geological time, through rocks deposited, warped, eroded and redeposited over unimaginably long periods. Spectacular volcanoes, tropical seas and vast sheets of ice have all played major roles in the development of this landscape. The river rises at Coquet Head, within an outcrop of ancient rock from the period referred to by geologists as the Silurian. Silurian sedimentary rock underlies most of Northumberland, but outcrops in only a few places where earth movements and erosion have conspired to leave it exposed at the surface. It was laid down within a deep ocean at an incomprehensibly ancient time when Northumberland lay near the equator. The Silurian ocean was home to a wide variety of bizarre looking creatures, including primitive forms of fish. Out of the ocean, however, life was apparently restricted largely to primitive plants such as ferns, although a few tiny sea creatures, looking a bit like millipedes or woodlice, may have begun to crawl out of the water to experiment with living on the land.

Archaeological time can be difficult to comprehend, but geological time is virtually impossible for the human mind to fathom. Just as archaeologists have invented their 'Ages' of Stone, Bronze and Iron to help them study the past few thousand years, so the geologists have designed their own chronological framework, but theirs is measured in hundreds of millions of years. The Silurian rocks of Upper Coquetdale were originally formed some 400 million years ago. In order to try to comprehend this vast period of time, we could represent it in

linear form as a journey from central London to Rothbury church: one year would be represented by every single millimetre of this journey. (Incidentally, a journey back to the origins of the earth - c4,600 million years ago - at the same scale of 1 year to 1 millimetre, would extend from Rothbury all the way to New York!)

After leaving its Silurian source, the Coquet flows amongst the distinctive rolling hills of the Cheviots (fig. 2.1). These hills are of volcanic origin, formed of lava and rock spewed out of massive volcanoes during the Devonian period, some 380 million years ago. Most are of andesite, formed of molten lava which flowed slowly out of the volcanoes and other vents in the earth's surface, while a few, such as Thirl Moor, are of pyroclast, made up largely of rocks and ash hurled spectacularly out of the volcanoes during massive eruptions. In contrast to these surrounding hills, the central Cheviots are of granite, formed of molten rock which cooled and solidified deep beneath the earth's surface, only to be exposed after millions of years of erosion of the overlying andesites. Today, these high granite hills are generally covered with peat and heather, giving them a dark appearance in marked contrast to the 'white land' of the lower, less acidic, grassy andesite hills of Upper Coquetdale. Further volcanic activity gave rise to other 'intrusions', including the distinctive porphyrite (or 'red whinstone') of Harden Quarry (fig 2.2), which now graces the Mall in London and numerous 'red' cycleways, hard shoulders and other road surfaces throughout Britain and elsewhere. (When forced to spend a day or two amidst the chaos and smog of our capital city, it is reassuring to wander down the Mall and think that I am actually walking on a little bit of the Cheviots!).

By 340 million years ago, this volcanic activity had ceased. During the subsequent

2.1 Aerial view northwards over the Coquet towards the Border Ridge at Windy Gyle. Barrowburn and Windyhaugh are visible on the valley floor in the middle distance.
Photo: AirFotos.

2.2 The unmistakeable exposure of 'red whinstone' at Harden Quarry. The quarry has expanded since this view was taken in 1985.

Carboniferous period, alternating layers of sand and mud were deposited in wide deltas in the shallow sea south and east of the old volcanoes, forming sandstones and shales. As sediments were laid down, their weight forced the seabed to subside, enabling further deposits to build up. On occasions, the deltas were inundated by the sea, resulting in the build up of the crushed remnants of billions of seashells which eventually formed bands of limestone. Collectively, these alternating beds of limestone, sandstone and shale are known as 'cementstones'. They form the low hills between Hepple and Whittingham, and an impressive, 45 metre high vertical exposure of them can be seen adjacent to the Coquet at Barrow Scar (fig. 2.3).

2.3 Exposure of cementsones at Barrow Scar.
Photo: Tony Hopkins.

The massive and often spectacular outcrops of Fell Sandstone, such as Simonside (fig. 2.4) and Harbottle Crags, were deposited a little later, by powerful rivers eroding a massive landmass and redepositing up to 300 metres of eroded material onto the gradually subsiding sea floor. The subsequent uplift of the Cheviot core, as overlying volcanic rocks were eroded, caused the tilting of surrounding rock strata, leaving the distinctive arc of crags facing in towards the Cheviots, from the southern fringes of Coquetdale, at Harbottle and Simonside, round as far as the north-eastern rim of the Milfield Basin, north of Wooler. The acid soils of the Fell Sandstones support heather, like the granite of the Cheviot core, but in contrast to the grassy andesite hills of Upper Coquetdale. This contrast is particularly clear when looking towards Alwinton from the east: the Coquet bisects the dark, angular, heather clad Fell Sandstones to the south, and the bright, smooth, grassy Cheviot hills to the north.

Over the next 300 million years, fish left the sea and became amphibians, some of which evolved into reptiles (the best known of which, the dinosaurs, ruled the earth from 250 to 65 million years ago, representing almost 50% of our imaginary 400 million year journey from London to Rothbury). The dinosaurs became extinct (although a few species may have evolved into birds), and the mammals gradually took over the earth. Early humans started to walk on two legs between 3 and 2 million years ago in Africa, with anatomically modern man appearing only some 50,000 years ago. Throughout all this time, no further major rock formations were deposited in Upper Coquetdale, where rivers and other erosive forces continued to eat away at the ancient rocks, as they still do today. At some unknown point during this vast period of time, the Coquet began flowing along something approximating to its current course.

By 1 million years ago (or just 1km from Rothbury on our imaginary journey) the whole of Upper Coquetdale was buried beneath a massive ice sheet, perhaps over a kilometre thick (fig. 2.5). Northern Europe was gripped by the Ice Age, which actually consisted of very cold periods interspersed with warm 'interglacial' phases. Many scientists believe that the Ice Age is not over, and that we are currently within an interglacial: whether or not the ice ever returns

2.4 Aerial view over Simonside, formed of 300 million year old sandstone, towards Coquetdale and the distant Cheviots.

2.5 Although modified by more recent erosive processes, including the activities of man, the present-day Upper Coquetdale landscape owes much to the effects of glacial erosion during the 'Ice Age', from 2 million to about 12,000 years ago. This period included many 'interglacial' periods, when the climate was warmer than today's, but also periods when even the highest hills were buried beneath slowly moving ice-sheets up to several hundred metres thick. This ice did much to mould the landscape that we treasure today.

2.6 The landscape of Upper Coquetdale that greeted the first settlers, at the end of the Ice Age, may have superficially resembled today's vast, open, grass covered hills (but with mosses and lichens rather than grass, and grazing reindeer rather than sheep, which were not introduced until much later). *Photo: Simon Fraser.*

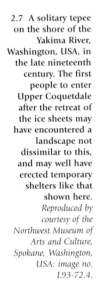

2.7 A solitary tepee on the shore of the Yakima River, Washington, USA, in the late nineteenth century. The first people to enter Upper Coquetdale after the retreat of the ice sheets may have encountered a landscape not dissimilar to this, and may well have erected temporary shelters like that shown here. *Reproduced by courtesy of the Northwest Museum of Arts and Culture, Spokane, Washington, USA: image no. L93-72.4.*

will depend on the balance between natural processes and the 'greenhouse effect' arising from man-induced pollution. The giant ice sheets scoured the landscape of softer rocks and soil, and smoothed the profile of the Cheviot Hills. The ice eventually melted away about 12,000 years ago, dumping vast quantities of 'boulder clay' on the lower ground surrounding the Cheviots, and leaving an open, tundra landscape rather like that to be seen today in parts of Iceland or Greenland. This was the landscape into which people arrived, probably between 12,000 and 10,000 years ago, to begin the period of continuous human presence in Upper Coquetdale which extends to this day (fig. 2.6). On our imaginary journey from central London to Rothbury church, representing the time from the deposition of the earliest rocks in Upper Coquetdale to the present day, these first people arrived in the valley well within the shadow of All Saints Church, only about ten paces from its front door. The rest of this book is all about these final ten paces: in geological time but the blink of an eye, but a blink which represents the entire story of human activity in Coquetdale.

Colonising Coquetdale

Settling Upper Coquetdale for the first time must have generated both exhilaration and trepidation. Getting to know a new landscape is not straightforward when there is no local tradition to follow, no parents or grandparents to learn from. Perhaps we feel a faint echo of the exhilaration felt by these early settlers when we wander unaccompanied into a vast, open, uninhabited landscape, such as can still be experienced in the more remote areas of Upper Coquetdale. However, this is probably a far from satisfactory analogy as we know that, all being well, we will be returning to our cosy homes at the end of the day. Something of the trepidation felt by Mesolithic settlers may perhaps be felt when we do get lost, perhaps in mist or in the depths of a modern forestry plantation: something that has happened to me on more than one occasion, often as the weather closes in and usually in areas where modern technology in the form of the mobile phone is rendered useless. In spite of such potential problems, however, the landscape must gradually have been 'learned' by the early settlers and their descendants. This process of learning would be slow at first, as the main landscape features were given names and no doubt became enmeshed within creation myths that would be retold and embellished by future generations.

We currently have no archaeological evidence for the presence of people in Upper Coquetdale during early post-glacial times. However, occasional discoveries of their stone tools have demonstrated that people were present just a little to the south, in Cumbria, Durham and Yorkshire, so it is reasonable to assume that some communities must also have existed in Northumberland by about 10,000BC. The first post-Ice Age settlers probably paddled up the river in canoes manufactured from hollowed-out tree trunks, or in small timber-framed boats with leather or birch bark skins, perhaps setting up small camps of temporary shelters not unlike the native American tepee shown in fig. 2.7. The landscape at the time was open tundra with few trees, although clumps of birch scrub were established in sheltered locations from which they would eventually expand to colonise most of the land as the climate gradually warmed up. The local fauna probably included wild cattle, wild horse, giant deer (with an amazing antler span of up to 3 metres), elk, reindeer and saiga antelope (a small antelope about the size of a modern sheep). Birds, including grouse, ptarmigan, ducks, swans and geese also provided much needed food, as did fish in the Coquet and its tributaries. Indeed, fish may have represented the major food resource to Mesolithic people, especially during the late summer and autumn months when the salmon returned to their traditional spawning grounds. People may have moved seasonally to the coast, where marine resources such as sea fish, seals and shellfish could be exploited. These early people also had competitors in the natural world,

2.8 Today, mixed woodland survives in carefully managed patches throughout Upper Coquetdale, such as here at Billsmoor, but in about 6,000BC most of the valley, including the high hills, would have been largely covered with inpenetrable woodland.
Photo: Simon Fraser.

as brown bears, spotted hyaena, lynx and wolf also required food, and no doubt also took the occasional person. At some point, the wolf was domesticated: Mesolithic people certainly had domestic dogs that could help with the hunt as well as provide company. Present-day shepherds may be interested to learn that the special relationship between man and dog stretches back to these distant times.

Mesolithic people would have used a variety of hunting and fishing strategies, including stalking and trapping, using spears and arrows of wood, flint and bone. The population density must have been very low: the average over the whole of Britain (which must have varied substantially from region to region) has been estimated at less than one person per square kilometre. The population growth rate would also have been low, with birth rates perhaps not greatly exceeding death rates, and little danger of over-exploitation of the environment.

A complex series of changes in sea level accompanied the fluctuating climate during the Ice Age. As water was locked into the ice, the sea level fell, but as ice built up over the land its weight forced the land down. The reverse occurred each time the ice melted. About 18,000 years ago, at the height of the last glacial phase when Coquetdale was engulfed by ice, the sea level was some 140 metres lower than at present, and the North Sea was dry land. By about 8,500 years ago, the British Isles had become separated from Europe as the North Sea rose, and Britain and Ireland were pretty much as they are today by about 6,500 years ago. The rising sea level meant that old traditional hunting grounds, including potential sources of flint for tool production, were now submerged. It must be doubtful whether this rising sea level, or the expansion of woodland as the land warmed up, would have been discernable within individual lifetimes. However, communal memory must have referred back to earlier times, when the land was both more open and more extensive. Fortunately, Mesolithic people were resilient and adapted, as they had to, to the changing environment.

The people of the wildwood

As the climate warmed up following the melting of the ice, the landscape became clothed in scrub consisting of birch with low shrubs such as bilberry and crowberry. These shrubs provided some seasonal food, but people must have lived primarily by hunting and fishing. The birch scrub was gradually replaced by mixed woodland, and by about 6,000BC all but the highest hills were clothed in varying combinations of birch, pine, hazel, oak, elm and lime, with alder in wet places (fig. 2.8). As the woodland expanded, many of the large mammals of the tundra landscape gave way to beasts more suited to life in, or on the fringes of, the forest, including wild boar, red deer, roe deer, beaver, badger, fox and mountain hare. These mammals would have been hunted for their pelts as well as for meat.

The Caudhole Moss pollen diagram records mixed deciduous woodland from about 5800BC, with very little pollen from open ground plants suggesting that very limited, if any, woodland clearance was taking place locally. Stumps and cones of Scots pine have been recovered from the lower levels of the Caudhole sequence, and have been dated to about 5000BC. The onset of peat deposition at Caudhole Moss, and the vegetation record prior to about 5000BC are thought to be entirely natural, with no evidence suggesting human activity. This is not to say that people were not active in Upper Coquetdale at this time: they almost certainly were, although they do not seem to have begun clearing woodland in the area of Caudhole Moss. Later in the Mesolithic, increases in heather and various heathland species are suggestive of small scale clearings which were probably created by people to attract grazing animals. Such clearances may also have been associated with the management of the woodland fringe to encourage the growth of hazel scrub, thus helping to guarantee a plentiful supply of hazelnuts each autumn.

Mesolithic people built no great ritual monuments or substantial settlements as their descendants would do in due course, but we know that they were present in Upper Coquetdale as a few examples of their characteristic flint tools have been found. David Dippie Dixon did not make a habit of collecting flints himself, but he did acquire a small collection of artefacts given to him by others. He published details of these in a couple of papers, and includes a discussion of them (with some illustrations) in *Upper Coquetdale*. I was delighted to find his entire collection in the stores at the Newcastle Museum of Antiquities, where my colleague Rob Young has completed a brief examination of it. Most of the flints are of Neolithic or early Bronze Age date, and are discussed in Chapter 3, but there is certainly a Mesolithic element (consisting of blades and small cores) within the collection. There is little that can be said for certain about these flints, but their recovery demonstrates that many more must still await discovery. If a modern programme of fieldwalking (see Chapter 6) can be organised, then the remains of Mesolithic settlement sites may yet be discovered in ploughed fields throughout Coquetdale.

John Davies has recently found five tiny flint 'microliths' eroding out of the peat on Simonside (fig. 2.9). John is an amateur archaeologist who has spent countless hours walking over ploughed fields at various places in Northumberland, engaged in the back-breaking work of searching for prehistoric flint tools. His dedicated work has resulted in the discovery of concentrations of flints which have led to the identification and excavation of Mesolithic and Neolithic settlements over recent years. The microliths from Simonside are presumably evidence of a temporary hunting camp, perhaps occupied about 8,000 years ago. They may have been dropped here by accident, to remain hidden for thousands of years until John happened to walk by soon after they had been eroded from an overburden of peat. The fact that he found five on a single occasion suggests that many more, perhaps thousands more if the site was used over a long period, may still lie beneath the peat in the immediate locality. Alternatively, it is possible that they are the remains of a single arrow fired during a hunt, of which only the flints remained in the peat as the wooden shaft would soon have rotted away. It is hoped to set up a project to investigate the site in the near future.

Microliths are the most commonly found Mesolithic tools. They are small flakes which may have had a variety of uses. Some were mounted on timber hafts to make arrowheads (the bow-and-arrow was already widely used by this time), harpoons or spears (fig. 2.10), while others may have been mounted into wooden frames to process vegetables. Unfortunately, the timber and bone elements of the Mesolithic toolkit only survive in exceptional circumstances, and no such objects have been found in Northumberland. The production of microliths may have been restricted to specialists, but I suspect that most Mesolithic people were capable of their manufacture. We can imagine small children cutting their fingers while attempting to master the skill, and no doubt some people became more proficient than others.

2.9 Microliths from Simonside found by John Davies. (Scale in cms).

While occasional pieces of naturally occuring flint may be recovered from within boulder clay, no reliable flint sources exist anywhere in inland Northumberland. People living in Upper Coquetdale must have obtained their flint either from the coast (where pebbles can still be found washed up on the beach) or from further afield. There is some evidence to suggest that flint from the chalk deposits of the Yorkshire Wolds was finding its way to Northumberland as early as the Mesolithic, although such supplies may have been irregular and it seems that local people sometimes resorted to using inferior but locally available stone (such as chert or quartz) for the manufacture of some tools.

Although some way outside our area, another very important Mesolithic site was recently discovered by John Davies and has been excavated by Clive Waddington. This is on the coast at Howick (about 12km north of Amble where the Coquet flows into the North Sea) but is of such importance that its potential relevance to the Mesolithic of Upper Coquetdale must be considered.

Clive Waddington arrived in Northumberland like something of a whirlwind in the mid 1990s. After graduating from Newcastle University, he set about completing a PhD on the prehistory of the Milfield Basin, but also involved himself in numerous research and interpretive projects throughout Northumberland. His contribution to local prehistory is immense, as is his capacity for socialising. He is one of those intensely annoying people who can stay up drinking into the early hours, then be up at the crack of dawn cheerfully directing an excavation or working on a complex academic paper, something I gave up trying to do many years ago! Although some of his interpretive work has generated controversy amongst colleagues, Clive certainly cannot be criticised for his exemplary record of writing up his fieldwork for prompt publication: an interim report of the Howick excavation was submitted to *Archaeologia Aeliana* (the journal of the Society of Antiquaries of Newcastle upon Tyne) within a few months of the completion of fieldwork, and was published in 2003. The report explains how the meticulous investigation of the flint scatter first noted by John Davies uncovered the remains of a Mesolithic dwelling, dated by a series of radiocarbon determinations to c7,800BC: a time when a land bridge still existed between Northumberland and Denmark, and when mixed deciduous woodland was gradually replacing birch scrub over most of inland Northumberland.

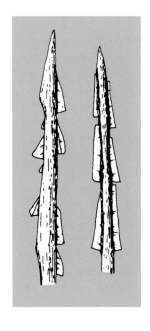

2.10 Reconstruction sketch of Mesolithic arrowheads, showing how the microliths were mounted on timber shafts.

Analysis of burnt bone from the hearths within this structure have demonstrated the presence of wild pig, fox, birds and either wolf or dog. Numerous hazelnut and acorn shells were also present. In excess of 18,000 pieces of worked flint were recovered from the excavation, and at the time of writing work is still in progress on these and on the numerous environmental samples from the project. Clive built a reconstruction of this Mesolithic house at Milfield (near Wooler) where visitors were able to visit it as part of an innovative archaeological trail (fig 2.11). I use the past tense, because, as I was putting the final touches to this book, Clive informed me that the house had burnt down as a result of his trying to light a fire within it! It was apparently a scary moment for those inside as the roof ignited with lightning speed. As Clive told me the story I found myself wondering how many Mesolithic people had endured similar misfortune: although they may have been more careful. Regardless of this, the Howick excavation is of great importance, and raises the possibility that similar structures of equivalent or later date could survive in Upper Coquetdale and elsewhere. Such sites may even survive better in more upland locations if they are buried beneath peat, but finding them will not be easy, and may depend upon the chance discovery of upland Mesolithic flint scatters.

Clive Waddington's work in the Milfield Basin, north of Wooler, has involved countless hours of fieldwalking by many committed volunteers, and has recovered much information about prehistoric settlement patterns in that region. Although there are reasons for regarding the Milfield area as 'special', similar results may well be recovered when a comparable campaign of fieldwork is eventually undertaken in Coquetdale, as there are many similarities between the landscapes around Rothbury and Wooler, and no real reason to suppose that prehistoric patterns of landscape exploitation would have varied greatly between them. Back in 1983, John Davies published a paper in *Northern Archaeology* (the journal of the Northumberland Archaeological Group) which included a distribution map of Mesolithic finds in Northumberland. Of seventy sites shown on this map, only one (relating to David Dippie Dixon's collection) was recorded in Upper Coquetdale. However, John observes in this paper that 'it has become increasingly apparent during the preparation of this article that the distribution of known Mesolithic sites must reflect recent activity, especially the work of

2.11 Northumberland National Park archaeologists Rob Young and Iain Hedley at the Mesolithic 'house' built by Clive Waddington at Milfield.

collectors and archaeologists, as much as the true pattern of Mesolithic settlement in Northumberland'. Early in 2006, members of the Upper Coquetdale Community Archaeology Project (see Chapter 6) found an important concentration of Mesolithic flints through fieldwalking at Low Trewhitt. At the time of writing, these finds have yet to be analysed in detail, but seem to represent the remains of a seasonal campsite which may have been occupied over hundreds if not thousands of years. It may be that many more such sites await discovery throughout the valley, but for now, in the absence of much hard evidence, we must content ourselves with a highly conjectural discussion of what life might have been like in Upper Coquetdale during the Mesolithic.

Mesolithic lives

Given such limited evidence, what can we say about the people of Mesolithic Upper Coquetdale? The evidence that we do have, coupled with archaeological evidence from elsewhere in Britain, can be used to offer a tentative interpretation of life in these distant times. In addition, ethnographic studies of pre-agricultural societies, such as native Americans, Australian aborigines or the San people of the Kalahari Desert, have much to tell us about how people may have lived in Coquetdale during the Mesolithic. It is important to remember, however, that all such societies are different, and that while generalisations may be appropriate, no direct parallels should be sought between any recent societies and the people of Mesolithic Coquetdale.

The first people to enter the valley after the retreat of the ice may well have done so in search of fish and other riverine resources. The well-known 'Coquetdale fishing songs' (collated into a beautiful little book by Thomas Doubleday in 1852) record the Coquet's long recognised fame as a fishing river. One of my favourite of these songs, 'The Coquet for Ever', closes with the following lines, giving a sense of the angler's love of both the river and its setting:

The Coquet for ever! The Coquet for aye!
The Coquet, the king o' the stream an' the brae,
Frae his high mountain throne to his bed in the sea,
Oh! Where shall we find such a river as he?
Then blessings be on him, and long may he glide,
The fisherman's home, and the fisherman's pride;
From Harden's green hill to old Warkworth sae grey-
The Coquet for ever! The Coquet for aye!

We can imagine the first settlers being largely reliant on the river. Perhaps they too enjoyed the challenge of catching fish in this glorious landscape setting, and no doubt they had their own stories and songs about the river. However, their attitude towards both fish and landscape would have been very different to those of modern people. The fish, along with most species of animals, birds and plants, would have had their own spirits which would have been respected by the people. The belief systems of these early settlers would have been based on

2.12 Reconstruction of a Mesolithic scene, based on evidence from several different sites throughout Britain, by Jim Proudfoot.

their homeland to the east, and their creation myths may well have included references to early post-glacial beasts such as wild horse, bison and giant deer. Such mythologies would gradually have been adapted to include references to distinctive local places, such as Simonside, and would have changed further as the open, tundra landscape gradually gave way to scrub and then to forest.

Five or six thousand years after the arrival of the first post-glacial settlers, the Upper Coquetdale landscape was smothered with dense mixed woodland. People would still have relied on fish and other riverine resources, but would also have hunted red deer, wild boar, wild cattle (aurochs) and wildfowl, and collected various nuts, berries and edible plants. Everything that people required (skins for clothing, timber for shelter and fuel, stone for tools and weapons) was provided by nature, and people lived in harmony with their environment. To begin with, there would have been very few people, but over time a complex system of base camps and seasonally occupied 'task camps' (for hunting, and the

2.13 Rock shelter adjacent to the Cambo bridleway, Simonside.

gathering of food and other materials) would have evolved. These base camps (fig. 2.12), in relatively sheltered spots close to the river, may have been occupied by mothers, young children and old folk throughout the year, and probably became home to everyone during the winter. During the warmer months, groups of people probably returned to a series of temporary upland camps to enable the exploitation of seasonal resources. In some places, the location of such camps would have been dictated by the presence of natural shelters in the form of caves or rock shelters (fig. 2.13), the examination of which must be a priority for local Mesolithic research.

Around the campsites, the vegetation may have been cleared through the controlled use of fire to encourage the growth of lush grass, and therefore attract red deer and other animals which could then be more easily hunted. Fire was probably also used at the forest margins to encourage the growth of hazel scrub, as nutritious hazel nuts were an important part of the Mesolithic diet. They could be gathered, roasted and stored in the autumn, providing a guaranteed resource for the long winter months when they may have been consumed as a type of paste or porridge. In addition, fish and meat would no doubt be dried or smoked and stored for consumption during the winter months, when natural resources were relatively scarce.

Ethnographic studies suggest that pre-agricultural people did not 'own' territories with defined boundaries like we do today. Rather, they exploited the landscape from a network of trackways, with different groups perhaps having access to different resources at different times. The lack of population pressure meant that there was no need for competition for resources: there was more than enough to go around. Under these circumstances, hunting and gathering can represent a very efficient way of life, and it is in some ways a mystery why agriculture, with its need for clearing, ploughing, sowing and harvesting, and the risks of disease, ever took off. It may be that access to some food sources was less predicable than would be the case once stock and cereals had been domesticated, but this would have been less of a problem if resources were shared between different groups, which they probably were.

In 1992, Christopher Smith, a lecturer in prehistoric archaeology at the University of Newcastle, published an excellent summary of the British Mesolithic (entitled *Late Stone Age Hunters of the British Isles*). On the basis of an analysis of different tribal groups in North America, Smith suggests a basic social structure that may have applied to the population of Mesolithic Britain. The basic unit is the 'family', a small group of individuals of various generations that we might describe today as an 'extended family'. Particular individuals from related families would join together to form 'task groups' at different times of year (for example, for hunting, gathering or flint procurement). Such task groups could vary in size according to the task in hand. Several families were grouped together as a 'band', usually linked to a particular territory. According to Smith, these bands could vary in size from 'less than 50 to over 2,000, with an average of about 300'. Perhaps Upper Coquetdale was occupied by one such band during the Mesolithic. The bands had no aristocratic chiefs or rigid social heirachy, although some individuals might assume dominant roles from time to time on the basis of their particular knowledge or experience. Every person would have played an important role within society. Women must have undertaken a variety of tasks. In addition to their crucial role in childbirth and the rearing of the young, they may also have been involved in hunting, fishing, trapping and gathering. Hunting for large game may well have been a prestigious activity, as well as being essential for the provision of meat, skins, bone and other materials. Without doubt, the hunters would have been accompanied by their faithful hounds, which were the first truly domesticated animals.

The bands were generally exogamous, meaning that members had to seek marriage partners from other bands, and bands in the same 'mating network', which probably spoke a common dialect, were linked together as a 'tribe'. These tribes could number several thousand individuals, and would come together at particular times of year for seasonal ceremonies. Whether or not any form of warfare existed from time to time between different tribal groups is not known, but the lack of pressure on resources during the Mesolithic might suggest that conflict was neither desirable (as many think it to have been amongst the warrior aristocracies of later prehistory) nor necessary.

Few people would have lived past thirty years of age, and those that did would probably have been held in high regard due to their knowledge and experience of what must have seemed to most people like ancient times. Seasonal gatherings would have become established in the calendar, with different groups coming together to exchange goods and arrange marriages. Such occasions must have provided great opportunities to meet old friends and tell stories, no doubt amidst much feasting. Some ceremonies would have included initiation rites, as individuals moved from one stage of life into the next: for example, from adolescence into adulthood. Ethnographic studies suggest that such ceremonies were probably regarded as potentially dangerous, and the tried and tested rites and rituals would need to be performed with great care. Amongst some native American societies, individuals were required to adopt a completely different name after undergoing some rites: our tradition of retaining the same name for life (allowing only for a change at marriage) may not have applied back in the Mesolithic.

Again borrowing from ethnographic studies, it seems that pre-agricultural people tend to regard themselves as part of the natural environment, rather than as separate from nature as seems to be the case in later prehistory, when people were more in control of food production. Inland from the sea, the all-enveloping wildwood, once established, must have seemed almost infinite in both time and space. It provided not only wood and food for the people, but must also have provided spiritual fulfilment. The Mesolithic in Northumberland was an 'untamed' world of sacred mystery within which the spirits and ancestors must have been ever-present. People had a respect for the environment which is sadly lacking in today's world: trendy modern concepts like 'biodiversity' and 'sustainability' would have been second nature to Mesolithic people. Although animals had to be killed for food, they would have been treated with respect, in stark contrast to present day attitudes towards animals as represented by our hideous factory farms. Indeed, some bands or tribes probably had 'totem' animals, which were treated with special respect even though they would on occasion be eaten. Particular animals may have represented special spirits relating to their particular strengths. Such spirits would have been everywhere, and although they were not 'worshipped', in a Christian sense, they certainly had to be constantly respected, as to upset the spirits at any time could bring misfortune on all the people. Whereas Christianity stresses the 'specialness' of mankind, Mesolithic religion may well have placed greater emphasis on the place of human beings *within* the natural world. Mesolithic religion was 'lived' rather than 'thought': people did not go to church on Sundays and forget about their religion for the rest of the week (indeed, the very concept of a 'week' would have been alien to a Mesolithic person).

These issues can be difficult for the modern western mind to grasp, but an insight is given in a recent fascinating account by an Australian aboriginal elder, Max Dulumunmun Harrison of the Yuin Nation. He explains that people he refers to as 'non-indigenous' will only be able to understand aboriginal culture and belief:

by walking the land with Aboriginal people and understanding their spirituality to the land; understanding why a tree is important, why a tree is sacred; understanding why the rivers and the

2.14 Simonside from the north.
Photo: Tony Hopkins.

waters become sacred; understanding why the wind is sacred; understanding all the animals that they share this planet with......By walking hand in hand and listening to the sacred text of the land, the sacred text is every facet of the land, the story of the land, every dreaming of the land. A text is a story, a dreaming! It's the same as the text that white man brings to us in a bible, if you can put it into those Christian terms. I believe that's where something went wrong because Christianity is man-made, spirituality is god-given.

I believe that Aboriginal spirituality probably shares many basic concepts with the attitudes of the inhabitants of Mesolithic Upper Coquetdale to their world. It is, in my view, quite probable that the Mesolithic landscape was understood by reference to a system of traditional 'song lines' akin to that of today's aborigines in Australia, and it may well be that Simonside, with its distinctive profile whether seen from north or south (figs. 2.14, 2.15) may have acted as a 'sacred mountain', rather like a local *Uluru* (Ayers Rock). There can be no proof of this, but unusual rock formations and high places throughout the world have been (and in many cases still are) of ritual significance to people. High places are often thought to link earth and sky, and are central to local creation myths. The sky, and the spirits associated with it, must have been of fundamental importance to people from the earliest times, and we will suggest later in this book that it remained of key importance throughout later prehistory. The sun, moon, planets and stars, and everyday weather phenomena, are all linked with the sky. Special events, such as eclipses, planetary conjunctions, and unusual weather patterns such as droughts, extreme thunderstorms, or very cold spells, would all have been understood by reference to the spirits, to whom offerings were probably made at regular seasonal gatherings to ensure that nature's infinitely reliable cycles continued to operate. Perhaps the return of the first salmon in the Coquet each year was an occasion for great celebration, as the fish, once dried, would provide essential nourishment for the forthcoming winter as well as providing for more immediate feasts. We can imagine the people giving thanks to the river spirits as part of such celebrations.

I suspect that any Mesolithic person seeing Simonside for the first time would have been drawn to its summit, just as people are today. The strange, eroded rock outcrops to be encountered here (fig. 2.16) would have invited the invention of creation myths and other

2.15 Simonside from the south.

stories, subsequently to be embellished as they were handed down by word of mouth through the generations. Once established, such sacred places help to provide people, both individually and collectively, with an identity. They are places where myth and 'history' become merged, places where shamans (or witch-doctors) may seek visions, and people may go on pilgrimages. I put 'history' in inverted commas because Mesolithic people probably had no concept of history as we understand it: indeed, the way we understand our world by reference to abstract concepts like history, culture, landscape or religion would certainly have seemed foreign to a Mesolithic individual, who would have regarded them all as inextricably linked together within the complex web of the everyday world. To Mesolithic folk, dreams, which may have provided links with the spirit world, were probably every bit as 'real' as our comparatively rather mundane 'real world' is to us. Mesolithic people certainly did not have geologists to provide them with 'factual' explanations for the origins of landscape features, and their explanations would undoubtedly have been rather more poetic than the account of the Upper Coquetdale landscape offered at the start of this chapter. We will see in Chapter 3 that Simonside certainly seems to have been of special importance in later prehistory, and the legends still associated with it today just might have very ancient origins.

Although they lived long ago, we must avoid any temptation to regard Mesolithic people as 'savages', like conventional cartoon images of cavemen. They were physically just like us, though no doubt, on average, considerably stronger and fitter. Their brains were the same size as ours, but they no doubt thought very differently. Their language would have been full of words and phrases linked to the natural environment. They were intelligent people living complex lives tuned to their particular environment, and capable of adapting as that environment changed. They would have observed how changes in the heavens related to the seasons on earth, and without doubt their 'real' world would have become merged with their cosmology, developed over the generations to account for the mysteries of life and the universe. They may have had shamans (or witch doctors) to mediate between the living and the ancestors: if so then these individuals may have been the most respected members of society. Shamans are known from various places around the world, where they are thought to be able to commune with the 'otherworld', often as part of communal events, by going into a trance induced through rhythmic chanting or dancing, or through the ingestion of hallucinogenic

2.16 left
The natural feature known as Little Church Rock on the northern flank of Simonside.

Centre and right
Weathered rock exposures on Simonside.
Central photo: Simon Fraser.

Today, such features are explained by the science of geology, but prehistoric people probably accounted for them by reference to a variety of creation myths.

substances. One cannot help but wonder what a Mesolithic shaman would have made of a modern acid house party! We will have more to say about shamans when we come to consider rock art in Chapter 3.

At Star Carr in Yorkshire, excavations recovered more than twenty examples of modified red deer skull fragments, with the antlers still attached. These appear to have been worn as head-dresses, perhaps by shamans and others during rituals and/or by hunters while stalking deer. These were only preserved at Star Carr due to the wet conditions of the site, and. although nothing similar has been found in Northumberland, it is not unreasonable to assume that people here would have produced and used similar objects. Unfortunately, many of the objects which would have been central to the identity of people living in Coquetdale are not recoverable through archaeology. Ethnographic work, however, leaves us in little doubt that the complex spirituality of the Mesolithic inhabitants of Upper Coquetdale would have been symbolically embedded within everyday objects such as clothing, personal ornaments and weapons, and in everyday activities such as hunting and cooking.

We have no evidence from Northumberland of Mesolithic burial, and may well never find any. Perhaps bodies were disposed of in ways which leave no trace in the archaeological record, for example they may have been put out to decompose in special places: a process, followed until relatively recently in some native American societies, known as 'excarnation'. Certainly, the lack of burials must not be taken to imply the lack of a complex spiritual life, and in some parts of Europe Mesolithic burials have been excavated, apparently demonstrating concern for the dead and belief in some form of afterlife in the realm of the ancestors. No doubt, just as individual native American tribes had their own creation myths which differed from those of their neighbours, so beliefs would have varied from group to group in Mesolithic times. However, it is probable, in my view at least, that all Mesolithic people believed in some way in the immortality of the soul.

Today, millions of people believe, to varying degrees of orthodoxy, in the Bible and the myths of the Christian Church. Whatever beliefs our Mesolithic ancestors may have had, they would have been intimately bound up with their world, providing explanations for things which were

otherwise inexplicable. Many within today's Christian church are convinced that their religion somehow represents 'the truth', but several festivals in the modern Christian calendar clearly have prehistoric origins. Christmas, for example, has evolved out of the pagan celebration of midwinter and the annual rebirth of the sun, something that would surely have been an important annual event in the lives of Mesolithic people. It is sobering to think that our modern Christmas celebrations may ultimately be rooted in local Mesolithic sun worship, rather than in the birth of a mythical Messiah in a distant land.

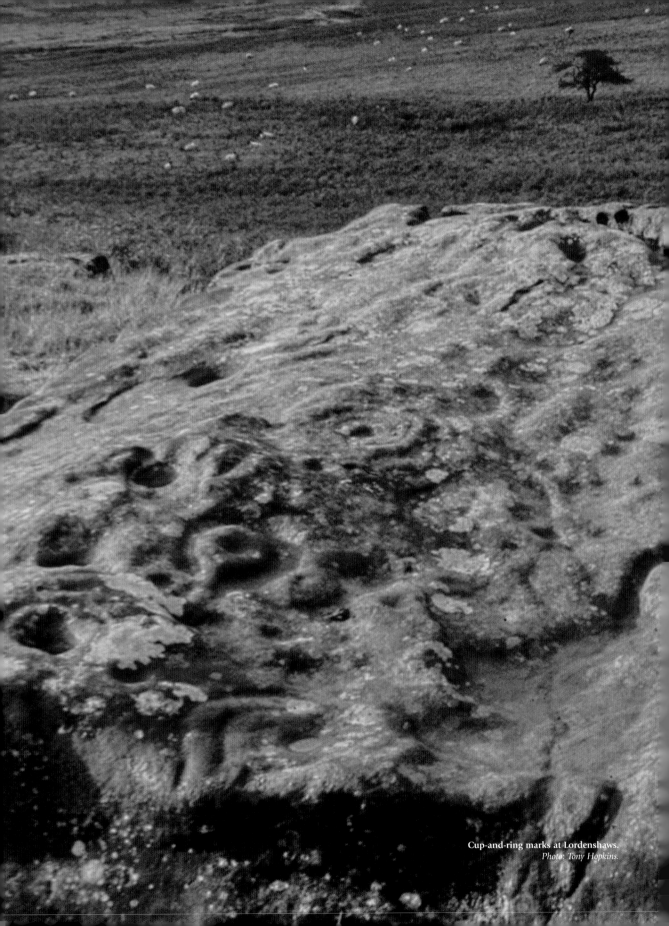

Cup-and-ring marks at Lordenshaws.
Photo: Tony Hopkins.

Chapter 3

An Ancestral Landscape
The Neolithic and earlier Bronze Age (c4000 - 1500BC)

Introduction

The New Stone Age, or Neolithic, saw one of the most fundamental developments in the story of mankind. This was the adoption of agriculture, often referred to in the literature as the 'Neolithic Revolution'. Prior to about 4,000BC, all people in Britain had survived by exploiting natural resources, and had lived tried and tested lifestyles based on the exploitation of seasonally available foods. In contrast, the initial adoption of agriculture was a risky business. Traditional ways of life developed over thousands of years were gradually abandoned as the emphasis gave way from the hunting of wild animals to the keeping of 'domesticated' beasts, and from the gathering of wild produce to the planting and harvesting of cereals and vegetables. Not only are archaeologists unsure as to how agriculture was adopted in an area like Upper Coquetdale, but, given the sheer hard work involved in the initial preparation of the land for farming, they are also far from clear about why this development should have taken place at all. Whatever the explanation, after thousands of years of hunting and gathering, it was during the Neolithic that people began the move towards the factory farming and numerous food crises of the modern age.

Today, most archaeologists account for the spread of agriculture as a gradual adoption by Mesolithic populations of the 'new way of life' that they would have become aware of through trading contacts. Instead of simply following herds of wild animals around the landscape, people began actively 'herding' domesticated animals, leading eventually to the development of permanent settlements with paddocks and fields. Other archaeologists prefer to see the development of farming as the result of folk movements, as early agriculturalists left their homelands on the continent in search of new farmland. This could have resulted in conflict with native Mesolithic people as the natural woodland cover was gradually cut down to make way for fields. The current crises in the rainforests of South America perhaps offer parallels, as native populations see their environments destroyed and find themselves gradually integrated into western culture. Native Americans suffered similarly as western settlers set up ranches on their sacred landscapes throughout the nineteenth century, and Australian aborigines are losing their traditional way of life as western culture and technology take over their world.

Once farming was successfully established, populations expanded and there was a constant demand for new agricultural land, putting increasing pressure on the 'natural' landscape as more and more woodland was cleared. However, there must have been much continuity between late Mesolithic life and that of the early Neolithic, and changes in the way that people perceived their world and their place in it must have been gradual. Indeed, it is quite conceivable that different groups, even within an area like Upper Coquetdale, lived in

different, perhaps complementary ways for several centuries. Some groups may have continued with a traditional, mobile, Mesolithic way of life, while others adopted new ways and became gradually more sedentary, with all congregating together for festivals at particular times (fig. 3.1).We should avoid the temptation to try and provide universally applicable models for all groups of people just because they happened to be living at the same time. By way of example, Romany Gypsies have maintained a mobile lifestyle for centuries alongside the essentially sedentary populations of Europe, and some Northumberland farmers and their families moved seasonally into the hills with their flocks as recently as three or four hundred years ago, when most people were living in towns and villages.

As the Mesolithic world gradually gave way to that of the Neolithic, some old practices and beliefs thrived and expanded, while others stagnated and died out as people thought of new ways of doing things or copied ideas developed elsewhere. We should not forget that the complex ceremonial world of the Mesolithic described in Chapter 2 would have influenced the ways in which agriculture was adopted by native people, and everything to do with early agriculture may have been highly charged with symbolic value. In some native American societies it is women who do much of the planting and harvesting, as there is thought to be a strong link between the fertility of women and that of the fields. This may well have been the case in early Neolithic Upper Coquetdale. The management of fields, which had to be prepared and sown, weeded, and harvested, must have led to new forms of land ownership and consequently new concepts of 'place'. Whereas earlier people may have spent little time in any one place throughout the year, the fields were now a focus of activity throughout spring, summer and autumn.

Cereals, which could be used for the baking of bread and the brewing of beer, were probably introduced to Northumberland soon after 4000BC. Although we have no direct evidence for Neolithic cultivation in Upper Coquetdale, palaeoenvironmental research has demonstrated that people were growing cereals (probably early forms of wheat and barley) during the fourth millennium BC in lowland areas to the north (eg around Milfield) and south (eg near Otterburn). Consequently, there is good reason to believe that early cultivation may have been practised in the fertile lowlands around Rothbury, if not in the surrounding uplands. At Bloody Moss, peat formation began in about 3,700BC, possibly as the result of artificial woodland clearance in the immediate locality. Pollen of meadowsweet and dock is probably indicative of such clearance, and the presence of charcoal suggests that people may have been creating and maintaining woodland clearances through the controlled use of fire. These upland clearances are perhaps most likely to have been made by essentially Mesolithic communities to attract wild animals, but their date implies that they could be related to the introduction of domestic beasts. It is just possible that some such early upland clearances could have been for the cultivation of cereals, but the currently available pollen evidence suggests that cultivation in the uplands of Northumberland did not commence until much later (see Chapter 4).

Neolithic fields, such as those we have suggested may have existed around Rothbury, would have been prepared by breaking up the ground surface using primitive ploughs, known as 'ards', which were dragged across the ground in a criss-cross pattern. These fields may have looked rather like allotments within woodland clearings, and may have been abandoned after just one or two seasons. The crops grown by these early farmers must have been afforded special symbolic status. They grew like natural plants, yet they were controlled by people. This conflict between 'nature' and 'culture' is an interesting theme in Neolithic studies, and some archaeologists have argued that a whole series of binary oppositions may have been key to Neolithic peoples' understanding of their world: for example, culture-nature, domestic-wild, inside-outside, life-death, sun-moon. These may also have been linked to less tangible, but no less important, concepts such as good-evil or love-hate. This is an interesting idea, but, like so much in prehistoric studies, is ultimately unprovable.

The introduction of domestic beasts, including cattle, sheep, goats and pigs, was probably of greater significance in early Neolithic Upper Coquetdale than that that of domestic crops. These beasts could be integrated into a traditional mobile lifestyle, with people still moving seasonally around the landscape but now herding their stock rather than following wild herds. A system of transhumance (whereby people moved into the uplands with their beasts in the spring before returning to more lowland areas for the winter) was probably in place during the Neolithic: remnants of this system are still in place on many farms today, where the cattle are turned out onto the hills for the summer, although the presence of four-wheel drive vehicles means that there is now no longer a need for farmers to spend their summers up in the hills

3.2 A reconstruction of the Balbridie Neolithic 'house', Aberdeenshire, by David Hogg.

like their Neolithic ancestors. Animals were kept for much more than just meat. Skins would have been used for clothing, shelter, bedding and for the manufacture of a variety of receptacles, while many tools must have been made from bone. Oxen could be used for pulling ploughs in the fields, or as pack animals for moving goods along the network of tracks that must have existed between different settlement foci.

Exactly what these different settlements would have looked like is not known. Some were almost certainly seasonal camps, like those of the preceding Mesolithic. Others were probably permanently occupied throughout the year, and the degree of sedentism would have grown as more and more emphasis was gradually placed on farming. A recently discovered Neolithic 'house' in Scotland (fig. 3.2), dating from about 3600 BC, proved to be a substantial timber hall 25 metres in length, not unlike the great Dark Age halls of post-Roman times, such as Beowulf's *Heorot*. This Neolithic hall could have housed an extended family in as much comfort as that provided by most nineteenth-century rural cottages, and there is no reason why such buildings should not have existed in Neolithic Coquetdale. There is some doubt as to whether they were actually 'domestic' or were primarily 'ceremonial', but I doubt whether the people who lived in them made much of a distinction between the 'domestic' and 'ceremonial' aspects of their lives.

There were, of course, great changes in all aspects of life during the two and a half millennia covered by this chapter. However, it was the construction of a variety of ceremonial monuments, linked to the burial of the dead and the worship of the ancestors, which represents the greatest contribution of Neolithic and early Bronze Age people to today's archaeological landscapes (fig. 3.3). This is why I have labelled this chapter 'An Ancestral Landscape' and reserved the title 'An Agricultural Landscape' for Chapter 4, which covers the intensification of agriculture during the Bronze Age and subsequent Iron Age. While both arable and pastoral agriculture were introduced during the Neolithic, they were, I believe, only adopted on a relatively small scale, alongside traditional hunting and gathering strategies, prior

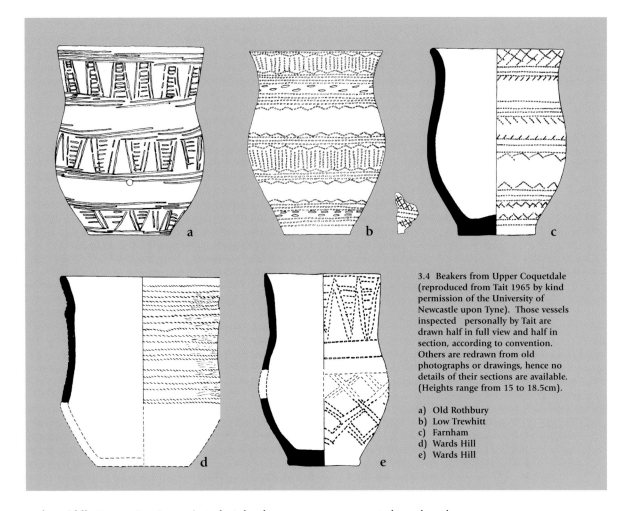

3.4 Beakers from Upper Coquetdale (reproduced from Tait 1965 by kind permission of the University of Newcastle upon Tyne). Those vessels inspected personally by Tait are drawn half in full view and half in section, according to convention. Others are redrawn from old photographs or drawings, hence no details of their sections are available. (Heights range from 15 to 18.5cm).

a) Old Rothbury
b) Low Trewhitt
c) Farnham
d) Wards Hill
e) Wards Hill

to the middle Bronze Age. Just as in today's landscape, some areas must always have been more suitable for grazing and/or hunting than for arable cultivation. These variations in landscape, coupled with differing attitudes towards farming between different groups of people, would have resulted in varying patterns of land use throughout different regions of Upper Coquetdale at any one time.

The Neolithic period saw the introduction of pottery. Fragments of pottery vessels are frequently recovered during archaeological excavations, and these can be crucial in dating sites from various periods of prehistory. In addition, the form and decoration of ceramic vessels reflect various aspects of the lives of the people who made and used them, and thus offer the archaeologist much potential for interpretation. Perhaps surprisingly, not even a single sherd of Neolithic pottery is known from Upper Coquetdale. We know from finds of flint and stone tools (discussed later in this Chapter) that Neolithic people were present here, but, due to its inherent fragility in comparison to stone, pot is rarely found other than through excavation. When we manage to locate and excavate some Neolithic settlements, we will find some Neolithic pottery, but as no such finds have yet been made we will not consider Neolithic pottery further in this volume. In contrast, many beautiful examples of early Bronze Age

3.5 This food vessel, found near Rothbury in the nineteenth century, is now in Alnwick Castle Museum. The splendid Alnwick Castle Catalogue of Antiquities, published in 1880, records it as 'a small, heavy urn formed of coarse materials, and apparently badly baked. It was found in 1876 in digging a drain near the Bull Bush Cottage, on Mr. Stephenson's Farm in Rothbury South Forest. It was in a cist formed of flat stones, having a flag both at bottom and top, and covered above by about six inches of gravel. Calcined bones were found in it; some are in it now. Height four inches, width at top four inches and a half, at bottom three inches.'

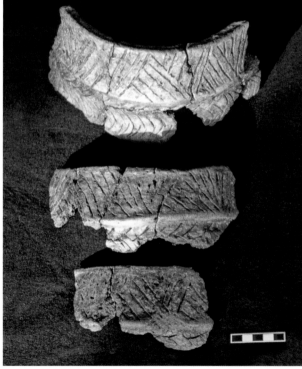

3.6 Rim fragments of a fine collared urn, now in the Newcastle upon Tyne Museum of Antiquities. Nothing is known of the context of this particular vessel, other than it was found 'near Rothbury'. (Scale in cms).

pottery have been recovered from burial sites throughout Upper Coquetdale.

The centuries around 2000BC represent the 'golden age' of prehistoric pottery production in Northumberland. Much effort was expended on the production of various forms of often very attractively decorated vessels, the classification of which can appear bewildering. The known examples from Upper Coquetdale fall largely into three general categories. The earliest of these are 'beakers', a distinctive group of often stunningly decorated vessels of elegant form which seem to have been introduced from the continent from about 2,400BC. Their name reflects the belief amongst nineteenth-century antiquarians that they were drinking vessels and were placed in the grave, possibly full of some form of alcoholic drink, to provide sustenance for the journey to the next world. The beakers may indeed have been prestigious drinking vessels, but exactly why they appeared in Britain at this time remains unknown. Some archaeologists believe that they were related to the widespread adoption of a new cult which involved communal drinking, but this theory might say more about the lifestyles of the archaeologists themselves than the ancient communities they study! In 1965, John Tait published a very useful little book cataloguing and illustrating all the known beakers from Northumberland and Durham (fig. 3.4). Out of a total of 106 finds, ten are from Upper Coquetdale, suggesting that this was an important region in the centuries from about 2,400BC.

While the beakers were thought by the early antiquarians to be for liquid sustenance, the next class of early Bronze Age funerary vessel commonly found in our region was thought to be for food, hence the rather uninspiring name 'food vessels' (fig. 3.5). Unlike the beakers, which were of an altogether alien form, the food vessels appear to have evolved out of native late Neolithic pottery traditions. They seem to have come into use slightly later than beakers, but were being placed with burials by c2,200BC. These often very attractive vessels display much variation in form and decoration, but generally have the shape of small bowls in contrast to the more upright form of the beakers. In 1978, Alex Gibson published an important corpus of all known early Bronze Age pottery in north-east England. His food vessel distribution map shows 122 sites, of which 13 (more than 10%) are in Upper Coquetdale. There are also larger vessels, which actually contained, rather than just accompanied, cremation burials. These are termed 'cinerary urns'. 90 such vessels are shown on Gibson's published distribution map, covering all of Northumberland and Durham, and 14 of these (more than 15%) are from Upper Coquetdale. These 14 examples are all 'collared urns', named (again, with little imagination!) after their characteristic, heavy collars (fig. 3.6). Collared urns seem to have been present in Britain from as early as the food vessels. There are also four examples of miniature vessels, sometimes known as 'incense cups', recorded as having been found in Upper Coquetdale (fig. 3.7). These are sometimes found within larger vessels, but their function is not known. It is unclear whether the beakers, food vessels, collared urns and miniature vessels had everyday uses on settlement sites (eg for cooking or storage), whether they were only used on special occasions, or whether they were intended primarily as funerary vessels. Answers to such questions will only be ascertained when a number of settlement sites are located and excavated. A number of pots from local early Bronze Age burials are illustrated and discussed later in this chapter.

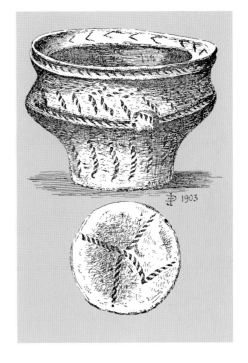

3.7 'Incense cup' from Hepple, drawn by John Turnbull Dixon. (Height 4 cm).

Ancestral monuments of the Neolithic

Although the adoption of agriculture was a milestone in the evolution of human society, it would be very wrong to think of it as the only major development in the Neolithic. In fact, recent accounts have suggested that the main single characteristic of the Neolithic was the development of a whole new way of living in, and thinking about, the world. It saw the building of the first great architectural monuments. In Britain, the earliest of these seem to have been the so-called 'causewayed enclosures' (large banked and ditched enclosures with many gaps or causeways providing access to a central area) and a variety of communal tombs. Later Neolithic monuments include stone circles and banked and ditched enclosures known as henges, which probably functioned as great open-air temples. Stonehenge, although in many ways atypical, is the best-known example.

Neolithic monuments may have been built as part of the process of claiming territory for a

3.8 The 1994 excavation trench at Harehaugh Camp. Although the results of such 'keyhole' excavations can be misleading, especially on complex sites like Harehaugh, this investigation led to a fascinating suggestion. The excavator, Clive Waddington, recognised an early bank, the construction of which was dated to about 3,100BC, sealed beneath the hillfort rampart. Clive interprets this as probable evidence for a Neolithic enclosure on the site, although he is the first to agree that further work is needed to test this hypothesis.

particular community: once the bones of the ancestors had been placed within a tomb, or used to sanctify a temple, then those ancestors perhaps laid claim to that land for their descendants for all time. In what must have been very superstitious times, most people looking for new land on which to settle would search elsewhere rather than risk incurring the wrath of the all-powerful ancestors by challenging the status quo. However they 'worked' and whatever they 'meant', the impact of these early monuments on the landscape, and on the minds of the people who experienced that landscape, must have been profound, far exceeding the strange feeling that we may experience today if suddenly confronted with an incongruous nuclear power station or military establishment in an otherwise 'natural' landscape. Once these monuments were built, the world could never be the same again. They could be re-worked and extended, but they re-defined the places where they were built forever. People would increasingly come to understand their world, and their place within it, by reference to such artificial monuments rather than to natural places.

To date, not a single monument in Upper Coquetdale has been scientifically dated to the Neolithic. Tantalisingly, a radiocarbon date of c3,100BC was obtained from charcoal from a burnt land surface sealed beneath an early bank, which was in turn sealed by the great hillfort ramparts at Harehaugh Camp (fig 3.8). Unfortunately, this comes from a very small excavation trench and we cannot yet state with any certainty that there is a Neolithic monument beneath the hillfort. On balance, given its critical position in the landscape above the natural pass into Redesdale, and the recovery of probable Neolithic flints from the site, I believe that there probably is a Neolithic monument or settlement of some kind at Harehaugh, perhaps a communal meeting place where representatives of local groups came together at certain times of year to engage in seasonal ceremonies and settle disputes, but more excavation will be necessary if this is ever to be proved or disproved. Within a few hundred metres of Harehaugh Camp are the Five Kings (of which only four remain, the fifth having been removed and

3.9a The Five Kings stone row, drawn by John Turnbull Dixon.

3.9b The site of the 'Five Kings' stone row can feel rather claustrophobic due to the adjacent conifer plantation, although a fine view eastwards down Coquetdale, which must surely have been of significance to those who built and used the monument, can still be enjoyed from the stones. *Photo: Matt Offer.*

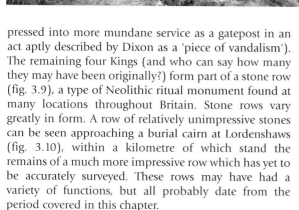

pressed into more mundane service as a gatepost in an act aptly described by Dixon as a 'piece of vandalism'). The remaining four Kings (and who can say how many they may have been originally?) form part of a stone row (fig. 3.9), a type of Neolithic ritual monument found at many locations throughout Britain. Stone rows vary greatly in form. A row of relatively unimpressive stones can be seen approaching a burial cairn at Lordenshaws (fig. 3.10), within a kilometre of which stand the remains of a much more impressive row which has yet to be accurately surveyed. These rows may have had a variety of functions, but all probably date from the period covered in this chapter.

Many stone rows, stone circles and tombs throughout

3.10 A row of small standing stones approaching a burial cairn at Lordenshaws.

Britain clearly have astronomical alignments built into them, for example towards the direction of midwinter sunrise or sunset. Much debate has raged amongst archaeologists as to the nature and purpose of these alignments. Some see Stonehenge as a great astronomical observatory, enabling astronomer-priests to predict events such as eclipses. Personally, and while not wishing to detract from the abilities of our Neolithic ancestors, I believe that such accounts are unrealistic in that they seek to impose elements of modern scientific enquiry on the ancient world. Certainly, people would have paid great attention to the movements of the stars and planets, as well as to those of the sun and moon, from the earliest times. My personal view is that alignments were not built into monuments to undertake 'scientific' observation of the heavens, but rather to provide a permanent bond between the eternal cycle of the heavens and the monuments (and through them the people) on earth.

Many people today tend to scoff at such things as the silly superstitions of ignorant, 'primitive' communities, but these people live in a world within which millions still pay serious attention to the complete absurdity of astrology. People pay money for experts to 'read their stars', and millions regularly read their horoscopes in newspapers and magazines. This is in spite of modern scientific knowledge, and really reflects nothing other than ignorance and superstitions. (Responsible editors who include such material in their otherwise respectable publications should perhaps reconsider why they do so: especially those who include horoscopes in children's magazines such as those I buy for my eight year-old daughter!) People back in prehistory would understandably look to the stars for all sorts of reasons. Today, we can ask different, and much more challenging, questions of those same stars, and to waste time and money on the nonsense of astrology is patently absurd.

3.11 The uninspiring mound on the near horizon in the centre of this view could be a Neolithic long cairn, perhaps the oldest surviving ancient monument in Upper Coquetdale. The Beacon, on which the cairn appears to be aligned, is in the background to the left.

The silent stones which survive today would once have been alive with myths and legends, constantly reminding people of their place within the world. The fact that many Neolithic tombs often contained disarticulated skeletons, often mixed up together, suggests that the community as a whole was regarded as of much greater significance than individuals. We don't know what proportion of people ended up in the tombs, but most bodies were probably disposed of by process known as 'excarnation', practised until recently by many native American societies. Bodies were put out into the landscape at special places, perhaps on timber scaffolds for crows and other birds to peck at, or buried in the ground for worms to eat, before a selection of bones was gathered up for incorporation into a communal tomb. Only much later, as we will see shortly, did people receive individual burials with grave goods which might represent 'superior' status in life. On balance, Neolithic society seems to have been

generally egalitarian, perhaps with 'elders' holding positions of authority on behalf of the community rather than to satisfy their own egos (a scenario which many present-day politicians might like to consider for a moment). These communities probably worked willingly together to build the great ceremonial monuments, and then benefited from them as a community rather than as individuals.

On the ridge across Harehaugh Hill, a short walk west of the hillfort, lies a much mutilated, turf-covered mound of stones about 30 metres in length (fig. 3.11). I first noted this many years ago, and was struck by the way its northern end was aligned with the distinctive summit of The Beacon (fig. 3.12). It was clearly a man-made structure, but surely it couldn't be a Neolithic long cairn? The surrounding area has been quarried for building stone and used for military training in more recent times, and my instinct was to account for this pile of stones as somehow related to this relatively recent activity. But it continued to niggle away at me, and I would visit it from time to time with different archaeologists, all of whom would reply 'yes, maybe'. Several years later, I took my newly appointed colleague Dr Rob Young to see this pile of stones. Rob is a nationally respected prehistorian who would surely have been a Professor of Archaeology by now, had he not opted to pack in the academic life and return to his native north-east to work for the Northumberland National Park Authority: his opinion on anything archaeological is one for which I have the utmost respect. Within seconds of walking up on to the mound of stones at Harehaugh, he pronounced, with some authority 'long cairn!'. That was good enough for me. The more we looked at it and discussed it, the more we convinced ourselves that it must be a long cairn, probably some 6,000 years old and quite probably the oldest visible ancient monument in Upper Coquetdale.

In summer 2005 the newly-founded Upper Coquetdale Community Archaeology Project (see Chapter 6) undertook a two week survey and excavation project here, under the direction of Peter Carne of Durham University. This work proved that the mound was at least partially

3.12 Sunset behind the Beacon, on which the Harehaugh 'long cairn' seems to have been aligned. The Beacon is crowned with a large round cairn, and may itself have been of considerable spiritual significance to local Neolithic people.
Photo: Matt Offer.

3.13 A well preserved burial cist was discovered during the 2005 excavation of the Harehaugh 'long cairn'. It may have been part of the original structure, or may have been added at a later stage. It was presumably constructed to hold a cremation, but no trace of a burial was found during the excavation.

3.14 Aerial view of
Bellshiel Law long
cairn.
Photo: Tim Gates.

artificial in origin, and, although not a typical long cairn, had functioned as a ceremonial site in Neolithic or Bronze Age times (fig. 3.13). However, the original form of the site, and its development through time, remains uncertain. This demonstrates both the fascination and the frustration of prehistory: we know we have discovered an important site, but its exact nature must await further excavation which is unlikely to take place in the near future.

Just over the watershed in neighbouring Redesdale, on the Otterburn Training Area, a great long cairn 112 metres in length survives at Bellshiel Law (fig. 3.14). This may originally have contained one or more chambers in which the dead were laid to rest during the earlier Neolithic, perhaps 6,000 years ago. It is also quite possible that some of the large round cairns in prominent landscape settings, such as those on Crigdon Hill and the Beacon, Simonside, may prove to be Neolithic. A large circular bank of stones more than ten metres in diameter can be seen a little to the west of the large round cairn on the Beacon. This is dismissed in the Northumberland Sites and Monuments Record as a collapsed sheep stell, but it may well be a Neolithic or Bronze Age ceremonial structure, perhaps a cremation cemetery.

The great stone circles of the Lake District, such as Long Meg, Castlerigg and Swinside have been much studied over the years, but their chronology and purpose are still not well understood. In Northumberland, only a few large stone circles are known, none of which approach those of the Lake District in the grandeur of their architecture. It is not known for sure whether these circles are of earlier or later Neolithic date, but they were probably constructed within a few centuries either side of 3000BC. About 30km north of Rothbury, in the Milfield Basin near Wooler, several henges have been discovered, dating to the late Neolithic or early Bronze Age (about 2000BC). Recent fieldwork by Clive Waddington has begun to provide a landscape context for these henges, demonstrating that contemporary settlements were also located here. The evidence for these settlements comes largely in the form of worked flint tools picked up from the surface of ploughed fields, a technique which has also borne fruit in Upper Coquetdale and which will be considered later in this Chapter. I am convinced that some Neolithic monuments, perhaps not unlike those of the Milfield Basin, must have been constructed in Upper Coquetdale, but many may have been destroyed by later agriculture, quarrying or building work. There is certainly still a chance that some such sites could be discovered here, either accidentally during construction or agricultural work, or through careful archaeological survey.

Rock art

Most archaeological monuments, and indeed finds, have a primary purpose that we can readily understand, even if we can't hope to know much of the detail about how such sites and finds were used by ancient people. Thus, houses are for shelter, tombs are for burials, axes are for chopping, and knives for cutting. Even

3.15 The 'main rock' at Lordenshaws, photographed by Tony Hopkins and drawn by Stan Beckensall.

mysterious sites such as henges and stone circles can be seen as places for communal ceremonies, even if we can never know the nature of the ceremonies. But what are we to make of the abstract rock carvings known as 'cup-and-ring marks' which litter the fell sandstones above Rothbury?

These rock carvings were first reported in Northumberland in the mid-nineteenth century, and

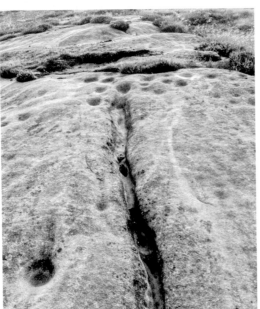

3.16 Various
examples of rock art
at Lordenshaws.

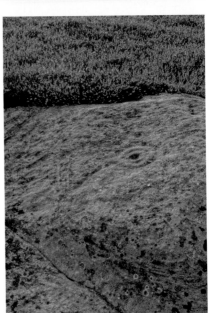

the great Alnwick antiquarian George Tate published a perceptive and beautifully illustrated book about them in 1865. In this, he makes mention of only one site in Coquetdale, the now destroyed decorated rock shelter of Cartington Cove (just south of Old Rothbury hillfort), observing that:

> concentric circles with central hollows were incised within this cave. Mr. Williamson of Alnwick, from whom I had this information, played around them when a boy more than fifty years ago; and they were then popularly called 'Cups and Saucers'. Nearly all of them have been destroyed by the wedges and hammers of quarrymen; but on visiting the spot in 1859, I found sufficient traces to confirm Mr. Williamson's testimony. This is the most southern locality in Northumberland, where inscriptions on a rock in situ have been discovered.

Today, it seems surprising that nobody had brought any of the decorated rocks at Lordenshaws (a little over 2km south of Cartington Cove) to Tate's attention. Some of the most spectacular and easily accessible rock art in the whole of Northumberland can be seen here (figs 3.15, 3.16). David Dippie Dixon had clearly inspected some of this, as he writes in *Upper Coquetdale* that 'Several large rocks in the vicinity of the camp bear those mysterious symbols found on sandstone rocks in the vicinity of other British camps in North Northumberland. These archaic sculptures consist of small pits or hollows and concentric circles with and without grooves, the meaning of which yet exercises the minds of many of our most eminent antiquarians.' Dixon, perhaps wisely, and in an approach adopted by many who came after him, avoided speculation as to the possible 'meaning' of the cup-and-ring marks. Having taken numerous guided walks around Lordenshaws, and delivered many public lectures on the subject throughout Northumberland, I am well aware that no archaeological subject generates greater fascination among people today than the mysteries of our cup-and-ring marks. I would be in trouble with some readers if I were to publish this book without offering some suggestions as to the 'meaning' of these ancient carvings, so I will set out some thoughts on this shortly.

The extraordinary variety and quality of rock carvings to be seen at Lordenshaws became more widely known with the publication of a paper by Edward Richmond Newbigin in the 1932 volume of *Archaeologia Aeliana*. This important paper, entitled *Notes on a series of unrecorded incised rocks at Lordenshaws*, describes seventeen previously unpublished sites at Lordenshaws and a number of others in the vicinity. It includes photographs of many of the carvings discussed. Some of the sites were discovered through the 'systematic uncovering and cleaning' of the rock surfaces, and a number of small mounds were excavated in an attempt to investigate a possible relationship between burials and rock art: 'the hope of establishing a connection was, however, entirely frustrated.' Newbigin observes that 'The number of marked rocks concentrated around Lordenshaws is greater than on any other site in Northumberland' and suggests that Lordenshaws may have been 'at some remote period something of a cult centre.' Unfortunately, though perhaps sensibly, he opts not to speculate as to the meaning of the markings, offering the familiar excuse that 'In what is intended to be only a descriptive account of hitherto unrecorded incised rocks, it would be out of place to make reference to the many unsolved problems which are raised by what has been discovered, and still more so to refer to any general theories on the subject of ancient cup markings'. He concludes:

> The question as to when and by whom these rock markings were made, what they originally signified, how their significance or associations were transferred from one object to another during the long centuries or even millenniums in which the cult prevailed here and elsewhere, are problems still awaiting investigation and solution by our archaeologists. Meantime, the raw material from which these conclusions will have to be drawn is by no means all in our possession, and the moors and hills of our

3.17 Two fine cup-and-ring marks near the intriguingly named Football Cairn on Cartington Moor. *Photo: Stan Beckensall.*

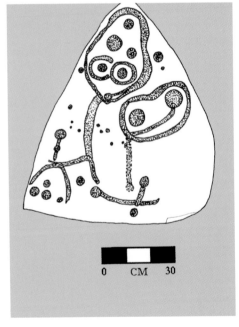

0   CM   30

3.18 The Cartington cist cover. *Drawn by Stan Beckensall.*

own area may still yield evidence of the activities of a forgotten age to those who care to occupy their time and energy in searching for them.

This brings us neatly to the one-man rock art phenomenon that is Stan Beckensall. Nobody has, or ever will, allocate more time and energy to the study of local rock art than Stan has done over the past four decades. Much of his work can be inspected on the recently completed Beckensall Archive Project website. This includes illustrations, including many of Stan's own drawings and photographs, of all known rock art sites in Northumberland. The project was directed at Newcastle University by Aron Mazel, who was able to apply his vast experience of rock art in his native South Africa to the study of Northumberland. Anyone interested in local rock art should join the many thousands of people around the world who have already spent some time inspecting this website (http://rockart.ncl.ac.uk).

In the 1960s, Stan lived in Malta, where he developed an interest in the extraordinary Maltese Neolithic tombs and their unique rock art based on spirals and other motifs. In 1966 he returned to England to train teachers at Alnwick College of Education, subsequently becoming head teacher at Dr. Thomlinson Middle School, Rothbury. As he began to explore the Northumberland landscape, he became increasingly fascinated, perhaps even obsessed, by the unexplained rock art to be found throughout the surrounding hills. His one-man mission to accurately record (using a combination of careful wax rubbing, drawing and photography) every decorated rock in northern England was soon underway. He has written many books and papers on rock art, and, in addition, has recently published a wide-ranging book about prehistoric Northumberland and a highly readable and atmospheric account of some

3.19 Rock art at Scrainwood.
Photo: Stan Beckensall.

of his favourite places in Northumberland entitled *Northumberland: The Power of Place.* His recent three books on rock art in Northumberland, Cumbria and Britain as a whole (which I reviewed together in *Northern Archaeology* under the title 'Lord of the Cup-and-Rings: the Beckensall Trilogy'), represent an excellent introduction to the subject for those who wish to know more about it. All in all, Stan's achievement is phenomenal, especially when it is considered that he never had any formal archaeological training. Without his contribution, much of the recent research into the rock art of northern England would have been impossible.

In 1983, Stan published *Northumberland's Prehistoric Rock Carvings: A Mystery Explained.* This was a rather naughty title, as it misled some people into thinking that the book would solve the mystery rather than simply explain it. In reality, even the 'Lord of the Cups-and-Rings' himself would freely admit to being incapable of providing a satisfactory solution to this particular mystery. An updated and much improved version of this book was published in 2001 under the title *Prehistoric Rock Art in Northumberland.* This opens with a discussion of the main rock at Lordenshaws, and includes details of all known rock art sites in the county. Of particular relevance to the present discussion are the sections entitled 'North of Rothbury' and 'Lordenshaw' (which Stan opts to spell without its final 's'). The sites north of Rothbury (which are actually north-west rather than north of the town) include a beautiful example adjacent to a large burial cairn known for some reason as 'Football Cairn' (fig. 3.17). There are a number of less spectacular motifs on exposed rock surfaces on Chirnell's Moor, at Crocky's Heugh, adjacent to the track known as the Cartington Carriageway, in the grounds of Westcliffe House,

3.20 Stan Beckensall with a recently discovered cup-and-ring marked stone at Biddlestone.

3.21 Stan Beckensall and Richard Bradley pictured during a visit to Coquetdale in the early 1990s.

and around the Iron Age hillfort of West Hills. The sadly destroyed decorated rock shelter known as Cartington Cove has already been discussed: this may have been used for ceremonial activity of some kind and may even have contained burials. A decorated slab from Cartington (fig. 3.18), now in the Museum of Antiquities in Newcastle, was found face down in the ground: it may originally have been a cover-slab for a burial, although no evidence of a burial was recorded when the slab was found. Elsewhere in Upper Coquetdale, a few outlying decorated rocks have been recorded (at Alnham, Scrainwood (fig. 3.19), Biddlestone (fig. 3.20), Clennell and Debdon Moor), and more are bound to be found in future. Nowhere, however, does the concentration or the variety of sites approach that found at Lordenshaws.

Rock art studies, in Britain and throughout Europe, received a major boost when Professor Richard Bradley of Reading University became involved in the subject in the 1990s (fig. 3.21). Richard is one of the world's most able and popular prehistorians, and seems capable of coming up with new ways of thinking about just about any subject, enabling the development of new theories and the asking of previously unrehearsed questions. It is largely thanks to him that rock art is now taught in our universities alongside more conventional aspects of Neolithic and Bronze Age studies. I had the good fortune to study under Richard for a couple of years in the early 1990s, just at the time that he was getting stuck into his rock art research. In addition to being educational, his fieldwork campaigns were always great fun, with good accommodation and food - circumstances which certainly do not apply to all undergraduate fieldwork projects! One student told me that he preferred Richard's projects to others 'because it was much nicer walking round a beautiful landscape looking at rock art than the alternative of getting cold and muddy digging holes in the ground!' This rather negative attitude may have applied to a few students, but most benefited enormously from these projects, as indeed I did, by learning new ways of thinking about the landscape. In addition to running several rock art related fieldwork campaigns, in Britain and abroad, Richard Bradley has also published many thought-provoking papers on rock art, and his book *Rock Art and the Prehistory of Atlantic Europe: Signing the Land* is recommended reading for anyone requiring more than a superficial introduction to the subject.

My first experience of rock art in Upper Coquetdale was during a visit to Lordenshaws during

one of Richard's projects in summer 1992. Having familiarised myself with the area, I was most amused, a few months later, to find myself in exactly the same place during a trip organised as part of the interview process for the newly created post of Northumberland National Park Archaeologist. I doubt whether my pronouncements on the local rock art had much to do with my subsequent appointment, but they clearly didn't do me any harm! Subsequent visits to Lordenshaws, often while leading public walks or student trips, have done much to influence my own thinking about rock art. On one such visit, I noticed a previously unrecorded low cairn, presumably a burial cairn, partially overlying the well known 'Horseshoe Rock', and began to wonder about the relationship between rock art and burial cairns (fig. 3.22).

3.22 The Horseshoe Rock at Lordenshaws. A low circular mound, probably a burial cairn, lies immediately upslope of the decorated panel. The main decorated rock (fig. 3.15) at Lordenshaws can be seen on the horizon. *Photo: Aron Mazel.*

At Lordenshaws, several burial cairns were built adjacent to panels of rock art, and one cairn appears to have cup-marked kerbstones, but it is not possible to say much about the relationship between the cairns and the art on the basis of the surface evidence alone. Similar relationships have been recorded elsewhere in Northumberland and further afield, but the nature of the relationship between cairn and art can be difficult to establish even when sites are excavated. Rock art on, within, or beneath a cairn does not necessarily imply that the two are of the same date: on the one hand, already ancient decorated stones can be incorporated into a cairn, while on the other, decoration can be added to stones long after a cairn was originally constructed, perhaps during a later remodelling of a site.

Stan Beckensall and I recently examined the relationship between cairns and art in a *Northern Archaeology* paper entitled 'Questions of Chronology: the Case for Bronze Age Rock Art in Northern England'. In this, we concluded that there is no clear evidence for the production of cup-and-ring marks during the Bronze Age, and that all open air rock art on naturally occurring boulders and outcrops is probably of Neolithic date. However, we were unable to conclude with any degree of certainty when in the Neolithic the practice commenced, or when it ceased. Today, on balance, I believe that the practice of decorating exposed rock surfaces with cup-and-ring marks probably originated during the early Neolithic, perhaps in the centuries around 3500BC. They may originally have been produced in upland grazing areas, with their purpose, at least in part, perhaps being to define a particular group's rights to graze their cattle over a certain area during the summer months. During the early Bronze Age, as people began living in permanently occupied settlements throughout the landscape, ancient seasonal patterns of exploitation died out, and the old panels of rock art became redundant. They apparently retained some significance in some places, as panels were occasionally incorporated within later burial cairns, but their meaning in such contexts must have been very different from the thinking behind their original production. People in later prehistory must have regarded them as mysterious relics of an earlier time, just as we do today, but they would undoubtedly have had their own fascinating accounts of how the rock art came to be.

Regardless of their possible chronology and function, can we say anything of the original 'meaning' of these ancient motifs? As already discussed, this is dangerous ground for the archaeologist. Ever since the mid-nineteenth century many 'experts' have avoided being drawn into extended discussion of the subject for fear of damaging their reputations, often painstakingly built on more mundane but 'scientific' foundations. Nevertheless, I believe that we can usefully consider some possibilities, although we must, of course, accept that we will never know for sure what the motifs 'meant' to those who created them.

In 1979, the late Ronald Morris (who was, in effect, Stan Beckensall's equivalent in Scotland) published a list of 104 possible explanations of cup-and-ring marks that he had heard over the years. These range from the patently absurd to the eminently reasonable. Amongst the former we might list messages from outer space, breasts, sacred wine or sacrificial blood holders, tattooists' shop windows, copies of worm casts, clocks, maps of settlements or stars, gaming tables, and children's graffiti. My personal favourite on Morris' list is the suggestions that cup-and-ring marks might represent 'marks of sexual prowess - the Chief made a cup-and-ring to celebrate each female conquest he made'. While implying that all chiefs were male, which need not necessarily have been the case, this theory fails to account for the variation in rock art motifs: most sexual conquests apparently warranted only a simple cup-mark while a few resulted in great big motifs with multiple rings - the mind boggles! To be fair to Ronald Morris, he regarded this suggestion as most unlikely.

To search for simple meanings behind the cupmarks and cup-and-ring motifs is almost certainly misguided, as I have no doubt that the symbolism behind the motifs was complex. Richard Bradley summarises this point with his customary eloquence:

> By its very simplicity a cup and ring, breached by a radial line, could mean many different things, and those meanings might well have changed during the currency of British and Irish rock art. Thus it could have reflected the tunnel imagery experienced during states of altered consciousness and might also symbolise the characteristic ground plan of a passage tomb. In a later phase the same motif might signify the organisation of a henge or a setting of monoliths. It could also stand for a 'circular' perception of space that referred to the landscape extending out from those sites. Alternatively, we could think of the monuments themselves as an embodiment of the wider world, as a metaphor for that landscape and a model of the cosmos. If so, then each of the carvings concentrated those same ideas into an image that could be deployed in many different settings.

I must resist the temptation to enter into an extended discussion of this particular subject (that must await another book!), but, because I know that many readers will be fascinated by the possibilities, I will briefly review three of my own recent papers which sought, amongst other things to address the possible 'meaning' of cup-and-ring marks.

It is interesting to note that Ronald Morris' list, referred to above, includes many references to sex and fertility, by no means all of which are ridiculous. Just as with the identification of 'drinking vessels' discussed earlier, we must avoid the temptation to impose our own prejudices on prehistoric people. It is hard to believe, however, that sex and procreation were not of fundamental importance to people back in the Neolithic, even if the expression of that importance was reflected in different ways from those of the modern western world. This view is expressed in a fascinating but rarely quoted little book entitled *Archaic Rock Inscriptions*, published anonymously in 1891, which I recently reviewed in a paper entitled *The Phallic Explanation: A Late Nineteenth-Century Solution to the Cup-and-Ring Conundrum.* Having been published in 1891, this book might have been available to David Dippie Dixon, though we shall probably never know whether or not he had access to it. If he did, then given his religious views he may not have had much time for it, though I would like to think that he would have approached it with an open mind. The book was published as part of the 'Nature Worship and Mystical Series', with companion volumes covering such fascinating topics as 'the mysteries of sex worship', 'serpent worship', 'phallic objects', and 'phallic tree worship'. After a discussion of rock art throughout the world, the book concludes, perhaps not surprisingly, that the cup-and-rings marks are of a sexual nature. But this does not mean that they simply represent human copulation. Rather, the author of *Archaic Rock Inscriptions* believes that the symbols relate to 'the worship of the creative and regenerative forces of nature'. I believe that he is probably right, at least in part.

In 1996, at a conference covering British and American archaeology, I gave a paper entitled *Interpreting the Ambiguous: Prehistoric Rock Art in Northern England and the American South-West.* (This was later incorporated into an edited volume, also entitled *Interpreting the Ambiguous*, which covers archaeological interpretation generally). The reason for writing this paper was to examine the ways in which students of British rock art, such as that in Upper Coquetdale, might benefit from an understanding of American rock art, some of which is remarkably similar and which is still regarded by modern Native American communities as 'sacred messages from the ancestors'. Campbell Grant, a widely respected scholar of American art, tells us that 'the world of the aboriginal Indian, where the supernatural was as real as the natural, is a world we cannot enter but nothing prevents us from enjoying the intriguing pictures that still exist by the thousands in caves and on cliffs'. This is equally true of British rock art, but our enjoyment of the sites is all the more fulfilling if we can offer some possibilities.

The possibility of learning from ethnographic studies also underlay part of my 1996 *Northern Archaeology* paper entitled 'Spirals in Time: Morwick Mill and the Spiral Motif in the British Neolithic'. This started with a description of the most unusual site of Morwick, which consists of a variety of curvilinear motifs, including several spirals, on a river cliff above the Coquet near Warkworth. This is too far down the Coquet to be considered in detail in this volume, and the art here is very different from that of Upper Coquetdale, but some of the conclusions within the paper are of relevance to cup-and-ring art generally. Certain traits within contemporary or recent ethnic communities throughout the world that might be of relevance to British prehistory are sometimes termed 'ethnographic parallels', but I prefer to think of them as 'ethnographic possibilities'. The fact that rock art motifs in America or Australia are similar to some from Neolithic Britain does not mean that similar thought processes necessarily lay behind them all. However, our minds can be opened to some possibilities that may never have occurred to us without access to the ethnographic data.

As stated above, I believe that the symbolism enshrined within the cup-and-ring marks is probably complex and multi-facetted, but one element of it may be a concept of life on earth as a journey to a 'central place', perhaps the world of the ancestors. This view is based on the cosmology of the Zuni People in the American south-west, and, without going into detail here, I believe that it neatly complements other elements of British Neolithic archaeology. This last fact is important, and also reminds us that rock art must not be studied in isolation. In the past it was largely ignored by academics, but today, all of a sudden, rock art research seems to have a life all of its own, and there is a risk of it being studied without adequate reference to the wider Neolithic world. This must be avoided if we hope to make progress with both rock art studies and the wider study of the Neolithic. There is still much to be done, and Upper Coquetdale offers many opportunities to the field archaeologist with an interest in rock art. Why are the motifs where they are and not elsewhere? How does their distribution relate to contemporary patterns of settlement, or to the distribution of ceremonial sites or burials? Did their significance change through time? Does their location appear to have influenced subsequent activity, such as the location of later burial cairns? Such questions are of interest in their own right, but attempts to answer them should also be of value to wider studies of Neolithic people, both in Upper Coquetdale and elsewhere.

The motifs employed in rock art must have been used in other media: perhaps on clothing, as tattoos, in jewellery, and carved on a variety of wooden structures and implements. They would certainly have been linked with myths, and related to music, dance and storytelling, perhaps incorporated into fabulous masks and costumes for use on special occasions. The production of rock art may, however, have been of special significance, as cold, hard stone is linked in some societies with death, and consequently with the world of the dead and of the ancestors. Amongst native American communities, the circle is of special significance, signifying continuity and infinity, and encompassing a concept of cyclical time. This is in contrast to our modern concept of 'linear time', within which everything has a beginning and an end. It is possible, therefore, that the cup-and-ring marks symbolised time, by reference to the various never-ending cycles (eg solar, seasonal, lunar) within which people live their lives on earth. They may also have represented individual life cycles, from birth through life to death and possible rebirth, either here on earth or elsewhere.

One further issue which we should consider in relation to the cup-and-ring marks is that of shamanism and altered states of consciousness. Recent accounts of the magnificent Palaeolithic cave paintings of the Dordogne and elsewhere have stressed the probable role of shamanism in its origin, and this may be no less relevant to the abstract art of Neolithic Britain. Shamanic practices have been documented over the past couple of centuries in various societies throughout Australia, North and South America, Siberia and Africa. In all cases, there are certain underlying trends which are common to the role of Shamans. As mentioned in the previous chapter, these include going into trances which can be induced in various ways such as through the ingestion of hallucinogenic substances or by repetitive music and dancing. While in a trance, the shamans are often regarded by others as having temporarily left this world to commune with the ancestors. When they return, their 'visions' (that we would term 'hallucinations') are interpreted as messages from the ancestors. Often, these visions incorporate abstract images (known to science as 'entoptic images') which we now know are created by neurological action within the part of the brain concerned with vision. These images can include concentric arcs and circles, and also 'herring-bone' patterns very similar to some decoration on late Neolithic/early Bronze Age pottery.

I have far less personal experience of altered states of consciousness than some of my archaeological colleagues, and certainly cannot claim to have seen any entoptic imagery myself. However, the results of ethnographic studies, coupled with recent laboratory experiments, leave little doubt in my mind that cup-and-ring marks (and much decoration on prehistoric pottery) owe their origin ultimately to images generated within the mind while under trance conditions. This is certainly not to claim that all carvings were produced by shamans to record their trips to see the ancestors, but simply that the origins of the motifs may lie in such activity. Once established as somehow special, the motifs could be copied and embellished by anyone, and their 'meanings' could be ambiguous and could change through time. Several people have commented to me over the years that the great cup-and-ring panels of Northumberland seem 'other worldly'. Perhaps this is because that is precisely what they are. Not because they were created by aliens, but because their origin lies ultimately in shamanic trips away from this world into the world of the ancestors. While such suggestions may initially appear outrageous to most modern westerners, shamanism was undoubtedly important in prehistoric Britain and would have seemed quite normal to Neolithic and Bronze Age residents of Upper Coquetdale. Just think for a moment about how you would interpret dreams without access to modern scientific research. To prehistoric people, dreams may have been regarded as just as real as the everyday world, giving glimpses into other places which could never be visited in this life. The shamans did visit such places, on behalf of the community, and what they 'saw' while away must have been of great importance to everyone. Much of our understanding of prehistory today comes from 'textbook' analysis of sites and finds, but anyone truly wishing to develop an understanding of the ways in our Neolithic ancestors may have viewed their world could do a lot worse than to read some ethnographic studies of shamanism.

I always begin public lectures about rock art with an apology to those members of the audience who have come to hear a definitive statement about 'the meaning of the cup-and-ring marks'. It should be clear from the above discussion that the provision of such a statement is simply impossible. The Neolithic world was very different from ours, and it is doubtful whether we would fully comprehend the original significance of a panel of rock art even if a Neolithic person could somehow be brought back to life to explain it to us. It may well be that much of the significance of the art lay in the actual process of its production, rather than in the motifs that were left behind, although these would certainly have been of some importance. Much of the power of abstract rock art may always have rested in its very ambiguity. Symbols have the power to represent thoughts without the need to specify or restrict those thoughts through the use of words. They exist within the everyday world, but can represent concepts from another dimension, beyond space and time.

Stan Beckensall has many talents in addition to his knowledge of prehistoric archaeology, and one of these is poetry. In 2001, he published the following revised version of his poem *The Sculptured Rocks* (originally published in 1974) which effectively reminds us that the study of our prehistoric past must involve art as well as science:

In this design you petrified the language of your soul -
Your own symbolic logic;
Linked a little world with universe,
Arrested time with space.
You saw the cycle of your birth and death with clarity
As sun and moon spun round,
As buds burst into leaves and fell upon the nourished ground.
A rhythmic pulse beat out like water flow,
Rippled from your centre to the stars.
The living rocks bear traces of belief,
Knowing all you used to know.
The curlew cry spills out
A plaintive, bubbling message to the moors
Above the desecrated graves and broken stones
As it has always done.
Its curved beak swings down from the sun
To execute parabolas in heather-scented air,
Or sink in silence to an unresponsive earth.

Beakers and burials of the early Bronze Age

Conventionally, the Neolithic is regarded as having given way to the Bronze Age at some point between c2400BC and 2000BC. Bronze working was certainly introduced at this time, but many associated changes in society were gradual and can be seen to have their roots firmly in the native Neolithic. Archaeologists have now generally dismissed the old idea of an invading early Bronze Age 'warrior aristocracy', which displaced the native Neolithic communities by force and introduced metalworking, 'beakers' (supposedly for beer drinking) and other new forms of pottery, single burials in round cairns, and new types of settlement consisting of timber built round houses. This is not to deny, however, that there may have been some incomers at this time. Just as with the transition from Mesolithic to Neolithic, that from Neolithic to Bronze Age is not at all well understood and may have involved the movement of people as well as ideas.

The most common prehistoric monuments to be seen in today's landscape are round burial mounds, conventionally dated to the early Bronze Age (c2000BC). These are dome-shaped mounds of earth or stone, beneath and within which were placed burials. (In the uplands these monuments were usually built using mounds of stone and are known as 'cairns'; on lower land they were sometimes constructed using piles of earth or turf, in which case they are more normally referred to as 'barrows'). They vary substantially in form and situation: some, as discussed previously, may be of Neolithic date, but the vast majority date from the early Bronze Age. Some are massive, like the stunningly sited group of three cairns on Thirl Moor (fig. 3.23), near the Roman encampment at Chew Green, and the lonely Russell's Cairn (fig. 3.3), high on the Border Ridge (named after the unfortunate Lord Russell, who met his end near here in 1585, by which time the cairn must already have been standing for at least 3,500 years). Some incorporate interesting architectural features, such as the standing stones protruding from the turf-covered mound near Debdon Farm, on the south-east slopes of Cartington Hill. These may originally have formed a kerb around the cairn, or may have formed the inner face of a 'ring-mound' with an open centre. Such monuments are known elsewhere, and it seems that their interiors were sometimes used for cremation burials over long periods before eventually being infilled with rubble or earth. Some cairns are grouped in large cemeteries, such as the 'Five Barrows' cemetery on Holystone Common (fig. 3.24) where members of the Border Archaeological Society have recently recorded nearly fifty individual mounds, displaying much variation in form and size, all of which could contain burials. Such variation may relate to differences in date and function. Only careful excavation can untangle the often complex histories of both individual cairns and extensive cemeteries.

3.23 These three large round cairns occupy a commanding position on top of Thirl Moor, at a height in excess of 550m.
Photo:Tim Gates.

When discussing the detailed structure of these monuments, and the finds from them, it is easy to forget that they must have been very powerful sites for the people who built and used them. Attitudes to death must have been very different from those of today, but every death must have brought a degree of sadness, if not grief, to family and friends left behind. However, just as often happens today, mourners at a Bronze Age funeral ceremony probably used the occasion to celebrate the life of the deceased along with the fact that he or she would now be heading for a 'better place'. Funerals may not have been overly morbid affairs. Regardless of the nature of the ceremonies, they would presumably have been focussed on these now silent mounds of earth and stone, the careful examination of which can give us some clues to the burial rites of the time.

The cairns are conventionally assumed to be the final resting places of the Bronze Age elite, including chiefs, warriors and perhaps priests and metalsmiths. The fact that young children were occasionally buried within cairns has been used as evidence to argue that power may have become to an extent hereditary, with an emerging aristocracy holding sway over the masses. There may be something in this theory, but recent work suggests that things may never have been quite so clear-cut. For example, recent excavations at Ingram in the Breamish Valley, 15km north of Rothbury, have demonstrated that cremated remains were scattered over and within a cairn which contained earlier burials dating from a little before 2000BC. Perhaps the majority of people were cremated, after which their ashes were gathered up along with bits of pyre debris and simply scattered over the local sacred cairn, where one or more known ancestors, perhaps gradually retreating into myth as time went by, were also interred.

The emphasis placed by Neolithic and early Bronze Age people on burial monuments can appear morbid to our eyes, but we must not forget that the risk of death was ever present in their society. Infant mortality and death during childbirth would have been commonplace, and life expectancy was probably only about 35 years. This is very different from western society today, where we expect to live to a ripe old age and can live our entire lives without even seeing a dead body, other than on television.

The move towards single burial in round cairns has been linked by some archaeologists with a move towards a concept of a 'historic' rather than an 'ancestral' past. The dead, rather than being added to the bones of the ancestors in the communal tombs, now had their own

3.25 *Above:* An exposed cist within an excavated cairn at Lordenshaws.
Below: A massive cist within Football Cairn on Cartington Moor. *Photo: Stan Beckensall.*
These cists were probably opened in Victorian times, if not earlier, and it is not known what, if anything, was found within them. They would have originally contained one or more inhumation or cremation burials, and would have been the focus of funeral ceremonies such as that recreated by Jim Proudfoot *(opposite)*.

individual monuments: the emphasis was now on the individual rather than the community as a whole. These monuments may have been named after the person or group of people originally buried within them, and stories associated with these people presumably remained in communal memory for at least a few generations. So far as we know, however, these cairns had no equivalents of 'headstones', so knowledge of their original occupants must have faded with the passage of time. The cairns thus became, albeit on a more local level, the final resting place of the ancestors, just like the great Neolithic tombs of earlier times. They represented the dead within the everyday landscape, and were no doubt associated with stories held within communal memory and learned by generation after generation. The burial cairns linked the mythical past with the present, and helped to provide a stable platform on which to face the uncertainties of the future. It is, in my view, quite reasonable to consider these early Bronze Age cairns as part of the 'Ancestral Landscape', even though they differ in many respects from the great ancestral monuments of the Neolithic, some of which had been built 2000 years earlier.

Several Bronze Age cairns have been excavated in Upper Coquetdale, but it is important to note that most were examined in Victorian times, when methods of excavation and recording were rather less refined than those of today (fig. 3.25). Thus, whereas the recent excavation of a couple of cairns at Ingram took a team of twenty students some twelve weeks (spread over four years) to complete, followed by many more weeks of post-excavation work in the laboratory, a typical Victorian barrow dig could be over and done with in a morning. Barrow-digging was considered by some of its practitioners as a kind of aristocratic sport, the sole objective of which was to recover pots and any other artefacts (such as occasional bronze, jet or amber objects) to display on the mantelpiece. There are many cairns and barrows throughout Northumberland that have clearly been dug into, but from which we have no idea what may have been recovered. It is fortunate that David Dippie Dixon, and others like him in other areas, were around to record the investigation of some such sites for posterity.

The greatest of all barrow diggers in north-east England was Canon William Greenwell, who discusses the results of his fieldwork in a monumental 763 page volume entitled *British Barrows*, published in 1877. In addition to undertaking his own fieldwork, Greenwell was also an avid collector of prehistoric artefacts and his personal collection of objects from more than 400 sites, now in the British Museum, is one of British prehistory's most important reference collections. While preparing the lectures on which this account is based, I sought access to this

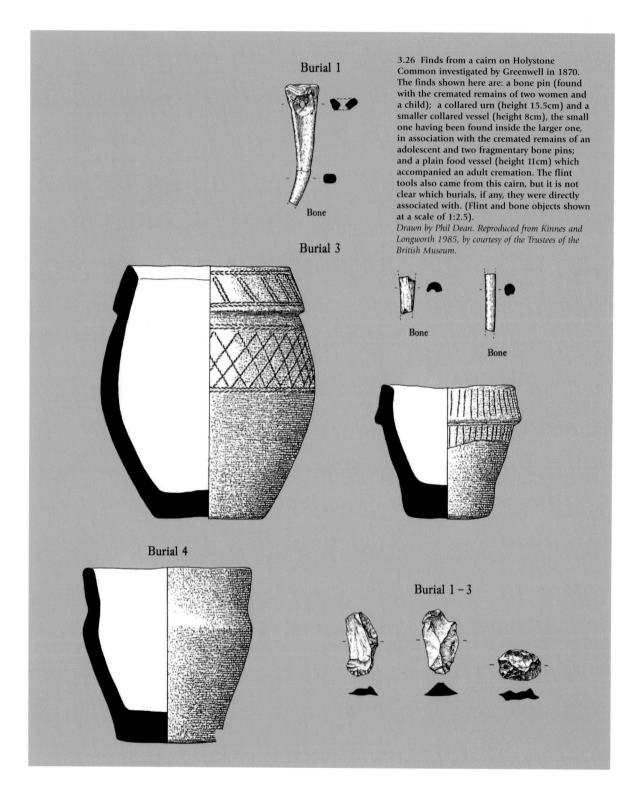

Burial 1

Bone

3.26 Finds from a cairn on Holystone Common investigated by Greenwell in 1870. The finds shown here are: a bone pin (found with the cremated remains of two women and a child); a collared urn (height 15.5cm) and a smaller collared vessel (height 8cm), the small one having been found inside the larger one, in association with the cremated remains of an adolescent and two fragmentary bone pins; and a plain food vessel (height 11cm) which accompanied an adult cremation. The flint tools also came from this cairn, but it is not clear which burials, if any, they were directly associated with. (Flint and bone objects shown at a scale of 1:2.5).
Drawn by Phil Dean. Reproduced from Kinnes and Longworth 1985, by courtesy of the Trustees of the British Museum.

Burial 3

Bone

Bone

Burial 4

Burial 1 – 3

collection in order to obtain photographs of some of the most beautiful specimens of early Bronze Age pots from Coquetdale. Regrettably, everything was in 'indefinite long-term storage' pending a possible reorganisation of the Museum's stores. It would be nice if some of this material could one day be put on permanent display in Northumberland, where it could be fully appreciated by local people as well as tourists. But I suppose the same argument applies to the Elgin Marbles and numerous other fabulous objects from the Ancient World, all of which seem destined to remain in London. In 1985, however, much to the British Museum's credit, it published a splendid volume describing and illustrating the entire Greenwell collection, including many finds from Upper Coquetdale. Unfortunately, this publication does not include photographs, but the pots are beautifully drawn in a traditional archaeological style to show their form (in section) and decoration (fig. 3.26).

Greenwell's *British Barrows* contains details of 220 excavated round barrows. Most of these (162) are in Yorkshire, but the book contains a chapter about Northumberland (31 sites),

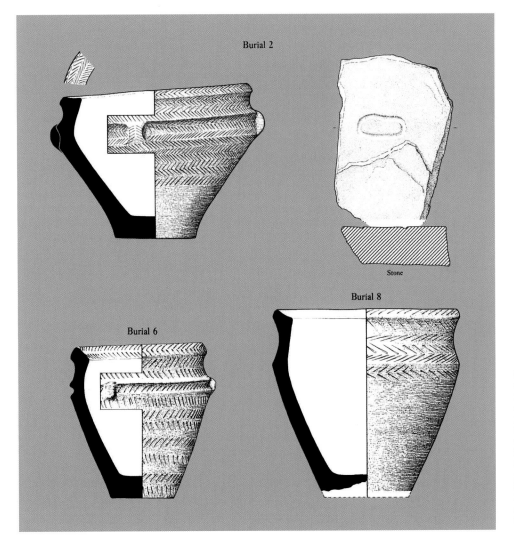

3.27 Three fine food vessels (heights 12.5, 13 and 16cm) and a curious carved stone (length c60cm) from the Harbottle Peels cairn.
Drawn by Phil Dean. Reproduced from Kinnes and Longworth 1985, by courtesy of the Trustees of the British Museum.
See also Fig. 3.28

within which are sections specifically about the parishes of Alwinton and Rothbury, each of which includes details of four excavated sites. These eight Upper Coquetdale sites are the fascinating cairn at Harbottle Peels, two cairns within the 'Five Barrows' cemetery on Holystone Common, one near Holystone Grange, two cairns at Lordenshaws/Burgh Hill, and two on Cartington Moor. Many attractive pots and other objects were recovered from these investigations. Interestingly, Greenwell records having found the burnt remains of a young sheep or goat amongst human remains at one of the Holystone Common cairns. Whether this was intended as food for the journey to the afterlife, or was the product of some other form of ritual activity, must remain open to conjecture. Greenwell also makes reference to other local sites examined by others, at Tosson and at Hepple. Dixon discusses Greenwell's excavations at some length in Chapter VII of *Upper Coquetdale*, so we will avoid repetition of the detail here, other than to give a flavour of his work by reference to his examination of the Harbottle Peels site (figs. 3.27, 3.28).

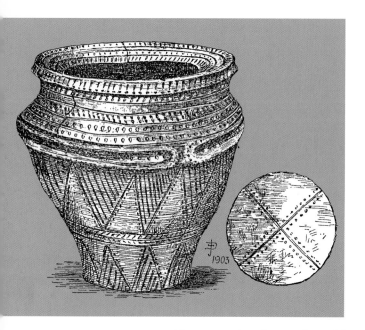

3.28 John Turnbull Dixon's drawing of the food vessel from Harbottle Peels which Canon Greenwell considered to be the second most beautiful of its class from the whole of Britain. (Height 12.5cm).

The Harbottle Peels cairn had been almost completely dismantled for walling stone when a stone cist was discovered, thus bringing the site to Greenwell's attention. The cairn was found to contain four separate stone-built cists, one of which had as one of its side-stones a sandstone slab with 'a very peculiar figure cut in outline with some fine-pointed tool, the marks left by which are as sharp as if made only yesterday. It is reniform or perhaps more like the shape of a human foot, $5^3/4$ in. long, and 3 in. wide at the broadest part.' The significance of this carving is unknown, but its freshness suggests that it was inscribed into the stone at the time the cist was constructed, as it had clearly undergone no weathering prior to deposition within the cairn. Greenwell considered the cairn to have contained the remains of at least nine individuals, three of which, including one child, were cremated. He recovered from this cairn a particularly fine food vessel (fig. 3.28) which he considered to be:

with one exception, the most beautiful specimen of its class, both in fabric and ornamentation, I have ever met with. The style of decoration will be best understood by a reference to the figure; the markings appear to be due to different applications of the same pointed instrument, which has sometimes been drawn over the moist clay, at other times inserted directly into it, by which means both lines and dots have been produced. It possesses the unusual feature of being ornamented on the bottom, where is a cross, formed by two transverse lines, with a series of dots along each side of the limbs.

Greenwell must have inspected many hundreds of food vessels from all over Britain and it is gratifying to think that his second favourite of the entire lot was found in Upper Coquetdale, where it was presumably designed and manufactured by a local person, some 4,000 years ago.

In 1858, four cists, apparently within a low cairn or barrow, and each containing a body, were uncovered by workmen quarrying limestone near Great Tosson, on the northern fringes of the Simonside Hills. The main finds from these cists found their way to Canon Greenwell's collection, and are now in the British Museum (fig. 3.29). They include two splendid food largely dismantled to provide stone for a nearby plantation wall in the nineteenth century, when three cists containing 'ashes and bones' were discovered. When visiting the site on a fine, clear day in early Summer 2002, I suddenly saw something I had never expected. Far away to the east, within the only long distance view obtainable from the cairn, was the distinctive profile of Black Stitchel, a remarkably regular natural little hill that looks for all the world like a large burial cairn. (Unfortunately it is unlikely to be investigated by archaeologists for some time as it lies within the OTA impact area, and is regularly targeted by tanks and missile launchers). But that was not all: Black Stitchel itself is framed in this view by the massive bulk of the Simonside range (fig. 3.34). Not the classic north or south elevation this time, but rather an oblique and very much less spectacular view that in itself would not justify comment. Nevertheless, it is still Simonside, and until or unless an alternative explanation is forthcoming from somewhere, I will continue to believe that the view in fig. 3.34 is crucial to an understanding of why this cairn was

3.34 Looking eastwards over one of the cists in Hare Cairn towards Simonside, with Black Stitchel just visible in the middle distance

3.35 The small stone circle at Fontburn, with the striking profile of Simonside just appearing over the near horizon.
Photo: Ian Hobson.

3.36 The 1908 excavation of the Low Trewhitt burial mound was directed by Dorothea M. A. Bate, who worked for the British Museum (Natural History) in the Department of Geology. Bate's excavation report includes some fascinating photographs which illustrate the rather crude excavation techniques of the day.

Above: The mound before excavation.

Left: An exposed cist within the mound.

Below: The fine beaker (carefully reconstructed using all the excavated fragments) from the mound's central cist.

built where it is. I am also aware of other monuments which appear to be located by reference to Simonside (fig. 3.35), and it may be that a student with an understanding of geographical information systems and nothing better to do could one day attempt a computer analysis of Neolithic and early Bronze Age monuments within the general vicinity to see whether any real patterns emerge: I would not be at all surprised if some did.

A small number of early Bronze Age burials have been investigated in the century since publication of *Upper Coquetdale*. A site at Low Trewhitt was excavated in 1908, and found to contain three large burial cists, the central one of which contained a fine beaker the location of which is currently unknown. Also found here were unburnt bones (suggesting that the original burial, with the beaker, may have been an inhumation rather than a cremation), further pot fragments and flint chips. The splendid photographs accompanying the published excavation report (fig. 3.36) give a flavour of the nature of archaeological investigations in the first decade of the twentieth century. Fragments of three further beakers, together with a beautiful barbed and tanged flint arrowhead, two flint scrapers, and a shale whetstone (presumably used to sharpen metal knives or daggers) were recovered from Wards Hill (above the Forest Burn, about 5km south of Rothbury) during quarrying in 1937 (fig. 3.37). Unfortunately, little is known of the context of these objects, but the recovery of some fragments of bone from the site suggests that they may all have been interred together within a burial cairn.

3.37. Fragments of beakers from Wards Hill (Scale in cm).

An extraordinary early Bronze Age burial was discovered within a 'tree-trunk coffin' at Cartington in 1913 (figs. 3.38, 3.39). In *A History of Northumberland* (volume XV) we learn that 'though the discovery was accidental, the late D D Dixon was early on the spot and collected particulars'. Dixon contributed a paper about the discovery to that year's *Proceedings of the Society of Antiquaries of Newcastle.* In this he tells us that:

Like many of the rarest finds, the discovery of this 'Tree Burial' was quite accidental. A farm servant, in the employ of the Messrs. Crawford was ploughing in a field on Cartington farm, when the plough struck against a large block of the local freestone. He immediately informed his masters, Mr. Edwin and Mr. Fred Crawford. These two gentlemen at once set to work and removed the stone, with the aid of iron pinches; when there appeared an opening through which water was visible some feet below the surface. A number of other large stones were then removed, when, at a depth of about four feet, a wooden trough-like object was seen lying east and west, this proved to be an oak tree coffin. The

3.38 John Turnbull Dixon's drawing of the Cartington tree trunk coffin.

J. Turnbull Dixon. 1913. June 21st.

coffin had been hewn out of a solid oak tree trunk about seven feet in circumference, by splitting it length-wise, one half being used for the coffin, the other half for the cover.

A carved platform at one end of the coffin is not unreasonably interpreted by Dixon as a 'pillow'. A few teeth found in this part of the coffin would seem to suggest that the deceased individual was indeed laid to rest with his or her head on this platform. Also found within the coffin were some flints and a beaker, which now seem to be lost. The body was apparently clad in a stitched garment, possibly of goatskin, and laid to rest on a bed of bracken. Sadly, the technology of the day did not allow for the preservation of the fragments of clothing that were recovered, so it will never be possible to subject them to modern analysis. Fortunately, however, the bottom half of the coffin does survive, and currently resides in a specially made timber 'coffin' of its own in a storeroom at the Museum of Antiquities in Newcastle. It is incredibly heavy, and while no account of its journey from Cartington to Newcastle survives, it is reasonable to suggest that this may not have been without incident.

3.39 The Cartington tree trunk coffin, photographed in 2003 in the Newcastle Museum of Antiquities store. Museum technician, Edwin Evans, points towards the carved 'pillow' within the coffin.

The coffin has a 'handle' carved into one corner, which was presumably for the attachment of a rope when it was first transported to its burial place. Recent radiocarbon analysis has dated the death of the tree from which the coffin was made to about 2,300BC, which sounds just about right for this burial as we have already noted that beakers, like the one from the Cartington coffin, are thought to have been introduced from about 2,400BC. Ambitious plans are currently being developed for the Museum of Antiquities, and its curator, Lindsay Allason-Jones, assures me that the Cartington coffin, as possibly her favourite object in the entire collection (which is saying something, given that her specialised field is Roman archaeology) will be given pride of place in the proposed new galleries.

After carefully describing the coffin and all the associated finds, Dixon allows himself his usual degree of informed and eloquent speculation:

Buried with such care, on the summit of an eminence, commanding an extensive view of

Coquetdale, and apparently a solitary burial, it has we doubt not been the last resting place of a person of some note, who might have held sway over the district, and who in his lifetime hunted the wild ox, the red deer, the wild boar, and the wolf amid the hills and dells of upper Coquet.

He may be right, but may equally well be very wrong. For all we know, the Cartington burial may have been of a woman, and until or unless we find more tree-trunk burials and subject them to modern analysis, we will not be able to say whether or not people afforded such burials were of some special status. In passing, we may also note the insight that Dixon's accounts relating to the discovery of the Simonside and the Cartington burials give into late nineteenth - and early twentieth-century society in Upper Coquetdale. The references to 'workmen', 'farm servants' and 'gentlemen' remind us that it is perhaps better that some things have changed over the past 100 years, at least to some extent. They should also serve to remind us that it is dangerous to impose, albeit often subconsciously, our current understandings of the world on the distant past, when things may have been very, very different.

3.40 Roger Miket's excavation of an inverted collared urn containing cremations at Kirkhill, West Hepple, 1972. *Photo: Roger Miket.*

Much more recently, in 1972, Roger Miket employed rather more careful techniques than those employed at Low Trewhitt when excavating the Old Chapel at Kirkhill, West Hepple. Roger was one of Northumberland's best known archaeologists in the 1970s and 1980s before he left the area to work in Scotland: fortunately, he has recently returned and is again actively involved in local prehistory. His excavation at Kirkhill was undertaken in order to investigate the chapel, but also uncovered a Bronze Age burial which thus became the only such burial to have been excavated in Upper Coquetdale in modern times. It consisted of a large collared urn (figs. 3.40, 3.41), placed upside down into a pit in the ground, which contained the jumbled up, cremated remains of at least three adults and a child aged about eight at the time of its death. Analysis of the bones suggested that one of the adults had suffered from rickets. Why so many individuals should have been placed together in this single urn will remain forever a mystery.

3.41 Diggers with treasure! Archaeologists Derek Cutts, Chris Leblique and Adam Welfare shortly after excavating the Kirkhill collared urn. *Photo: Roger Miket.*

Perhaps they were related, or perhaps they all simply had the misfortune to die at around about the same time. A single radiocarbon date suggests that this burial took place in the mid second millennium BC, nearly a thousand years after the earliest beaker burials in the valley. It must be amongst the latest early Bronze Age burials in our area, as the use of cairns for burial seems to have waned from about 1500BC, after which the dead were disposed of in a way which leaves no obvious trace in the archaeological record. We will consider this further in Chapter 4.

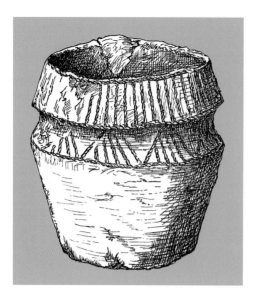

3.42 The Scrainwood urn drawn by John Turnbull Dixon. (Height 12.5cm).

Interestingly, antiquarian references dating back to about 1820 record the finding of several other burials in the immediate vicinity of Miket's excavation at Kirkhill: this may once have been an extensive Bronze Age cemetery, perhaps consisting of a number of cairns or barrows and some flat, unmarked graves. It is fascinating that a chapel, built more than two millennia later, was constructed on the same site. While it is tempting to suggest that the location of the chapel may relate to some faint folk-memory that the place had been of special spiritual significance in the far distant past, it probably owes more to coincidence.

A further excavated Bronze Age burial, worthy of brief mention here, is that from Scrainwood. This is of interest primarily because of its fine collared urn which was lost and 'rediscovered' during the twentieth century. The story is told in a fascinating paper by Adam Welfare in the first volume of the journal *Northern Archaeology* (published in 1980). David Dippie Dixon gave an account of the original discovery of this urn to a meeting of the Berwickshire Naturalists' Club on 24th September 1884: the published version of this account includes a fine drawing of the urn by John Turnbull Dixon (fig. 3.42) which was subsequently reproduced in *Upper Coquetdale*. The urn was found in a stone cist, disturbed during quarrying. Dixon regrets in his account that when this cist was found 'no person interested in such matters was present, to note its position or other articles contained therein'. After being in the possession of a Netherton innkeeper, the urn had found its way to Cragside by 1902. Subsequently, it was referred to as 'lost', until its rediscovery, in April 1979, at the back of a cupboard at Cragside! It has since been conserved and is now safe in the Newcastle Museum of Antiquities. Perhaps there is still hope for some of our other Bronze Age pots known only from secondary sources and currently listed as 'missing' or 'presumed destroyed'.

3.43 The ruins of a 'tri-radial cairn' at Lordenshaws, with Simonside in the background.

Before leaving the subject of burial cairns, we must briefly consider a recently recognised phenomenon which has caused much controversy amongst archaeologists: the so-called 'tri-radial cairn'. Several of these structures, which consist of three low stone-walls radiating from a central point, have recently been recorded by members of the Border Archaeological Society, including half a dozen probable examples, in various stages of preservation, at Lordenshaws (fig. 3.43). Although explained away by some archaeologists as post-medieval sheep shelters, the evidence from two recently excavated examples elsewhere in Northumberland (including several finds, burials and radiocarbon dates in the third millennium BC) certainly suggests that they are prehistoric structures. They vary considerably in size: some have arms several metres long, but one of the Lordenshaws examples is so small that any post-medieval sheep seeking shelter within it must have been no more than about six inches tall! Clearly, more work is needed on these enigmatic structures in order to approach an understanding of their chronology and function, after which it might be possible to offer some informed speculation as to the thinking behind their architecture. Surveys undertaken by the Border Archaeological Society suggest that many tri-radial cairns incorporate astronomical alignments (to the north, and perhaps also to sunrise and sunset at midwinter and midsummer). Such characteristics recall the alignments built into Neolithic monuments discussed earlier, and would surely have been of little consequence to post-medieval sheep!

Intervisible with the Lordenshaws tri-radials, on a plateau high on the northern-east flank of the Beacon, towards the eastern edge of the Simonside range, is another site of potential astronomical interest. This is an extraordinary 'holed stone': an enormous boulder with a 1.67 metre long shaft running right through it. What makes it extraordinary is that the shaft is aligned with the midsummer sunset over Yarnspath Law in the Cheviots to the north west (fig. 3.44), and also, in the opposite direction, with the rising of the midwinter sun in line with Tynemouth Priory on the distant North Sea coast. While the shaft may well be entirely natural in origin, it is hard to believe that it could have acquired its

Fig. 3.44. The midsummer setting sun shines through the holed stone on the Beacon, Simonside.
The inset, taken at the same time, shows the ray of sunlight actually within the shaft in the stone.
Photos: Crispian Oates.

link with the solstices entirely by chance. It may well be that the boulder was manoeuvred into its present position by Neolithic or Bronze Age people, perhaps at about the same time as the tri-radial cairns were being constructed.

The site was discovered in 1987 by the late David Thompson, a computer scientist at Newcastle General Hospital, and has subsequently been studied in great detail by his colleague Crispian Oates. Crispian has calculated that the alignment in both directions would have worked in 2000BC, but that the stone may have shifted very slightly over the intervening centuries so that the midwinter alignment is now out by just a couple of centimetres. He has recorded the boulders in the surrounding landscape in great detail and suggests that some kind of ritual centre, linked with the seasonal movements of the sun, may have existed here. It may never be possible to prove this one way or the other, but if such a centre did exist in Coquetdale then it would come as no surprise to find it located here on Simonside.

Stone tools and settlement sites

Most of what we have discussed so far in this chapter relates to monuments built for ceremonial or burial purposes. This is because these are the most obvious remnants of this 'Age of the Ancestors' in today's landscape. The people alive in the Neolithic and Bronze Age did not, however, spend all of their time engaged in ritual activities or dying, and more mundane everyday tasks had to be undertaken. Evidence of settlement and food production from this time is not easily found, but there are some clues. These come largely in the form of flint tools, picked up from the surface of freshly ploughed fields by eagle-eyed 'fieldwalkers'. Of course, prehistoric people made many things from wood, bone and other biodegradable materials, but these do not generally survive. During nineteenth-century drainage operations at a site called Ehenside Tarn, near Sellafield in Cumbria, several Neolithic wooden objects were found in a remarkable state of preservation due to the continuously wet nature of the ground within which they had become buried. These included a club, a spade or paddle, and axe-haft and a bowl. Similar objects would undoubtedly have been made and used by Neolithic people in Upper Coquetdale, but we are unlikely to find any unless we are very fortunate and manage to locate a local version of the Ehenside Tarn site. Other than occasional sherds of pottery, it is generally only the stone objects which survive in the soil, and consequently it is on these that we must base our interpretation of settlement patterns in the ancestral landscape of the Neolithic and early Bronze Age.

Today, most fieldwalking is professionally organised, and all finds are carefully recorded and the results statistically analysed. In the past, however, most fieldwalking was done by on an entirely amateur basis. We have already referred, in Chapter 2, to David Dippie Dixons's flint collection, now in the Newcastle Museum of Antiquities. In addition to the Mesolithic component, this collection contains assemblages which Rob Young considers, on the basis of a brief examination, to date from all periods from the early Neolithic to the early Bronze Age (from c4000 - 1500BC). The most interesting assemblage is from Low Farnham Farm, which Dixon discusses in a brief paper published in the *Proceedings of the Berwickshire Naturalists' Club* for 1883. Interestingly, this paper contains two plates by John Turnbull Dixon, illustrating sixteen of the flints from Low Farnham (fig. 3.45a): his drawings compare very favourably with the original artefacts in the museum (fig. 3.45b). Dixon records that a further fifty flints, in addition to those illustrated by his brother, have been found here, and these are all now in the museum. They were all picked up by Mr John Nicholson, having been turned up by the plough. This assemblage is important in its own right, but also because it demonstrates the potential for further fieldwalking at Low Farnham: if 66 flints were picked up by Nicholson, then there

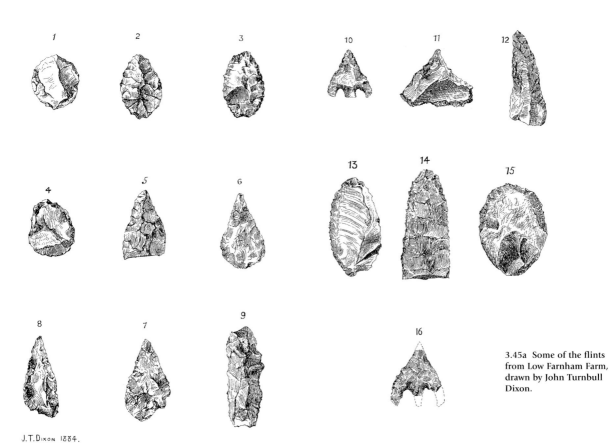

J.T. DIXON 1884.

3.45a Some of the flints
from Low Farnham Farm,
drawn by John Turnbull
Dixon.

3.45b A tray of flints
from Low Farnham Farm,
from the Dixon
collection, now in the
Museum of Antiquities,
Newcastle upon Tyne.

will undoubtedly be many hundreds more still in the ploughsoil awaiting a modern programme of fieldwalking. If such a campaign of fieldwalking can be mounted, and concentrations of artefacts identified, then there may yet be a chance to locate and excavate some surviving remains of local Neolithic or Bronze Age settlements. Such settlements would have been built of timber, and the postholes of houses and other buildings may well still survive beneath the ploughsoil.

In addition to the flints from Low Farnham, the Dixon collection also includes two boxes labelled 'flints from the neighbourhood of Rothbury' and two bags of 'unworked' and 'roughly worked' flints also from Rothbury. The exact provenance of these finds is not clear, but they demonstrate that the potential for future fieldwalking is not restricted to Low Farnham. Some of them may be from Newtown Farm near Great Tosson, as Dixon tells us in *Upper Coquetdale* that 'in the cultivated fields on the lower slopes of Newtown farm a number of flint arrow-points and 'scrapers' have been picked up by the work-people, one of the best collectors being Miss. Mary Bootieman, who periodically brings her 'finds' to the writer.'

The curator of the Newcastle Museum of Antiquities, J D Cowen, presented a paper about Dixon's flint collection to the Society of Antiquaries on 30th March 1932. This paper was later published in the Proceedings of the Society. In it, he records that:

> *During the course of his long life in the Rothbury district the late David Dippie Dixon, F.S.A., made a small collection of prehistoric antiquities. He was not, strictly, a collector on his own account, and many of the objects he was instrumental in bringing to notice found their way into the hands of others - Lord Armstrong, Canon Greenwell, and our own Society. He did, however, accumulate a certain number of local objects of this class, and eventually he acquired the excellent collection of flints found on Low Farnham Farm by the tenant, John Nicholson. In his later years he parted with the whole series to our member Dr. Wilfred Hall, by whose kindness it has now been placed on exhibition in our Museum.*

The Dixon collection certainly includes some exquisitely beautiful flint objects, the colours of which range from black through brown, honey, pink and grey to white. This suggests that the flint may have been obtained from a variety of different sources. Rob Young has identified the following artefacts within the collection:

From Low Farnham Farm:
    15 leaf-shaped arrowheads and points (Neolithic)
    4 'petit-tranchet-derivative' arrowheads (late Neolithic)
    3 barbed and tanged arrowheads (late Neolithic/early Bronze Age)
    5 bladelike flakes
    2 tanged artefacts
    1 probable dagger blade
    11 scrapers
    12 small blade and flake fragments (probably Mesolithic)

From the 'vicinity of Rothbury' (Box 1):
    5 leaf shaped arrowheads (including one tiny, 1 cm long, exquisitely manufactured example)
    2 definite and 1 possible barbed and tanged arrowheads
    10 bladelike pieces, several with areas of retouch
    3 large flakes, all retouched
    1 greenstone axe (probably of Langdale tuff)

3.46 Some flint arrowheads from the Dixon collection. (Scale in cms).

1 flint axe (very rare in Northumberland)
5 small cores (probably discarded at end of useful life)
1 scraper

During the later twentieth century, the late Dr. Joan Weyman undertook some fieldwalking in and around Upper Coquetdale, recovering worked flints at Flotterton, Thrunton, Biddlestone Edge, Bickerton, Tosson Tower, Farnham, Low Farnham and Trewhitt. Weyman's finds are now held with Dixon's collection at the Newcastle Museum of Antiquities, and they clearly demonstrate the potential for future work.

3.47 Sue Brophy with her barbed and tanged flint arrowhead from Simonside.

Of all the flint tools, it is the arrowheads (fig. 3.46) that always demand attention due to their often (to our eyes) exquisitely beautiful form. While they may have been primarily functional objects to the people who made them, I can't help believing that prehistoric people must also have gained some pleasure from the aesthetics of a well-made arrowhead. Most arrowheads must have been used in the hunt, although a few may have been directed at human targets, perhaps as a result of territorial disputes or other conflicts. There is little suggestion, however, that Neolithic society was outwardly aggressive as seems to have been the case in later prehistory when much effort was expended on the construction of 'hillforts' and the manufacture of swords and other weapons (see Chapter 4). In about 4,000BC, the composite arrowhead of the Mesolithic was gradually replaced with the leaf-shaped arrowhead knapped from

3.48 Three small Neolithic axes (one of which is flint) from the Dixon collection. (Scale in cms).

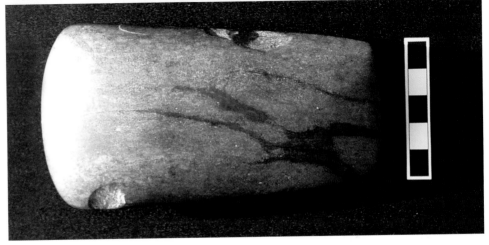

3.49 This fine Neolithic axe, now in Alnwick Castle Museum, was found in the nineteenth century in Rothbury. It is made from stone quarried in Northern Ireland. (Scale in cms).

a single flint flake. During the later Neolithic, this was in turn replaced by the 'barbed-and-tanged' arrowhead which remained in use well into the Bronze Age. Clive Waddington has made the interesting suggestion that this change from a 'natural', rounded, leaf-shaped point to the wholly artificial, angular, 'barbed-and-tanged' form could relate to a perceived greater degree of control by people over their environment: people no longer had to seek inspiration in the natural world. This is an interesting theory, especially as a similar change can be recognised in the decoration applied to pottery (eg beakers) at about the same time.

In addition to planned programmes of fieldwalking, stray finds will continue to turn up from time to time and it is important that the location of these is recorded. One such example is the splendid arrowhead (perhaps a remnant of a hunting expedition of some 4,000 years ago) recently found by Sue Brophy on Simonside (fig. 3.47). Sue tells me that she was walking down the footpath towards Lordenshaws when she momentarily lost her footing and looked down at the ground. She could not believe her eyes as she noticed the arrowhead lying on the ground right in front of her, having been washed out of the peat by a severe rainstorm earlier that day. Perhaps we should all keep our eyes to the ground, as well as on the fabulous views, when out walking in Upper Coquetdale!

Flint was not the only stone used for the manufacture of tools during the Neolithic. Over the years, in excess of a dozen polished stone axes of Neolithic date have been found in Upper Coquetdale, proving that Neolithic people were active here, probably using those very axes to chop down trees in the business of creating fresh agricultural land. In *Upper Coquetdale*, Dixon discusses the discovery of several such axes, and illustrates a flint example found by a workman on Cragside Hill in 1889. A small axe from Low Burradon Farm, now in the Dixon collection (fig. 3.48, left) has a slightly damaged blade, demonstrating that it was used for chopping; its butt end is also worn, suggesting that it was also used as a hammer. Many of these axes must simply have been lost, perhaps flying off their wooden handles and becoming lost in undergrowth: we can imagine the uttering of Neolithic expletives as subsequent seaching proved fruitless.

Many axes found in Northumberland were made of stone quarried from a remote source high above Langdale in the Lake District, while the flint used here was probably imported from the coast or from Yorkshire. One axe from Rothbury, now in the Alnwick Castle Museum, has been sourced to a known axe quarry site in northern Ireland (fig. 3.49). There were clearly complex exchange networks in place by the Neolithic, although we are far from sure exactly how these operated.

A survey of Neolithic axes from Northumberland, published jointly by Colin Burgess and three colleagues in 1981, notes that 'the whole length of the Coquet valley is rich in finds, especially its upper end around Holystone'. The accompanying distribution map shows 14 polished stone axes from Upper Coquetdale, to which we can now add a couple more. One of these (fig. 3.50) was found by Jim Miller while out for an afternoon stroll one Boxing Day in the early 1970s. He noticed it lying in the upcast from a recently dug gas pipeline trench on the eastern fringes of Rothbury. It is always worth inspecting areas of disturbed ground in the hope of making such discoveries, as many more axes and other artefacts undoubtedly lie concealed in the soil awaiting discovery throughout Upper Coquetdale.

Another 'new' axe was shown to me in 2004 by Michael Davy of Warton Farm. It is a beautiful little specimen, about 7cm in length, but is manufactured from quite soft rock which could not have made for a practical implement. This axe was apparently a 'ritual' rather than a

3.50 Jim Miller with his stone axe from Rothbury.

3.51 This little axe (7cm in length) was found on Warton Farm. It is a very attractive object, but is of a soft rock and would have been quite useless as a functional axe: it was presumably of ritual importance.

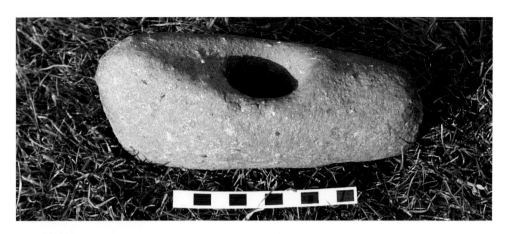

3.52 This late Neolithic 'axe hammer' is now in Alnwick Castle Museum. The museum catalogue records that it was found 'about 200 yards north-west of East Bank, Burradon, Alwinton, and was presented by Mr. Thomas Walby, 1859'. (Scale in cms).

3.53 John Turnbull Dixon's drawing of the early Bronze Age flanged axe (c12cm in length) from Burgh Hill, Tosson. This is the earliest known metal object from Upper Coquetdale.

practical object, a suggestion reinforced by the way in which it was carefully designed to incorporate a pattern of concentric circles occurring naturally within the rock (fig. 3.51). This is not as unusual as might be thought, as there is much other evidence to suggest that axes were indeed of symbolic importance as well as having functional value. Some axes were carefully buried in special places, such as within ceremonial or burial monuments, and many were made of stone quarried from spectacular and relatively inaccessible locations, such as the previously mentioned Langdale quarries in the Lake District. One further fact which may not be irrelevant here is the remarkable similarity in form between some of the most important early Neolithic monuments, the long cairns, and arguably the most important contemporary tools, the stone axes. Both are trapezoidal in outline and, although rarely commented on by archaeologists, it seems to me that this similarity must have been apparent, and possibly of considerable ritual significance, to Neolithic people.

Assuming all the polished stone axes to be of Neolithic date (and there is no reason to assume otherwise) then they provide clear evidence for the presence of Neolithic communities in Upper Coquetdale. Unfortunately, these axes were produced to a uniform design over a very long time period, perhaps from before 4,000 through until after 2,000BC, so they cannot tell us a great deal about developments during the Neolithic. Also, we must always interpret distribution maps with caution, remembering that they reflect our *discovery* of axes rather than any genuine distribution of Neolithic activity. Towards the end of the Neolithic, the polished stone axes were superceded by the so-called 'battle axes' or 'axe-hammers', of which only about half a dozen are known from Upper Coquetdale (fig. 3.52). This low number does not mean that the axe-hammers were any less popular than the the polished axe had been in earlier times: the smaller number known to us probably reflects the fact that they only remained in use for a few centuries before being effectively replaced by bronze axes.

Perhaps surprisingly, we know of only one bronze object of probable early Bronze Age date with a firm provenance in Upper Coquetdale. This is a flanged axe found during trenching in the 'Long Planting' on Burgh Hill, Tosson, in 1890 (fig. 3.53). Another couple of early Bronze Age axes might have been found near Rothbury, but the references are frustratingly vague and the axes themselves are now apparently lost. There must have been many more such objects, and the initial appearance of metalworking must have had a dramatic effect on those privileged enough to have access to objects of copper, bronze or gold. It was later in the Bronze Age, however, that flint finally gave way to bronze for the large scale manufacture of tools and weapons, and for this reason the impact of metal working is considered in Chapter 4 rather than here.

Summary

This chapter began with the onset of the Neolithic, in about 4,000BC, when people were still living by hunting and gathering strategies developed throughout the preceding Mesolithic. The Neolithic saw people gradually taking control of their world, seeing themselves as increasingly separate from nature as agriculture replaced hunting and gathering. In Upper Coquetdale, arable agriculture was apparently not undertaken on a large scale in the period covered by this chapter, but domesticated livestock gradually increased in significance over wild beasts as time went by.

We know that people were present in Upper Coquetdale throughout the Neolithic and early Bronze Age, as many examples of stone axes and flint tools have been found here. However, no settlement sites from the period have yet been investigated, and we still have much to learn about the ways in which people lived in the valley prior to the setting up of small villages of round houses considered in the next chapter. It may be that people maintained a largely nomadic way of life throughout much of the Neolithic period.

Neolithic communities erected great monuments to house the remains of the ancestors, who were celebrated at open-air temples, some of which seem to have incorporated solar alignments. The ceremonies at such monuments served to link the ancestors with the eternal cycles of the heavens, probably linking the dead, the sun, the moon and the other heavenly bodies with the everyday lives of people on earth. Just as we seek to account for the inexplicable through modern day religions, so Neolithic people would have developed their own cosmologies to account for the mysteries in their lives. No local monuments have yet been dated unambiguously to the Neolithic, but the 'cup-and-ring' marked rocks at Lordenshaws and elsewhere, although strictly undated, must relate in some way to local Neolithic cosmology. As we have seen, the interpretation of this rock art is far from straightforward and continues to provide a challenge for anyone interested in local prehistory.

During the millennium from about 2,400 BC, thousands of round burial cairns were constructed throughout Britain. Several such sites have been investigated in Upper Coquetdale. These are conventionally regarded as the final resting places of important individuals, perhaps 'warrior-aristocrats'. While there are occasional rich burials with 'luxury' grave goods (of stone, bronze, jet or amber), many such cairns appear to have contained the cremated remains of ordinary folk. The cairns probably functioned as funerary monuments for specific communities, but we do not know whether or not burial in a cairn was restricted to specific classes of individual. Whatever the detail, these cairns certainly continued the Neolithic tradition of constructing funerary monuments for the ancestors, a tradition that, as we will see in Chapter 4, was not destined to survive into later prehistory.

Today's agricultural landscape is the result of more
or less continuous farming since Bronze Age times.
Photo: Tony Hopkins.

Chapter 4

An Agricultural Landscape

The later Bronze Age and Iron Age (c1800BC - AD100)

Introduction

In Chapter 3 we observed that most Neolithic and early Bronze Age monuments surviving in today's landscape appear to have been originally concerned with ritual and/or burial. We then looked at the discovery of stone tools and used this information to investigate possible patterns of settlement throughout the landscape. The structure of this chapter is, to an extent, a mirror image of that of Chapter 3. We will first examine the most obvious features surviving in the landscape, which, in marked contrast to earlier times, appear to relate primarily to settlement and agriculture. We will then discuss artefacts, this time of metal, before using these to make suggestions regarding possible ritual practice. Without doubt, prehistoric people would not have made rigid distinctions between these different classes of evidence, but I consider this to be the best way to present the various strands of archaeological information available to us.

Clearly, any division between the 'ancestral landscape' of Chapter 3, and the period covered in this chapter is to an extent arbitrary. I have reflected this by deliberately leaving a large overlap between the dates of the two chapters. Someone who saw a draft of this text asked me if this was a mistake, but it is actually a deliberate and carefully considered decision. I think we sometimes worry a bit too much about exactly when certain changes occurred, and sometimes seek to group changes together and attempt clever but perhaps misguided all-encompassing explanations as to why everything changed at once. In fact, things were changing constantly throughout prehistory, and while there were undeniably major developments from time to time, such as the introduction of metal working or defended settlements, many of these developments were introduced gradually rather than overnight. Nevertheless, the millennium between c1800BC and c800BC undeniably witnessed fundamental changes in most aspects of everyday life in Upper Coquetdale and surrounding areas. These changes must have been to an extent interrelated, but it is rarely a straightforward exercise to determine which event was cause, and which was effect.

Prior to 1500BC, most surviving ancient monuments, such as burial cairns, standing stones and rock art, seem to relate primarily to ritual and burial, hence I have referred to it as an 'ancestral landscape'. After about 1500BC, the emphasis in the archaeological record moves away from ritual and burial to settlements and agriculture, and we have hardly any evidence for specifically ceremonial monuments or for burial. I must stress that this certainly does not mean that people now had no ritual beliefs, but their beliefs were now being expressed in different ways. Whereas I believe that people had previously looked back to the ancestors as the main focus of their religious belief, people from now on sought religious inspiration in natural places within the land of the living, and symbolic architecture was built into domestic structures and settlements, rather than being concentrated into specially constructed 'ceremonial' monuments. Agriculture, in the form of domesticated cattle, sheep, pigs, and cereals, had been introduced into the region during the Neolithic, but, so far as we know, permanent, self-sufficient agricultural settlements only began to appear in upland regions like the hills of Upper Coquetdale during the second millennium BC. The chronology of this process cannot be known until a sample of sites has been excavated: it may have begun closer to 2000BC than 1500BC, and may have occurred gradually over several generations, perhaps over two or three centuries. Regardless of the detailed chronology, the general pattern of events during what are conventionally termed the later Bronze Age and the Iron Age seems reasonably clear and will be outlined in this chapter.

Farmsteads and fields

The known distribution of archaeological sites in upland areas throughout Northumberland is largely based on discoveries made by aerial photography, and owes much to the astonishing efforts of one man. In the days before County Archaeologists, back in the 1970s, Tim Gates was effectively the County Archaeologist for Northumberland. He had an office at Newcastle University, and worked tirelessly to protect archaeological sites throughout the Cheviots and elsewhere from threats such as large scale afforestation. With his colleague, Stewart Ainsworth (now of TV 'Time Team' fame) he surveyed many such sites on the ground, and a quarter of a century later these surveys are still the best available. Tim's main contribution to the cause, however, has been his skill as an aerial photographer. He has discovered hundreds of sites over the years, and has enabled many other known sites, such as extensive fieldsystems which can be hard to see on the ground even when one is walking over them, to be properly recorded.

In the 1990s, Tim was commissioned to undertake an aerial photographic survey of the Otterburn Training Area as part of an initiative by the National Park Authority and the Ministry of Defence to ensure that no unnecessary damage was done to ancient monuments through military training, agriculture or forestry. One of the most interesting discoveries that Tim made during his survey of the OTA is at Crane Sike (fig. 4.1), exposed in a recently burnt patch of heather a little over 2km south-west of Harbottle. Although I have yet to visit this site on the ground, it looks very much as though it could be a middle Bronze Age settlement of two or

4.1 Aerial view of the Crane Sike settlement, taken at the time of its discovery on 4th June, 1996. The remnants of a couple of round houses together with associated field walls can be seen towards the centre of the photograph.
Photo: Tim Gates.

more timber roundhouses surrounded by small paddocks or fields. It could well be the source of the earliest cereal pollen recorded in the pollen diagram from Bloody Moss (discussed later in this chapter), which is only about a kilometre away to the south. Many similar settlements are known from further north in the Cheviots, and other examples almost certainly await discovery in Upper Coquetdale. Two interesting examples at Kidlandlee Dean will be described in the discussion of Clennell Street, below. These undefended homesteads were built by the first farmers to live and farm permanently in the hills. Most were probably founded between 2000 and 1500 BC, and some may have been continuously occupied for several centuries. It has been suggested that many of these settlements, and especially those on higher ground, were eventually abandoned in the face of deteriorating climatic conditions after about 1200BC. This climatic deterioration has been linked by some archaeologists to the massive eruption of the Icelandic volcano, Hekla, which it is known occurred in 1159BC. This must have thrown vast quantities of ash and dust up into the atmosphere and may have affected the climate for several years. Whether or not the actual abandonment of villages in Upper Coquetdale can be linked precisely to this event, however, must await further research.

No Bronze Age settlements have been excavated in Upper Coquetdale, but two have been investigated a little further to the north. These were excavated by two of Northumberland's most distinguished archaeologists, George Jobey and Colin Burgess, both of whom were based at the University of Newcastle. In the late 1960s, George Jobey (known to his colleagues as a 'one man Royal Commission' due to the phenomenal amount of site survey work he completed) excavated at the Bronze Age settlement of Standrop Rigg, high in the Breamish Valley. Here, at least six timber roundhouses clustered within a system of small, irregular, stone-walled fields rather like those that can be seen on the air photograph of Crane Sike.

4.2 Jim Proudfoot's reconstruction of a typical Cheviot Bronze Age village in about 1800BC. People are living in small villages of roundhouses surrounded by fields, but are still burying their dead in cairns in the traditional manner.

Colin Burgess was one of Britain's foremost prehistorians in the 1970s and 1980s, and undertook several excavations in Northumberland with his extra-mural students from Newcastle (this group is still active today as the Northumberland Archaeological Group). One of these sites was the Bronze Age settlement at Houseledge, in the northern Cheviots near Yeavering. As at Standrop Rigg, this consisted of half a dozen timber houses within a surrounding field system. The Houseledge settlement seems to have been associated with nearby burial cairns, suggesting that this new way of life in the uplands was still linked, at least initially, with the old traditions of burying the dead in round cairns. We observed in Chapter 3 that some such burial cairns may have originated as the final resting places of a new, early Bronze Age aristocratic elite. We should stress, however, that no evidence for such an elite exits in the settlement record: no particularly large or imposing homes have been recognised. It may be that many cairns were constructed initially for the 'founding fathers' (or mothers) of new upland settlements, and do not actually reflect any great aristocratic status at all.

In some places it is impossible to distinguish between small burial cairns and so-called 'field clearance cairns'. This could be because there was not always a clear distinction between the two: if an individual died then he or she may have been buried within a cairn built of stones recently cleared from the community's fields. Thus, cairns could relate to both burial and field clearance: the dead received a suitable burial and the stones were removed from the fields either to improve pasture or to help facilitate the next ploughing episode. If it did indeed exist then such an arrangement would have made practical sense, and must also have been laden with potent symbolism linking the agricultural landscape to the ancestral world of the dead.

Despite their importance over many centuries, interest in the old cairns was waning by the middle Bronze Age, when religious practice seems to have become intimately bound up with natural wet places rather than artificially constructed burial monuments. This interest in wet places will be considered later in this chapter.

From homesteads to hillforts

There is no clear division between a late Bronze Age and an early Iron Age in Upper Coquetdale, but what is clear is that a decline in the climate, leading to colder and wetter conditions, occurred in the centuries from about 1200BC. Associated with this change in climate are major changes in the pattern of settlement in the Cheviots. Some Bronze Age settlements on higher ground seem to have been abandoned, and at one time it was thought that the entire uplands were abandoned at this time. However, the Bloody Moss pollen sequence provides no suggestion of any such abandonment. Also, it should be pointed out that the abandonment of a long established settlement, with its own identity and social history, would not be undertaken lightly. Despite this, it does seem that the declining climate must have influenced the abandonment of the more marginal settlements. It would also have resulted in greater pressure on good agricultural land, and seems to have led to the first defended settlements and eventually to the great hillforts discussed below. It should be emphasised, though, that not all settlements in the hills were abandoned in the centuries around 1000BC. For example, Tim Gates excavated a late Bronze Age/early Iron Age farmstead at Hallshill, in neighbouring Redesdale, which seems to have been occupied throughout the period from about 1200 to 600BC.

The earliest defended settlements are surrounded by timber stockades and are known to archaeologists as palisaded settlements or 'palisades'. They are recognisable as slight grooves in the turf, in which the timbers of the defensive circuit were originally set. The few excavations

4.3 Trows Law palisade with overlying cord rig: clearly, the site was cultivated at some point after the abandonment of the settlement.
Photo: Tim Gates.

of palisades undertaken in north-east England and southern Scotland suggest that they may have been built from about 800BC, although it would come as no surprise if some were eventually dated to about 1000BC. If their origin is related to the deterioration in climate that seems to have set in from about 1200BC, then we would expect something of a time-lag as, as noted above, people would be reluctant to leave their homes and would only do so when it became impossible to stay, perhaps after a few generations of struggle. However, it may be that changes in settlement pattern in about 800BC occurred due to other factors, rather than simply in response to a deteriorating climate. This is the precisely the time that iron technology was introduced, and it may be that changes in society due to the introduction of iron had more of an impact on settlement patterns than climatic deterioration. It may also be at about this time that horse riding became widespread throughout Britain, enabling effective transport and communication over wider areas than had previously been possible, thus bringing communities closer together and offering opportunities for powerful individuals to exercise power over larger territories.

At some palisades, aerial photography suggests that the actual palisade overlies some pre-existing timber houses, suggesting that an existing settlement may have been 'defended' by the addition of a defensive circuit. This has recently been demonstrated by excavation at Wether Hill, Ingram, where the palisade and overlying hillfort enjoy magnificent views in all directions, including southwards over Coquetdale towards Simonside. A fine palisade, which once contained at least two timber houses, can be seen on Trows Law, high in the hills above the Trows Burn, near the Border Ridge (fig. 4.3). Another fine example, also with evidence of internal houses, survives above Biddlestone Quarry (fig. 4.4). A little further to the north, but still within the Coquet catchment, are two sites on High Knowes above Alnham (fig. 4.5). These were investigated by

George Jobey in 1962 and 1963. The first of these (Jobey's 'Site A') consists of double palisade trenches, with an entrance in the east, containing an internal area of 0.15 hectares. Within the interior are the remains of four circular timber buildings: two large examples about 15 metres in diameter, and two smaller ones with diameters of 8 metres. One of the large buildings was excavated and was found to consist of a solid timber wall with two internal rings of substantial timbers which supported the roof. A circular ditch around the internal perimeter of the house has been interpreted as evidence of 'mucking out', and consequently as evidence of cattle being kept on the ground floor of the house, perhaps with people occupying an upstairs for which there is, of course, no archaeological evidence. These internal ditches have been recorded at many other sites throughout Northumberland, and their actual purpose remains unproven. If they are evidence for cattle, then the house could have functioned rather like a medieval bastle, with beasts down below and people living upstairs. This would have provided an effective, if slightly smelly, heating system during the cold winter months. One of the smaller buildings was also excavated and this had only a single ring of internal roof supports. We cannot be certain of the appearance of these buildings, but they probably looked something like the reconstructed examples in fig. 4.6.

Unfortunately there were no finds from Jobey's excavation to help date the site or provide information about the use of the different buildings. However, a modern excavation would almost certainly be able to provide dates as Jobey records having found lots of 'burnt wood': it is not clear from the excavation report why no radiocarbon dates were obtained. The second site at High Knowes ('Site B') consists of another double palisade, with a larger internal area of 0.23 hectares within which are the visible remains of sixteen closely packed, round, timber buildings ranging from 8 to 12 metres in diameter. Given the lack of finds from Site A, the original intention to excavate part of Site B was abandoned. Although there is no dating evidence, Jobey suggests that the High Knowes palisades may have been abandoned when the nearby Castlehill hillfort was constructed. This is certainly an attractive hypothesis, but it will not be possible to prove or disprove it without further fieldwork at both the palisades and the

hillfort.

Three further palisades are described in the section on Clennell Street, below. Several other examples probably survive sealed beneath later hillfort ramparts, as seems to have been the case at Witchy Neuk (also described below).

The second half of the first millennium BC is sometimes termed the 'Celtic Age', but who were the Celts? The word 'Celtic' derives from the Greek 'Keltoi', which dates back at least as far as 500BC. The Greeks believed that most of central and western Europe was occupied by people they referred to collectively as the Celts. The Iron Age Celts left no written evidence of how they regarded themselves, and all contemporary written sources derive from Greek and Roman sources. Thus it was the Greeks and Romans rather than the 'Celts' themselves who lumped together a number of tribal groups, over a vast geographical area, as 'Celtic'. Nevertheless, and despite much regional variation, there does appear to be a degree of cultural homogeneity which does allow us to talk of 'the Celtic Iron Age' as a Europe-wide phenomenon. Classical sources and archaeology combine to suggest that the characteristics of this Celtic Iron Age include:

A stratified society dominated by an aristocratic warrior elite.
Defended settlements, sometimes quite large, often in apparently defensive positions.
Iron working, for everyday tools and prestige objects.
Widespread use of horse riding, and chariots.
A distinctive style of 'Celtic' artwork.

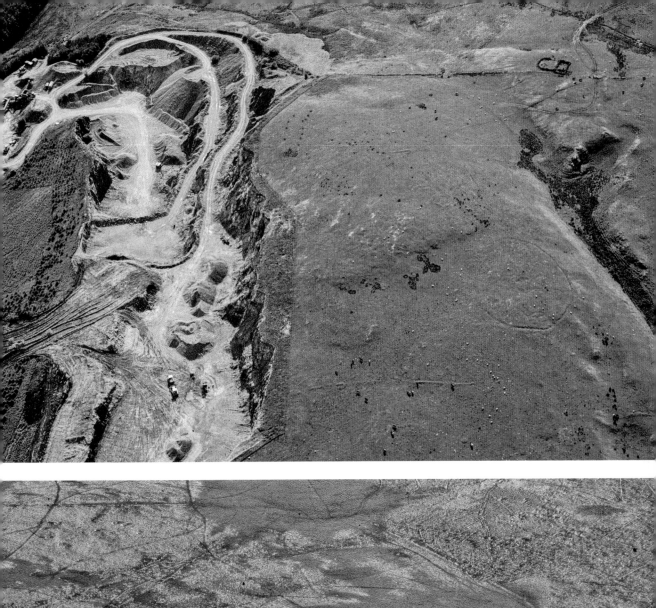

4.6 *Above:*
Reconstructed timber roundhouses at Castell Henllys in the Brecon Beacons National Park, South Wales.

Right:
The interiors of such houses were spacious. The central hearth provided warmth and was also used for cooking.

Classical sources, and later Irish sources which refer back to earlier times, paint a picture of a heroic society, continually engaged in cattle raiding and feasting, with warriors well provided with spears, swords and shields. Society was apparently hierarchical, with kings (or queens) at the top, followed by nobles, warriors, priests and craftsmen, all supported ultimately by the agricultural surplus generated by the peasant masses. Families belonged to particular tribes, with different tribes bound to each other through marriage alliances and oaths of allegiance.

How does the archaeological evidence from Upper Coquetdale equate with this general picture of life in the latter half of the first millennium BC? This is not an easy question to answer given the lack of relevant archaeological excavations in our area. However, we do have evidence of defended settlements in the form of hillforts, and of skilfully manufactured swords, both of which could be interpreted as evidence of a warrior aristocracy. We will first consider the hillforts, before discussing other aspects of life such as agriculture, metal working and religion.

While the palisades discussed above generally consist of quite slight surface features, and were only recognised recently through aerial photography, the monuments which succeeded them, the hillforts, often still survive as impressive earthwork sites (fig. 4.7), many of which were known to David Dippie Dixon. In 1915, Dixon and Parker Brewis jointly published a report in the *Proceedings of the Society of Antiquaries of Newcastle* entitled 'Pre-Roman remains in Upper Coquetdale'. This lists a large number of sites, including hillforts, burial cairns, and cup-and-ring marked rocks. It begins with a list of 'camps', most of which would be classified today as 'hillforts', in the parishes of Alwinton and Rothbury. It is an impressive list:

Alwinton Parish:
Gallow Law Camp
Campville Camp
Harehaugh Camp
Roberts Law Camp (now destroyed)

Rothbury Parish:
Witchy Neuk/Whitefield Camp
Hetchester Camp (now destroyed)
Caistron Camp
Bickerton Camp
Tosson Burgh Camp
Newtown Camp
Lordenshaws Camp
Pike House Camp
Craghead Camp
Old Rothbury
West Hills Camp

4.7 The ramparts of Campville hillfort, Holystone, survive today as impressive earthworks. This photograph was taken during a survey project undertaken by UCCAP (see Chapter 6) volunteers.

While all of these sites are of interest in their own right, the possible nature of relationships between them (or rather, between the communities which built and lived in them) is a subject that would repay much careful study. In *A History of Northumberland* volume XV it is observed that:

....we cannot leave Coquetdale without drawing attention to the magnificent series of earthworks with which the pleasant and fertile vale immediately above Rothbury is completely encircled. Starting from Old Rothbury the ring passes in a great sweep by West Hills, and the destroyed camp on Trewhitt, Robert's Law to Hetchester; thence in a straighter line and in closer array stand Harehaugh, Witchy

Neuk, and Tosson Burgh, with their satellites at Soldier's Fold, Bickerton, and Newtown; and so by Lordenshaws to close the circuit. But whether chance or purpose designed this grand display of primitive strength we shall never know.

I do not believe that these sites were ever part of some centrally organised 'grand plan', but that they were founded independently by different groups as the trend towards hillfort construction gathered pace, probably in the centuries around 300BC. It is interesting to note the variation in the form of the Coquetdale hillforts. Lordenshaws is a classic 'Cheviot fort', roughly circular in plan, whereas Harehaugh is 'pear-shaped', Tosson Burgh is oval, and Witchy Neuk is 'D'-shaped. Such variation, however, probably reflects nothing other than the local topography at each site: the forts were constructed in the most suitable form for their particular locations.

Today we can suggest a couple of additions to the Dixon/Brewis list. Ward Law, impressively located at a height of almost 400 metres, within a couple of kilometres of the Border Ridge at Windy Gyle, must be one of the most stunningly sited of all hillforts. Harbottle Castle, given its strategic position above the Coquet, must almost certainly be on the site of a hillfort, although evidence of prehistoric activity here may have been destroyed during the construction of the medieval castle in the twelfth century AD. In addition, the magnificent Castlehill fort at Alnham (fig. 4.8), not usually regarded as a Coquetdale site, actually lies within the Coquet catchment and must be considered within any study of Iron Age Coquetdale. It may be that a few other 'unclassified enclosures' should also be considered as small hillforts but deciding which sites to classify as hillforts is not at all straightforward. Sites were probably enclosed by earthworks for a variety of reasons, and at different times. Dixon and Brewis note that some of the sites listed (eg Bickerton and Newtown) probably functioned as cattle enclosures, while others are apparently settlement sites.

Visitors to hillforts often ask why Iron Age people chose to live on exposed hilltops when the lowlands must have been much more hospitable, and often express surprise that people chose to live with no immediate access to a constant supply of fresh water. In fact, during the Iron Age many lowland areas would have been susceptible to flooding, and good pasture and cultivable soils were available in abundance in many upland areas. With regard to water, much rainwater was probably collected within settlement sites, and people would have thought nothing of travelling a few hundred metres to a nearby burn to collect fresh water on a daily basis, as people still do today in some parts of the world. Today, we have become conditioned

4.9 Looking over the ramparts of Old Rothbury hillfort towards Simonside.
Photo: Stan Beckensall.

into thinking of the lowlands as 'home territory', but this may have been a relatively recent development, perhaps following the setting up of many lowland villages during Anglo-Saxon times. Iron Age people would have thought differently, and to live in a hillfort would have seemed perfectly normal to them, as indeed would the fantastic views to be enjoyed each morning as they emerged from the shelter of their cosy roundhouses.

Although its original form is now hard to appreciate due to recent disturbance, Old Rothbury is the largest Coquetdale hillfort with an internal area of nearly 1.5 hectares (fig. 4.9). The site is impressively located above Rothbury, but, as Dixon and Brewis observe, this location could not have been chosen solely on the grounds of defensibility: 'The situation is naturally a strong one, on its northern and western sides. To the east it is sheltered by a higher plateau…but this shelter is gained at the expense of security, as the site is overlooked and commanded from this plateau within bowshot of the ramparts.' This is an important observation which has recently

4.10 Looking south over the ramparts of West Hills, Rothbury. Tosson Burgh Camp is on the flat-topped green hill in the middle distance, just right of centre in this view.

4.11 Aerial view of Tosson Burgh Camp.
Photo: Tim Gates.

been repeated at several hillforts throughout the Cheviots, surveyed as part of the National Park Authority's *Discovering our Hillfort Heritage* project. A similar situation occurs at West Hills, just 800 metres west of Old Rothbury (fig. 4.10). Just across the valley from West Hills, the Tosson Burgh fort (fig. 4.11) appears dramatically sited when seen from the valley floor, but is actually overlooked by higher ground to its south.

It appears that many hillforts were located to give an *impression* of strength from particular viewpoints, and that ramparts may have been as much symbolic as functional. Such observations are important when trying to recreate Iron Age society, conventionally viewed as a 'warrior aristocracy', with warriors and their entourages living in hillforts: the more spectacular the hillfort, the more powerful the particular group. There may well be something in this, and the presence of splendid bronze swords in the artefact record might seem to back up such a view. However, the observation that many hillforts are not in prime defensive positions, but were built to look impressive from below, and the fact that the swords and other artefacts could have been used for show as much as for fighting, might also suggest that a lot of Iron Age bravado was about the display of wealth and power rather than actual warfare. Regardless of this, the hillforts remain in today's landscape as magnificent monuments to their time.

None of the sites on the Dixon/Brewis list had been excavated at the time that the list was compiled, and no finds from any of the sites are recorded other than 'a number of querns' from Roberts Law and 'several querns and a large quantity of antlers of the red deer' from Hetchester. Half a dozen excavations have taken place at Northumberland hillforts over the past few decades, and these seem to suggest that most hillforts were built a century or two either side of 300BC. I think it highly likely that the largest Cheviot hillforts were the earliest (with Yeavering Bell, by far the largest, possibly dating back to 1000BC), and that smaller, local versions were constructed throughout the landscape by local groups over subsequent centuries. The possible relevance of such a model for Upper Coquetdale must await much further fieldwork, which, sadly, is unlikely to take place in the near future.

In addition to the palisades and hillforts, we should note that there are several sites where unenclosed timber or stone built roundhouses exist, either singly or in small groups of up to half a dozen. Until a sample of these is excavated, we cannot be sure about their date, but they probably belong to a general late Iron Age/Romano-British horizon. Some may have been occupied at the same time as the hillforts, while others may not have been founded until the Roman period and thus should belong in Chapter 5 of this book. Some may have been occupied throughout the late Iron Age and much of the Roman period. It was twentieth-century archaeologists that invented the term 'Romano-British', not people who were alive at the time: everyday life in Upper Coquetdale may have changed little, if at all, in the decades following the arrival of the Roman army in the region.

Clearly we do not have space here to discuss all the Upper Coquetdale hillforts in any detail, so we will concentrate on three sites at which fieldwork has taken place since Dixon's time (Lordenshaws, Witchy Neuk, and Harehaugh) together with a brief examination of the cluster of sites along Clennell Street. Along with our discussion of Harehaugh, we will also consider the sadly destroyed site of Hetchester, which demonstrates very clearly the need for effective conservation policies if we wish to preserve such sites for the future.

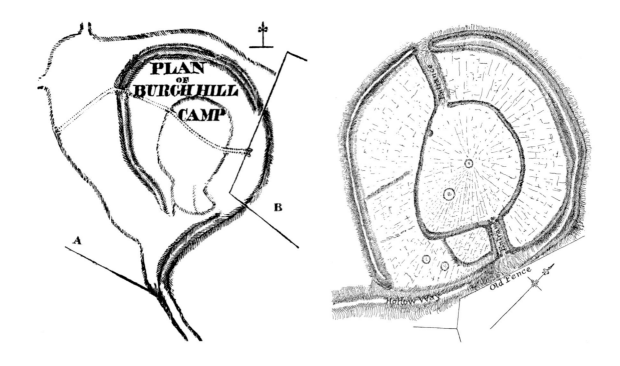

4.12 Surveys of Lordenshaws.

Above left:
a) Survey of the hillfort by E. Smith of Rothbury, published by Mackenzie in 1825 (although misleadingly labelled 'Burgh Hill Camp', this plan is clearly of Lordenshaws).

Above right:
b) R. C. Hedley's 1888 survey of the hillfort, published in Dixon's *Upper Coquetdale* in 1903.

Right:
c) The first survey to show the fort within its landscape setting, published within volume XV of *A History of Northumberland* in 1940.

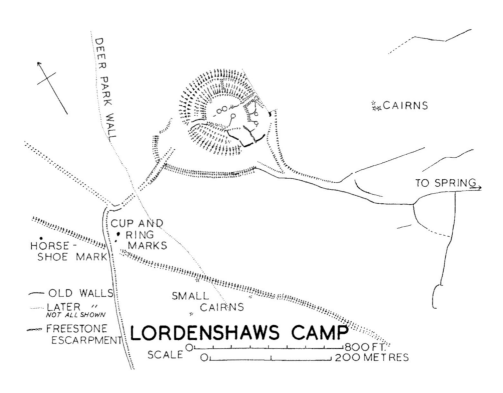

Lordenshaws

Excavation is not the only method of investigation that can be usefully employed on hillforts. As noted in the introduction to this volume, detailed topographic survey (careful recording and accurate large scale mapping of all features visible above ground) can tell us a great deal without recourse to shovel or trowel. Such survey work is a very specialised skill, necessitating the recognition of relevant features on the ground, the accurate recording of these using complex scientific instruments, and the artistic representation of the recorded features on the printed page. The Lordenshaws hillfort and surrounding area were subjected to such survey in 1990, and the results are presented in a paper by Peter Topping in the 1993 volume of *Archaeologia Aeliana*. Peter is a native north-eastener who has maintained an active interest in the region since his enforced transfer to the Cambridge office of English Heritage. He has continued to direct excavations for the Northumberland Archaeological Group during his summer 'holidays', and, due to his decades of experience and extensive list of publications, must now be considered amongst Northumberland's most illustrious prehistorians.

The 1990 survey is by no means the first to have been undertaken at Lordenshaws. In fact, surveys have been completed here roughly every 50 years since the 1820s, and these document the development of archaeological survey techniques over the past couple of centuries (fig. 4.12). Peter Topping's paper includes a very detailed description of the visible remains of the hillfort, and demonstrates the benefits of recording the landscape around ancient sites rather than just recording sites in isolation. The following excerpts from the report (see also fig. 4.12d) give a flavour of the site, without going into any great detail.

Lordenshaws is a sub-circular, multivallate work with two opposing entrances which has an overall diameter of some 140m. The inner enclosure has a sub-oval, almost D-shaped plan, measuring internally roughly 70m from NW to SE by 45m transversly.

The outermost defences, though partly disturbed by later features in the E and SE, are the best-preserved and most prominent,

Two opposing entrances cut through the defences and are embanked on both sides. The better-preserved E entrance is 4.8m wide, between walls 3.0m wide and up to 1.5m high. Some facing stones are visible, particularly where the entrance cuts through rampart 2; here a series of upright orthostats standing 0.8m high still survives. (Fig. 4.13).

The interior of the fort lies on two levels, the N part rising up to 1.3m above that on the S. This division is clearly defined by a prominent natural scarp running across the centre of the site roughly from E to W.....In the N part of the interior are at least two hut-circles....Several lengths of poorly-preserved curving banks, no more than 0.3m high, protrude from beneath the two hut-circles, perhaps representing the foundations of earlier huts or small enclosures.

The S part of the interior contains a particularly prominent hut-circle, the interior of which has been cleared probably by antiquarian activity.

Overlying the SE quadrant of the defences are the remains of a later settlement, suggesting population growth, settlement shift, or a new requirement for shelter rather than strength of fortification. The defences seem to have been almost levelled in this area....

In summary the fort would appear to have had a complex development. The variously preserved and

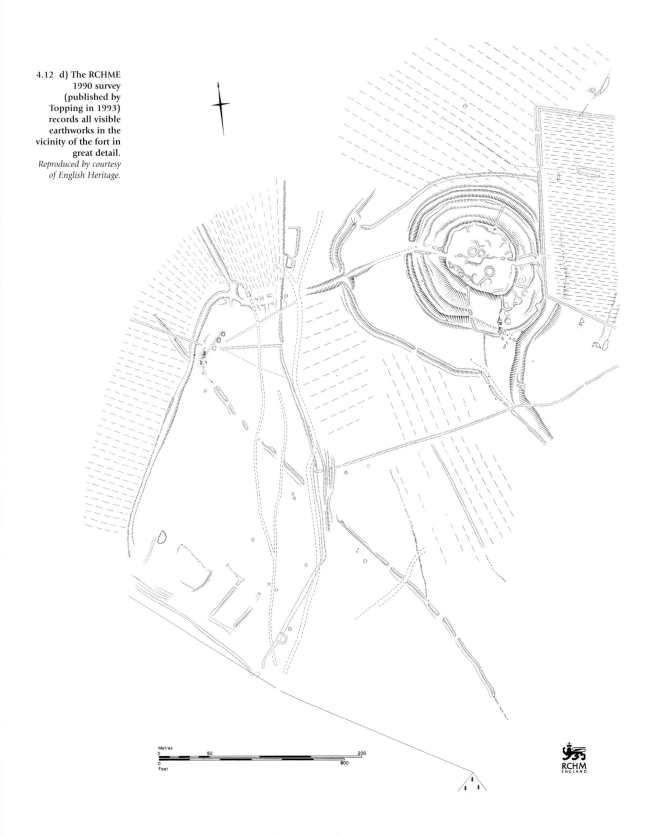

4.12 d) The RCHME 1990 survey (published by Topping in 1993) records all visible earthworks in the vicinity of the fort in great detail. *Reproduced by courtesy of English Heritage.*

Metres
0   50   200
0   600
Feet

RCHM
ENGLAND

4.13 John Turnbull Dixon's sketch of the eastern entrance into Lordenshaws hillfort, together with a recent photograph of the same view.

partly overlapping defences suggest reuse and possibly expansion before parts of the defensive circuit became obsolete and were overlain by a later settlement in the SE.

Topping's report also provides detailed discussion of other remains surrounding the hillfort, including a substantial outer earthwork, trackways and field systems. Some of these are probably contemporary with the hillfort, while others are clearly later.

At virtually all hillforts where modern surveys, such as that at Lordenshaws, have been completed, it has been demonstrated that what were often previously classified simply as 'Iron Age hillforts' are actually complex monuments with more than one architectural phase. Often, evidence is uncovered of activity both before and after the hillfort itself was occupied. Such observations are important, but if we wish to fully understand the chronology of these sites then there will always be a need to resort to excavation to supplement the information derived from survey.

Witchy Neuk

In the following wonderfully evocative passage from *Upper Coquetdale*, Dixon records an address he gave to members of the Newcastle Society of Antiquaries on site at Witchy Neuk in 1901, during which a number of prehistoric artefacts were also examined:

This camp, in its primitive state, would be surrounded by a massive rampart of earth and stones, surmounted by a high strong fence. Arranged within the rampart there would be a number of circular huts, with small doorways facing the south, having pointed roofs covered with sods and heather; a fire of wood burning on the large stone flag, usually found in the centre of each hut circle, the smoke escaping as best it could; a numerous colony of men, women, and children, moving hither and thither, using such domestic implements and tools, weapons of war and of the chase, as the members are now inspecting. With weapons such as these flint arrowheads, spear heads, and bronze axes, did the pre-historic inhabitants of the valley fight their battles, hunt the British ox in the woodland glades along the banks of the Coquet, the wild boar among the thickets of Swindon burn, the red deer on the heights of Kill-buck, the wild cat on Cat's-law, the prowling wolf in his lair at Wolfershiel, the raven on the lofty cliffs of Ravensheugh, or the eagle on Earnslaw. This hillfort is known as Whitefield camp, or Soldiers'-fauld, and Witches'-neuk. The latter is derived from a legend that 'Meg o' Meldon,' in one of her midnight flights on broom shank or stalk of ragwort, rested on the rocks that form its northern defence.

Present-day interpretation officers would charge a fortune for such powerful prose, were any capable of it. Having said that, the passage is a little chronologically confusing, as it merges discussion of the Iron Age hillfort with much earlier flint tools, but it seems trivial to criticise such splendid scene-setting on the basis of mere facts!

Partial excavation of the 'Witchy Neuk' enclosure was undertaken for the Northumberland County History Committee by Thomas Wake, Thomas Hepple and 'four local workmen' over a two week period in June 1936. A report of the excavation appears in the 1939 volume of *Archaeologia Aeliana*. The justification for the excavation is given as the 'lack of definite information as to the period of construction and purpose of this and similar works'. Interestingly, the first paragraph contains an acknowledgement of H.M Office of Works (Inspectorate of Ancient Monuments) for 'permitting the disturbance of a scheduled monument'. It may surprise some readers to learn that experienced archaeologists require special permission from the government to undertake excavations of scheduled sites (of which there are many thousand throughout England), and the account of the Harehaugh saga which follows will demonstrate how difficult it can be to obtain such consent. Some readers may question whether consent should be required from civil servants in London for professional archaeologists to investigate archaeological sites in Northumberland, but this is an issue way beyond the remit of this account. The Witchy Neuk report also makes reference to 'a heavy growth of bracken which made excavation difficult': a problem with which any modern archaeologist who has worked in a bracken infested landscape will readily sympathise. Invasive bracken roots are not merely inconvenient, but they can cause serious disturbance to fragile archaeological deposits. Under the circumstances, and judging by the photographs accompanying the published report, this seems to have been a very neat and tidy excavation.

4.15 Plan of the Witchy Neuk excavations, reproduced from the excavation report.

The Witchy Neuk site consists of a fortified 'D'-shaped enclosure of approximately 100 by 75 metres, sited on the edge of impressive sandstone crags with tremendous views over Coquetdale (figs. 4.14, 4.15). The excavation opened up three areas within the camp's interior, and also cut trenches across both entrances. As often happens, the true significance of some of the results was not realised at the time of the excavation, but thanks to the fine photographs accompanying the excavation report we can now suggest a rough framework for the chronological development of the site. The presence of a saddle quern, re-used as building stone in the structure of the rampart, suggests that occupation here might extend back into the Bronze Age, if not earlier. (Saddle querns were used during Neolithic and Bronze Age times,

4.16 Views of the Witchy Neuk excavations, reproduced from the published excavation report:

Above:
a) excavated house site, with stone flagging still extending over much of the house interior.

Right:
b) the outer face of the fort rampart adjacent to the west entrance, with the external ditch visible in the foreground.

and worked simply by providing a smooth surface on which grain was ground using a large pebble as a grinding stone. They were eventually replaced by rotary querns, discussed later in this chapter). Further evidence for pre-hillfort occupation may well lie concealed within the site. For example, the excavation uncovered a stone-filled trench running across the camp's west entrance. This is probably part of a construction trench for a palisaded enclosure that may have pre-dated the hillfort by a century or more, rather than part of a gate structure contemporary with the hillfort ramparts as suggested by the excavators.

The excavation uncovered two of the houses that Dixon had correctly predicted would be found here, and there may well be others outside the excavated areas. It is important to note that these were substantial structures, up to 7.5 metres in diameter, and would potentially have had two storeys: to refer to them simply as 'huts' is very misleading. When looking at the sterile images of these excavated structures, we should not forget that these were once the homes of real people: Dixon's 'colony of men, women and children, moving hither and thither'. In addition to their practical value, the houses would almost certainly have incorporated considerable ritual symbolism, with specific areas of their interiors having particular functions (eg sleeping or cooking) and also ritual associations (eg with death or fertility). The two timber-built roundhouses and associated areas of stone flagging (fig. 4.16a) may well be contemporary with the construction of the ramparts, perhaps dating from the third or second centuries BC. Judging by the photographic evidence in fig. 4.16b, Witchy Neuk must have been an impressive site, with its substantial ditch and formidable, stone-faced rampart.

The excavators report that 'the interest of the settlement with its varied structures was unfortunately mitigated by the paucity of datable artefacts'. This was always a major problem prior to the invention of radiocarbon dating in the 1950s: if no stratified, datable finds were encountered it could prove impossible to allocate even approximate dates to the various phases of occupation identified during an excavation. Today, radiocarbon dating could provide a series of dates from features like the cooking pits and hearths encountered within the roundhouses at Witchy Neuk, but unfortunately the only datable object found during the excavation was a single, small fragment of a glass jug, thought to date from the third century AD. While this might hint at occupation here extending into the Roman period, it was recovered from a rabbit barrow rather than a secure archaeological context, so is of dubious value to the interpretation of the site.

The report concludes that 'we cannot claim to have exhausted all the information to be obtained' from the site. Indeed, it might be fair to suggest that the 'lack of definite information' referred to in the introduction to the report remained pretty much unaffected by the excavation. However, Thomas Wake and his colleagues are to be congratulated for at least attempting to throw some light on the Iron Age of Upper Coquetdale, especially when it is considered that it was to be nearly sixty years until the next excavation of a local Iron Age site was attempted. The excavators of Witchy Neuk had 'hoped to resume further work later on', but circumstances arose which prevented this from happening. There is clearly much scope for further investigation here, and considerable potential for obtaining samples which, thanks to modern scientific techniques, could tell us much about the origins, occupation and abandonment of the site.

Harehaugh and Hetchester

Harehaugh Camp (fig. 4.17) is a stunningly sited hillfort at the junction of the Grasslees Burn and the Coquet, enjoying exquisite views over Coquetdale towards the distant Cheviot Hills. When I first visited the site, in the company of the then landowner Mr Guy Renwick of Holystone Grange, I was concerned about the rapidly deteriorating state of some sections of the generally extremely impressive turf-covered fort ramparts. These were being systematically destroyed by burrowing rabbits, in combination with sheep which took advantage of the ramparts to shelter from the occasionally inclement Northumberland weather, further scraping away the soil where it had already been exposed by the bunnies (fig. 4.18). There was also a serious problem of bracken infestation which meant that the impressive ramparts were almost hidden from view for much of the year. I remember being treated to a most enjoyable lunch of roast chicken in the impressive surrounds of Holystone Grange, during which Mr Renwick intimated that he would be quite happy to sign a management agreement ensuring the site's sympathetic management and eventually enabling public access. This agreement, one of many which are now in place at important archaeological sites throughout the National Park, was duly completed, and a comprehensive management plan for the site drawn up.

I could easily write an entire book about the ensuing 'Harehaugh saga', but will content myself here with are a few edited highlights. A casual observation that the site had 'managed to survive the Roman invasion and two world wars, but was now being systematically dismantled by bunnies which were gradually turning the site into something akin to a swiss cheese' was picked up by the press. Generally I find that members of the press are interested in archaeological stories, but where a site has a quirky aspect to it this interest can become overwhelming! I was called upon to give several interviews about Harehaugh for local and national media, and was informed that the story even appeared in the South African press! These interviews covered the background to hillforts, through the problems of managing sites in the modern landscape, to detailed discussions of rabbit contraceptives. Having noticed something on the news some time previously about the possibility of developing a rabbit contraceptive to help keep numbers down (an altogether more satisfactory option than the hideous myxomatosis which still returns from time to time), I decided to make enquiries about the possibility of holding a trial here at Harehaugh. I obtained some phone numbers from somewhere, and began several calls with 'I'm not sure if I'm in the right place, but I'm ringing to ask about contraceptives for rabbits...'. Responses were mixed, but believe it or not I did eventually find myself talking to someone at a laboratory near London where experiments were indeed being undertaken on the development of a chemical that could be sprayed around rabbit warrens to control the birth rate. Unfortunately, trials were to last about a decade before anything became available on the market, and we were not able to offer Harehaugh for trials as it was not a 'securely contained area'. I have no idea whether the experiments have been successful, but the story certainly made for good television (and radio!).

Throughout my archaeological career, I have always sought to achieve a sensible balance in the allocation of limited resources to the three related objectives of conservation, interpretation and research. Clearly, here at Harehaugh, there was a pressing need for conservation work to preserve the crumbling ramparts, and there was also a clear case for interpreting such an impressive site in such a beautiful location for the general public. There was also, in my view, a clear case for undertaking limited excavation in the attempt to better understand the history of the monument, the potential fragility of surviving archaeological deposits throughout the site, and the nature of the damage being done by the the bunnies and bracken. My recommendation was to undertake an archaeological evaluation (a small scale excavation) of the site and

4.18 The collapsing ramparts of Harehaugh Camp. The figure on the crest of the inner rampart gives an indication of the impressive scale of the surviving earthworks, while the damage to the ramparts caused by a combination of rabbits and sheep is clear.

consider the results of this before deciding on the best long-term management regime for the site. The Department of Archaeology at Newcastle University was prepared to undertake this evaluation, enabling students to learn the techniques of archaeological excavation while also completing a useful piece of work. However, there was a major problem to be overcome. Just like Witchy Neuk, Harehaugh is a scheduled ancient monument, so no work could take place here without special consent from the government.

Unfortunately, and very frustratingly for me, the archaeological climate in England in the mid 1990s did not encourage excavation. Instead, most resources were allocated to conservation in a well-intended (but in my view anti-academic and short-sighted) approach to conserve everything for the distant future when better techniques would be available for excavation. What the relevant authorities seemed incapable of realising was that archaeological research offered enormous potential for conservation and interpretation: as local people, including farmers and landowners, became aware of the importance of sites, they would become more concerned about the protection of similar sites elsewhere. Eminent academics were forced by sheer frustration to pack up working in England and to concentrate their fieldwork abroad

4.19 The detailed survey of Harehaugh Camp by RCHME. *Reproduced by kind permission of English Heritage.*

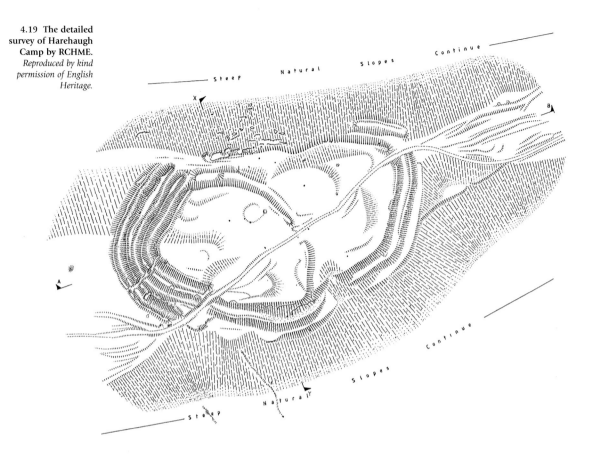

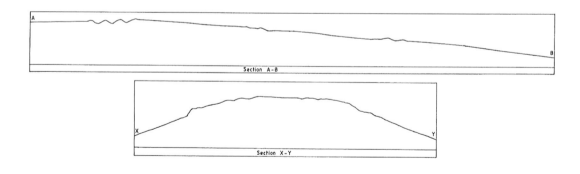

(even Scotland, with its more enlightened views on archaeological research, counted as 'abroad' at this time) while important and threatened sites in England remained uninvestigated. Eventually, permission was given for the excavation of a single, small trench at Harehaugh, primarily to 'investigate the levels of rabbit damage'. The erosion scars around the entire site were all photographed, and retired National Park head ranger Jimmy Givens was employed to control the bracken and the bunnies. Bracken spraying is normally undertaken over wide areas by helicopter, but for the relatively small area around Harehaugh Camp Jimmy dressed up in a protective 'space suit' and sprayed the entire site from a back-pack. He also returned to the site on a monthly basis to gas the rabbits in an attempt to control their rate of expansion. Gassing was never my preferred option, but is common practice where rabbit numbers have to be controlled on agricultural land. I recall being goaded into joining a discussion by a local newspaper reporter who had obtained a quote from a local wildlife officer to the effect that 'live rabbits are much more important than all that dead history': a variety of replies came immediately to mind, but I opted to maintain a diplomatic silence.

As the first stage of investigation at Harehaugh, prior to the excavation of the single permitted trial trench, the fort was surveyed (fig. 4.19) by staff from the Newcastle office (now sadly closed) of the Royal Commission on Historic Monuments of England (now subsumed within English Heritage). While planning this survey I remember walking round the site with Humphrey Welfare, then head of the Newcastle RCHME office. 'Hum', as he is affectionately known to colleagues, is an immensely knowledgeable and widely respected archaeologist who grew up in Coquetdale and is now very high within the echelons of English Heritage, though most unfortunately no longer directly involved with the north-east. While walking round the site, I remember suggesting to him the possibility of there being a Neolithic site here as well as the hillfort. His response, which struck me at the time as perhaps overly negative, was something along the lines of 'steady on, we're not in Wessex here' - a reference to the fact that some Iron Age sites in Wessex have been shown to have Neolithic precursors, but no examples of this phenomenon had been recognised in our region. Hum was being rightly cautious, but, as we suggested in Chapter 3, the Harehaugh ramparts may well conceal an important Neolithic site that could have major implications for Neolithic archaeology throughout Coquetdale and further afield.

The single excavation trench (fig. 3.8) was eventually dug by Newcastle University undergraduates in summer 1994, under the direction of Clive Waddington. Both Clive and I remember the Harehaugh trial project with some frustration, largely due to the restrictions placed on what we were allowed to do. Interpretations based on small-scale interventions can be notoriously difficult, often giving false impressions of what might be inferred from a larger excavation. The inability to excavate a section across the fort's ditches was also frustrating, as the fills of such ditches often hold the greatest clues as to the chronology and function of earthwork sites. Nevertheless, Clive attempted a plausible reconstruction of the fort ramparts based on this small excavation, and also obtained the Neolithic radiocarbon date discussed in Chapter 3. The English Heritage inspector of ancient monument, Mr Henry Owen John (who, extraordinarily, lived in Swansea, had his office in London, and was responsible for the archaeology of North-East England, but in my experience was never late for a single site meeting!) sympathised with my desire for further excavation here, but suggested, most sensibly as it turned out, that I should commission a survey of all the Park's hillforts so that the importance and deteriorating condition of Harehaugh could be considered in context.

Henry's suggestion to undertake a general survey of all the hillforts led the National Park Authority to commission Steve Speak, of Tyne & Wear Museums, to visit the fifty or so hillforts in the park and report on their condition. Steve has been active in local archaeology

4.20 Views of the 2002 Harehaugh Camp excavations.

Above: An early stage in the excavation of a section across the ramparts.

Below: An excavated section of ancient walling running along the crest of one of the fort's ramparts.

for many years, having worked on many of Colin Burgess' excavations back in the 1970s, and his expert knowledge of all the sites made him the ideal person to carry out this survey. He awarded points to every hillfort according to its perceived importance, its fragility and the apparent threat to it from any source of erosion. A league table was drawn up, and, surprise, surprise, Harehaugh Camp was the champion by a mile! At last, I thought, we will be able to undertake some investigation of the site.

The investigation that eventually took place was designed as part of the National Park Authority's *Discovering our Hillfort Heritage* (DoHH) project. This wide-ranging project attracted a little over £1 million of external funding from various sources (most notably the Heritage Lottery Fund and European Union) to complete work relating to the survey, research, conservation and interpretation of hillforts and prehistoric landscapes throughout Upper Coquetdale and the Cheviots. (At the time of writing a separate publication on the results of

the project is being prepared for publication by Alistair Oswald of English Heritage.) I had hoped that a Harehaugh excavation would develop into a major element of the DoHH initiative, perhaps spread over two or three years, but for various reasons it did not. There were major problems with project planning, with different 'experts' frustratingly offering conflicting opinions which inevitably led to delays. For example, having drawn up a project design for the proposed excavation, involving a combination of professional archaeologists and students from Newcastle University, I was informed by one 'expert' official that students would not be permitted to participate as it was not good practice to 'use' inexperienced diggers on scheduled monuments. A few days later I received a letter from another official of equal status, informing me that he 'particularly liked the educational aspects of the project' and wondered whether there was scope for including more places for students. The life of a National Park Archaeologist has its share of frustrations!

Fieldwork was originally scheduled for summer 2001, but was postponed due to the horrendous outbreak of foot and mouth disease that blighted the Northumberland countryside that year. Eventually, limited excavations (generously funded by English Heritage) were completed during summer 2002 (fig. 4.20). It was again frustrating not to be able to investigate the ditches, or to delve deeper into archaeological deposits encountered within the fort which might have included evidence of houses or other structures. Nevertheless, the results are of some interest, and certainly suggest that further work here would be worthwhile. The finds include two flint flakes which reinforce the case for a Neolithic presence here; several sherds of Iron Age pottery, probably of local manufacture; a shale armlet of probable second-to fourth-century AD date (suggestive of occupation during the Roman period); and several pieces of iron slag which appear to be evidence of on-site smithing. Unfortunately, the environmental samples collected during the excavation proved to be of little value, although small quantities of both hulled barley and hulled wheat were recovered and the presence of buttercup suggests that land in the vicinity of the fort was used for pasture. Thus, assuming these samples were all from Iron Age deposits, people in the vicinity of the fort appear to have been practising a mixed agricultural regime. We will consider further evidence for late prehistoric agriculture shortly.

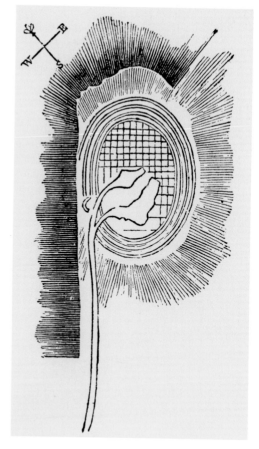

4.21 An early nineteenth-century plan of Hetchester Camp.
Reproduced from Mackenzie 1825.

Due to a combination of its strategic location and impressive form, I believe that Harehaugh may one day prove to be one of the most important prehistoric sites in the whole of Upper Coquetdale, assuming, of course, that the bunnies don't manage to destroy it before permission and funds are forthcoming for further investigations. On the subject of the destruction of hillforts, there is one further site which deserves special mention. I had occasionally wondered, while looking out over the Coquet from the splendid ramparts of Harehaugh, why no similarly impressive site existed to the north of the river. On checking the records, I found that such a site did indeed once exist here - Hetchester Camp. Ennias Mackenzie, in his brilliant *Historical, Topographical and Descriptive View of the County of Northumberland* (second edition - published 1825) describes this site (fig. 4.21) as follows:

At a short distance to the north-west of Hepple there is a British entrenched strong-hold, called Hetchester. The subjoined drawing will convey a correct idea of the form and strength of this ancient hill fortress. The interior length of the entrenchment is 140 yards, and the breadth 90 yards. The breadth of the inner ditch is 18 feet, and of the exterior ditch 15 feet. Each of the rampiers is 15 feet in height, and 6 feet in breadth. The hill being very steep and difficult of access on the north-west side, the fort has had but two ditches in that part. Most of the entrenchments have been levelled, and it is only on the north-west side that they remain in any degree of good preservation. The foundations of the ancient buildings are very perceptible within the entrenchment. But all traces of this remarkable castrametation will soon be obliterated, as excavations for lime are proceeding in the heart of the works.

In 1903, in *Upper Coquetdale*, Dixon notes that 'several querns, a few defaced Roman coins, and large quantities of antlers of the Red Deer, have from time to time been laid bare by the quarrymen when removing earth from the top of the limestone; this process, of many years' continuance, has almost destroyed the outline of the ramparts of Hetchester.' It is not clear from this account whether or not these finds came from the actual site of Hetchester, or from other quarries in the vicinity, but the reference to Roman coins is intriguing. I have no idea where these coins are now, but it would be fascinating to examine them if they ever come to light. Today, the Hetchester site is littered with quarry pits and spoil heaps, and according to recent accounts (I have not visited the site myself) there is now no sign whatsoever of the once mighty Iron Age ramparts.

Archaeologists are understandably tempted to concentrate on the best preserved sites when studying an area. We must never forget, however, that a now-destroyed site like Hetchester may have been of very great importance at the same time as other, now better preserved sites like Harehaugh, were occupied. I have little doubt that the occupants of Hetchester and Harehaugh must have been in regular contact. Perhaps the two camps somehow functioned together to control movement through this section of the Coquet Valley. Indeed, Harehaugh, Hetchester, Witchy Neuk and the nearby lowland site of Caistron Camp should really be considered together, as a group of probably contemporary sites, when seeking to interpret Iron Age life in this stretch of the valley. It would be foolish to attempt to interpret any of these sites without reference to the others.

The story of Hetchester demonstrates that even a huge site like a hillfort can be entirely destroyed by subsequent human activity, and this, sadly, is not the only such example in Upper Coquetdale. Another hillfort once existed on Robert's Law, just north of Trewhitt Hall. Antiquarian sources record that this had impressive stone-built ramparts, and several querns were apparently recovered from it. However, recent inspection of the site suggests that no trace of the fort survives above ground: perhaps the ramparts were dismantled and the stone re-used in nearby field walls or farm buildings.

Hetchester and Robert's Law serve to remind us that all ancient monuments need to be sensitively managed and conserved for the future. Tomorrow's threat might not be from something as obvious or as immediate as quarrying, but other threats such as rabbit burrowing, poaching by cattle or sheep, tree planting, or even perhaps too many tourists, all have the potential to cause serious damage to ancient monuments. We must seek to conserve all remaining prehistoric monuments as valuable elements of the beautiful Upper Coquetdale landscape, enabling them to be appreciated by everyone while also ensuring their survival for archaeological investigation in due course.

Clennell Street

Two splendid hillforts stand either side of the southern end of Clennell Street, one of the great ancient tracks across the Cheviot Hills. These tracks were probably in regular use by the Bronze Age, and three thousand years later, in the sixteenth century AD, were used as cross-border routes by raiding parties during the era of the border reivers (fig. 4.22). David Dippie Dixon notes in *Upper Coquetdale* that 'Immediately on emerging from amongst the densely packed hills around the upper sources of the Coquet into the more open valley near Alwinton, races of an early occupation are met with in greater abundance than amid those higher altitudes.' This observation is certainly reflected in the distribution of hillforts, only a couple of which are known higher up the valley than Alwinton. Clennell Street must have been a major route into and out of Upper Coquetdale during Iron Age times, and it may be that the upper reaches of the valley (above Alwinton) were something of a 'cultural backwater' in comparison to the fertile lowlands and surrounding hillfort-rich upland fringes between the southern end of Clennell Street and Rothbury.

There is certainly an extraordinary concentration of still visible prehistoric settlement sites towards the southern end of Clennell Street (fig. 4.23). None of these sites has been excavated, but by analogy with better known sites elsewhere we can place them into a general chronological sequence and thus gain an insight into patterns of settlement in this closely defined area over the entire period considered in this chapter. The earliest of the sites is probably that known as Kidlandlee Dean 1, on the grassy slopes between the line of Clennell Street and the edge of Kidland Forest. The site nestles into the east-facing slope to take advantage of whatever natural shelter was available from the prevailing westerly winds. The visible remains (fig. 4.24) consist of three platforms for timber roundhouses up to 8 metres in

4.22 Several popular walking routes in the Cheviots use tracks which date back to prehistoric times. *Photo: Tony Hopkins.*

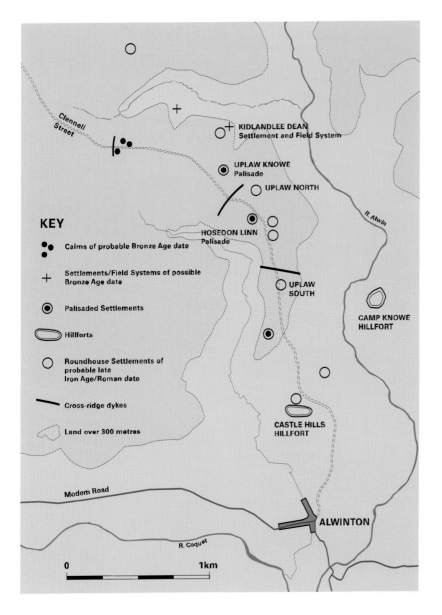

KEY

- **Cairns of probable Bronze Age date**
- **+ Settlements/Field Systems of possible Bronze Age date**
- **◉ Palisaded Settlements**
- **▭ Hillforts**
- **○ Roundhouse Settlements of probable late Iron Age/Roman date**
- **▬ Cross-ridge dykes**
- **⌂ Land over 300 metres**

0   1km

Labels on map: Clennell Street · KIDLANDLEE DEAN Settlement and Field System · UPLAW KNOWE Palisade · UPLAW NORTH · HOSEDON LINN Palisade · UPLAW SOUTH · R. Alwin · CAMP KNOWE HILLFORT · CASTLE HILLS HILLFORT · Modern Road · ALWINTON · R. Coquet

diameter, set within a complex of low banks and lynchets which form open-sided fields. It is possible that the nearby round cairns, immediately adjacent to the line of Clennell Street, may be the final resting places of some of the early farmers who ploughed these ancient fields. The Kidlandlee Dean 1 site is almost certainly of Bronze Age date, probably originating from the centuries between 2000 and 1500BC. Hopefully we will soon be able to say a great deal more about it as the Department of Archaeology at Durham University, under the direction of Peter Carne and Rachel Pope, began an excavation programme here in the summer of 2005. Although no results are available at the time of writing, Peter and Rachel intend to return to the site for at least one more season and will hopefully be able to ascertain the detailed chronology of the houses and fields, and discover much fascinating information about the lifestyle of the people who lived here. A nearby site, Kidlandlee Dean 2, contains fragmentary banks and lynchets which may also be Bronze Age, although the single house identified here is of 'ring-groove' type and therefore probably of Iron Age date.

4.23 Map showing the locations of prehistoric settlements along Clennell Street, north of Alwinton. *Drawn by Ian Scott.*

Three palisaded settlements, perhaps dating from as early as 800BC, but possibly as late as 300BC, have been recorded along this stretch of Clennell Street. The largest, known as Hosedon Linn (fig. 4.25), includes the ring-grooves of at least nine circular timber buildings, of which the largest two have 'double ring-grooves' and are 11 metres in diameter. Exactly why some buildings had double ring-grooves is not known, but they may well have been architecturally very grand structures, surrounded in this case by a cluster of lesser but still far from unimpressive buildings. They may have been the dwellings of particularly important individuals or families, but need not necessarily have been domestic buildings: some of the so-called 'roundhouses' may have been workshops, byres, stables, or communal buildings. The surrounding palisade trench at Hosedon Linn is only partially visible, but enough survives to

demonstrate that this was indeed a palisade rather than an unenclosed settlement. It remains possible, however, that some of the timber houses could initially have formed an unenclosed settlement, with the surrounding palisade added later. A second palisade, Uplaw Knowe, lies some 500 metres north-west of the Hoseden Linn site, again hard by the line of Clennell Street. This example consists of an egg-shaped palisade surrounding the ring-grooves of two large buildings, each about 14 metres in diameter. A third example, containing at least seven circular buildings, has been recorded 1km south of the Hosedon Linn site, again close to the line of Clennell Street.

The next phase in the sequence of prehistoric settlement along Clennell Street is represented by the two substantial hillforts: Camp Knowe and Castle Hills (also sometimes referred to as Gallow Law, suggesting a rather unpleasant alternative use of the site in more recent times). These two sites appear to stand guard over the southern end of the Alwin Valley, overlooking the junction of the Alwin and the Coquet at the village of Alwinton. However, whether their original purpose related to guarding the valley in any way must be open to doubt. It may be that they were constructed independently by two different groups, with their impressive form and location owing more to matters of group prestige than to any strictly defensive duties. Indeed, Camp Knowe is not really on the line of Clennell Street and may have related

4.24 Kidlandlee Dean I Bronze Age settlement and field system.
Photo: Tim Gates.

4.25 Hosedon Linn palisaded settlement.
Photo: Tim Gates.

4.26 Looking north up the Alwin Valley towards the ramparts of Camp Knowe hillfort. The impressive location of the hillfort, on a ledge above the steep valley side, can be readily appreciated from this view.

primarily to communities living on land to the east. Regardless of its possible link with Clennell Street, it is a very impressive site on a south-west spur of Clennell Hill high above the Alwin (fig. 4.26). Although it is separated from the main bulk of Clennell Hill by a slight saddle, it is nevertheless overlooked from this direction. We have observed earlier in this chapter that many Cheviot hillforts are in what may appear initially as strongly defensive positions, but are in fact overlooked by nearby higher ground. They were built to look impressive, but defence was apparently not the primary consideration in their design. The Camp Knowe fort may be another example of this phenomenon, although it does have a continuous double rampart of earth and stone (except along its north-west side where only a single bank was constructed above the precipitous drop down to the Alwin). The ramparts have been much damaged by later agricultural activity, but this must originally have been amongst the most impressive of all Northumberland hillforts. The low walls of stone houses and other structures still visible within the interior probably date from the Roman period, by which time the ramparts had fallen into disrepair.

The Castle Hills fort (fig. 4.27) is also impressively sited, on the crest of an elongated oval shaped hill, aligned east-west. The site appears to consist essentially of a single rampart enclosing an area of 170 by 60 metres, with an additional, internal rampart around the western side. Occasional facing stones have been noted within the tumbled ramparts, so it may be that the site was originally surrounded by great stone walls rather than today's relatively unimpressive banks of rubble. Such defences would have looked mightily impressive to anyone viewing them from the lower land to the south, or passing along Clennell Street to the east. There appear to be original entrances at the west and east ends. This site really should be subjected to modern topographic survey, which might clarify the nature of the defences and pick up slight undulations in the turf, suggestive of internal structures such as houses. Evidence

4.27 Aerial view of the Alwinton Castle Hills hillfort.
Photo: Tim Gates.

for such structures, which may have been built of timber or stone, probably lies safely buried beneath the turf, awaiting the time when this very important site eventually attracts the attention of the archaeologist's trowel.

Two further substantial ancient settlements can also be seen along this stretch of Clennell Street. These may belong in Chapter 5, but will be described here to complete the extraordinary sequence of visible late prehistoric settlements in this area. The sites consist of clusters of stone built roundhouses and stockyards, and must date originally from either late Iron Age or Roman times, with occupation possibly extending throughout (and perhaps even beyond) the Roman period. At the northernmost of these two sites, known as Uplaw North, careful ground survey has recorded at least eight circular buildings, most of which are probably houses. The second site, Uplaw South (fig. 4.28), is located only about 500 metres away along the line of Clennell Street. Sixteen probable house sites have been recorded here, ranging from about three to seven metres in diameter. A community of fifty or more individuals could have lived quite comfortably here, with a further two or three dozen at nearby Uplaw North (both sites may reasonably be assumed to be contemporary). Other smaller settlements in the immediate locality, of apparently similar date, suggest that a community of a hundred or more people may have lived on the southern edge of Clennell Street during late prehistoric times.

Why should this area have been so important throughout later prehistory? A major clue is offered in the form of the linear earthworks which cut across the line of the Clennell Street track in at least three places. These cross-ridge dykes are undated, but may well date originally from later prehistory. Their original form is also unknown: they may have been crowned with a timber palisade or a hedge. Regardless of this, their function must have been to help to

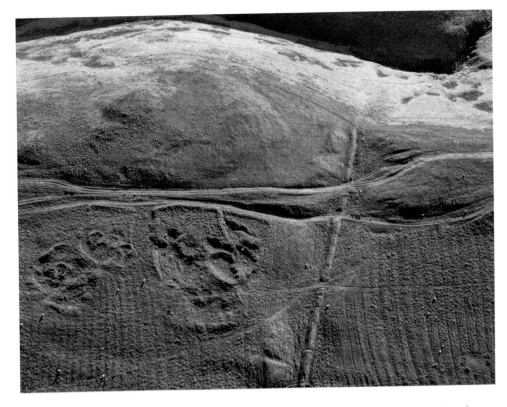

control movement of people and livestock along the line of Clennell Street. People on horseback, and all cattle and other livestock passing along the track, would have had to pass through narrow gaps in these dykes which would presumably have been gated. Thus, the dykes enabled a considerable degree of control over people entering and leaving Upper Coquetdale along what we have already suggested must have been one of the major routes into and out of the valley. The individual or community capable of controlling this traffic must have been of considerable status, status which would have been regularly reinforced as people passed along the route. Perhaps it was necessary to pay a form of tax or toll in order to pass this way. It is quite possible that someone living in the Castle Hills hillfort was in control of whatever system was in place, although this must remain conjecture at least until both the hillfort and the cross-ridge dykes are securely dated. Both Uplaw settlements are sited immediately adjacent to cross-ridge dykes, to which they must surely have been related in some way. As noted above, these settlements could have originated in Roman times, and thus should perhaps belong in Chapter 5. However, it is quite plausible in my view that their origins are earlier, and that they could have co-existed with the hillforts. Thus, the Uplaw dykes and settlements and the Castle Hills hillfort could all be bound up within a late Iron Age system of control over the ancient route of Clennell Street.

Celtic cowboys and cord rig fields
Agriculture in later prehistory

During the early Bronze Age, the Bloody Moss pollen sequence records an increase in heathland associated with a peak in charcoal, suggesting that people were burning the vegetation to promote the regrowth of heather for grazing animals: heather burning clearly has a long history in Upper Coquetdale. An upland site like Bloody Moss probably does not reflect what was being grown further down the valley, and it may be that crops were being grown here much earlier (as suggested in Chapter 3). Regardless of this, by about 1500BC, cereal pollen is recorded at Bloody Moss, indicating that people in the surrounding uplands were now engaged in arable agriculture. Unfortunately, it is not possible to identify the types of cereals being grown from pollen evidence alone, but it is likely that they included barley, which could be used for the baking of bread and the brewing of beer. Identification of particular types of cereal is normally only possible when actual grains or chaff are recovered from excavations. Not far from Coquetdale, an excavation at Hallshill, overlooking the Rede near West Woodburn, demonstrated that the residents of a small farmstead were apparently growing six-row barley, emmer wheat, spelt wheat and flax in the centuries around 1000BC. They were also collecting wild foodstuffs in the form of hazelnuts and blackberries or raspberries.

During the first millennium BC at Bloody Moss, although there are occasional indications of temporary recolonisation of hazel scrub, the pollen sequence records increasing levels of grass species and herbaceous plants associated with pasture (eg buttercup, ribwort plantain and various herbs). This suggests that more and more areas of upland were being used for grazing as time went by, a pattern which apparently intensified after about 450BC.

We must now consider the extent to which the archaeological record supports the picture painted by palaeoenvironmental evidence. In the past, archaeologists assumed that later prehistoric people of upland areas like Upper Coquetdale would have been primarily pastoralists. In 1958, Stuart Piggott (Professor of Prehistoric Archaeology at the University of Edinburgh) wrote of 'Celtic cow-boys and shepherds, footloose and unpredictable, moving with their animals over rough pasture and moorland', who 'could never adopt the Roman way of life in the manner of the settled farmers of the south.' The hillforts were generally regarded as safe havens for both people and stock when threatened by parties of cattle raiders. Although now outdated, and regarded as simplistic by many modern archaeologists, this picture may not be wholly inaccurate. I think it quite probable that large areas of upland were given over to extensive cattle ranching, and the hillforts may indeed have functioned on occasions as refuges, much as towers and bastles did in the medieval period. There may well have been a degree of transhumance, whereby people and stock moved into the high hills in summer, and back down to lower ground in winter. The cross-ridge dykes on Clennell Street may relate, at least in part, to the control of stock passing between lowland and upland pastures. Such a cycle, bearing an echo of the seasonal round of Mesolithic people thousands of years earlier, survived in Northumberland into the seventeenth century AD, so perhaps we should expect it to have been the norm during later prehistory. The form of the deep hollow-way approaching the fort at Lordenshaws certainly suggests that it was used for the funnelling of stock towards the fort, and the mysterious hollow-ways on Holystone Common (fig. 4.29), although undated, may also relate to stock movement over several centuries during later prehistory. It may well be that wealth was both stored and flaunted in the form of cattle, with the most wealthy individuals controlling the greatest herds, and cattle rustling a constant threat.

The image of the 'celtic cow-boy' has been tempered of late, however, through the discovery of extensive cultivation remains in the hills, as well as by the palaeoenvironmental evidence discussed above. In some places, clear lynchets are associated with settlements of probable Bronze Age date, providing unambiguous evidence of cultivation. A good example of such a field system can be seen at Kidlandlee (fig. 4.24). Elsewhere, as at Crane Sike (fig. 4.1), small, irregular fields are formed by linear banks of stone which may have supported hedges. Throughout the Cheviots, settlements of Bronze Age date are often accompanied by field clearance cairns, suggesting that the ground in the vicinity of the settlements was cultivated, or that pasture was being improved. Often, the field clearance cairns are the most obvious surviving features of such agricultural settlements. It is reasonable to assume that timber-built roundhouses (like those discussed earlier at Standrop Rigg and Houseledge) would have stood

4.29 Ancient hollow-ways of unknown date on Holystone Common.
Photo: Tim Gates.

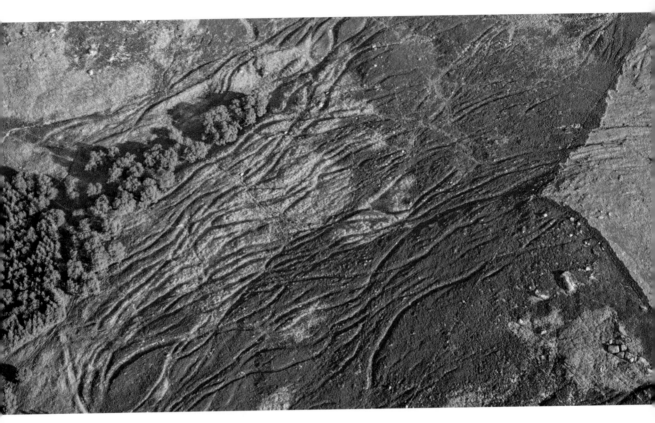

adjacent to, or within, such cairnfields, but it can be impossible to locate such structures from today's surface evidence. Sometimes, the experienced field archaeologist can identify tell-tale signs, such as platforms cut into hillsides or low rings of field clearance stone originally piled up outside the walls, which can prove the previous existence of timber houses. Often, however, no such traces are visible and the remains of timber houses, where they survive, will only ever be located by careful excavation.

Around the headwaters of the Black Burn, south-west of Debdon Whitefield, at least sixty small cairns and low banks, possibly field walls, provide evidence of agriculture of probable Bronze Age date. There are also some sepulchral cairns here (Dixon himself opened two examples, in 1902, one of which contained an urn. Another was excavated in 1969, and found to contain charcoal, flint tools and a fragment of a jet ring). There must also have been contemporary houses in this landscape, but these have yet to be identified. In the same location, there are several stone-built hut circles, almost certainly dating from late Iron Age or Romano-British times, and also the remains of a rectangular stone-built house of probable medieval date. This area contains evidence for settlement and farming extending back over perhaps 3,500 years: it would certainly repay more detailed archaeological investigation.

During the Iron Age, cultivation took place within sometimes extensive 'cord rig' field systems. Cord rig consists of narrow, ridged cultivation strips, with gaps of only about 1.5 metres between the centres of the ridges (fig. 4.30). It was recognised on air photographs at many sites in north-east England and southern Scotland during the 1980s. (The term 'cord rig' is alleged to have been invented by an archaeologist who happened to notice the similarity between it and the cordoroy trousers he was wearing while studying it. Types of archaeological sites and finds have acquired names for various reasons over the years, but I believe 'cord rig' is the first to have been named after a pair of trousers.) In 1989, Peter Topping published an important paper about cord rig in the *Proceedings of the Prehistoric Society*, a distinguished journal read by archaeologists throughout the world. Several Upper Coquetdale sites featured in this paper, including Trows Law (fig. 4.3) where people were clearly growing crops at an altitude of 420 metres above sea level. Since 1989, many more cord rig sites have been recorded, almost all from the air. Some of these sites are small plots, while others form extensive field systems (fig. 4.31, 4.32). Some cord rig occurs without any sign of adjacent settlement, while in other places it has been recorded close to settlement sites of presumed Bronze Age, Iron Age or Roman date. We know that some cord rig in Northumberland is of Iron Age or very early Roman date, as it has been recorded by excavation in sealed contexts beneath Roman military sites. Its overal chronology, however, is not known: cord rig cultivation may have been continuously or intermittently practised from the Bronze Age through into Roman times. It must originally have been far more widespread than the distribution of surviving sites might suggest, as many prehistoric field systems must have been destroyed by medieval ridge-and-furrow and other subsequent activity.

4.30 Cord rig adjacent to Clennell Street, seen from ground level.

The creation of ridges resulted in better drainage, raised the soil temperature markedly, and increased the depth of soil available for root growth. Some of the smaller cord rig plots may have been spade-dug, but the large field systems must have been worked with a plough of some kind. Scratching of the subsoil, evidence for the use of a simple plough, has been detected at some excavated sites. Perhaps future excavations, using new scientific techniques of investigation, will one day demonstrate not only the chronology of cord rig in Upper

4.31 An extensive tract of cord rig at Carshope. *Photo: Tim Gates.*

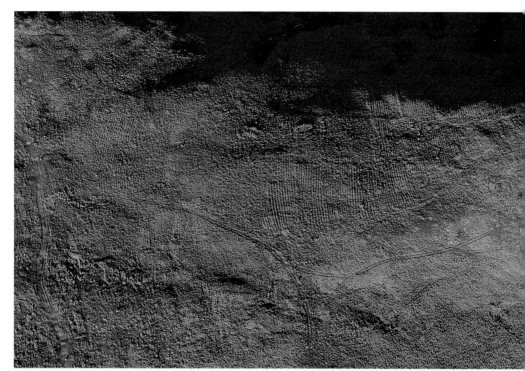

4.32 Aerial view of Ward Law, showing the hillfort towards the top-right corner, and remnants of a possibly contemporary cord rig field system towards the bottom-left. (The wider ridges in the right-hand half of the image relate to ploughing of much more recent date, which may well have destroyed more extensive remnants of cord rig cultivation). *Photo: Tim Gates.*

Coquetdale, but also the way in which it was cultivated and the range of crops grown on it.

The cord rig is not the only evidence for prehistoric cultivation. Elsewhere, there are cultivation terraces which, although strictly undated, most probably originated in late prehistoric times (fig. 4.33). Back in 1903, David Dippie Dixon observed that:

> *those narrow terraces seen cut into the face of Lord's Seat at Alwinton, their peculiar formation, their close proximity to Gallow Law camp, as well as the distance from the village - for the villagers would naturally prefer their cultivated strips on the surrounding alluvial flats - seem to point to their connection with a primitive system of cultivation, coeval with the occupation of the camps and hillforts in the immediate neighbourhood.*

Evidence for the processing of grain comes in the form of the ubiquitous quern-stones, for the grinding of grain into flour. These have been found on many excavations of Iron Age sites throughout Northumberland, and can be seen in museum displays where, in some cases, children are invited to partake in the messy practice of feeding grain into them and grinding it into flour, usually making a white, powdery mess of museum and child alike. Other querns have been turned up by the plough and are now preserved as ornamental features in farmhouse gardens. David Dippie Dixon tells us in Upper Coquetdale that 'querns are often seen on garden rockeries, where, as a rule, they are carefully preserved' (fig. 4.34a). A rather less well preserved, but still instantly recognisable, fragment of a rotary quern was recently discovered built into a field wall adjacent to the hillfort at Castlehill, Alnham. When this wall was dismantled in 2004, two further quern fragments were discovered within it (fig. 4.34b). The rotary querns must have been among the most essential domestic utensils of later prehistory, and their use extended well into Roman times. I have heard it suggested that some

4.33 Aerial view of the agricultural terraces on the 'Lord's Seat' at Alwinton.
Photo: Tim Gates.

4.34 Quern-stones are common finds on Iron Age and Roman-British settlement sites.

Above: **a)** This fine quern-stone now resides on a garden rockery at Warton Farm.

Left: **b)** National Park Archaeologist Rob Young with three quern-stones and a probable socket-stone for a door, all recently found in the field wall (visible in fig. 4.8) adjacent to the hillfort and Romano-British settlement at Castlehill, Alnham.

of them may also have been used to grind metal ores: an interesting suggestion though not yet, so far as I am aware, one with any firm evidence to support it.

The general picture painted by the palaeoenvironmental evidence appears, therefore, to receive support from the visible archaeological remains. This is only a very general picture, and further fieldwork will be necessary if we wish investigate regional variation throughout the valley and to firm up the chronological framework. We can be reasonably certain, however, that people in Upper Coquetdale were practicing mixed agriculture by about 1500BC, and that the extent of agricultural land, in the form of both arable fields and pasture, expanded steadily throughout the following 1500 years. An Iron Age farmer transported onto an early twentieth-century Coquetdale farm may have found little that he or she did not understand: many agricultural tools would have been familiar, and the annual farming calendar would have been little changed. Indeed, many aspects of hill farming in Upper Coquetdale probably changed more during the twentieth century than during the previous twenty centuries.

Axes, swords and ritual hoards
Metalwork and religion in later prehistory

On completing the first draft of this text, I was aware of only half a dozen finds of prehistoric bronze objects from Upper Coquetdale, all of which had been known to David Dippie Dixon a hundred years earlier. Amendment of the text became necessary after a visit to Michael and William Davy at Warton Farm in March 2004. Michael and William showed me two 3,000 year-old (late Bronze Age) axes which immediately doubled the number of such axes known to me from Upper Coquetdale (see fig. 6.10). Not a bad result for a chance meeting and casual conversation in a farmyard! Of the other two such axes known from Upper Coquetdale, one was also found on Warton Farm, back in 1897 (fig. 4.35). Was something special going on here at Warton, or are there many similar objects throughout the region awaiting discovery or identification? Such questions must await further work: for now we must concentrate on the few known local objects, but bearing in mind that the corpus of known objects is pitifully small and without doubt does not reflect the great importance of bronze in late prehistory.

4.35 A Bronze Age socketed bronze axe from Warton, now in the Newcastle Museum of Antiquities. (Scale in cms).

Before describing the known finds from Upper Coquetdale, we should briefly consider the impact of metalworking on society. Throughout the Stone Age, and well into the Bronze Age, there must always have been some people who were more proficient than others at the production of stone tools. I suspect, however, that most adults during the Neolithic could knock out a half decent flint scraper or arrowhead in a few minutes, and that most such artefacts were simply discarded if broken during manufacture or subsequent use. In contrast, bronze working is a much more specialist task, and valuable bronze objects could be melted down and recast if broken. Consequently, the introduction of bronze working brought about fundamental changes in the way that tools, weapons and other artefacts were procured.

The classification and chronology of bronze artefacts is a complex science in its own right, which we cannot cover in any detail here. However, we cannot ignore the probability that the introduction of metalworking may well have brought about profound changes in peoples' attitudes towards their world. (Such changes would presumably have begun with the introduction of the first metals, which may have reached our area a little before 2,000BC: a case could therefore be made for including this discussion in Chapter 3. However, as all but one of the known surviving prehistoric bronze objects from our region are of late Bronze Age date, and as I wish to link the discussion with a consideration of iron working, it is included in this chapter.) In Chapter 3 we noted that Neolithic axes were clearly of symbolic as well as functional importance: similarly, we will suggest here that Bronze Age axes, swords and other objects must have had more than just mundane practical value.

Bronze is an alloy of copper and tin, neither of which occurs naturally in the Upper Coquetdale area. Prehistoric copper mines have been investigated in Wales, and some may have existed closer to home in the Lake District. Most known deposits have been worked in historic times, and more recent workings may have destroyed any evidence of prehistoric mining. Consequently we may never know exactly where the copper used in Northumberland came from, although new technology may one day enable us to trace the copper in local objects back to its original source. The most likely source of tin is far away in south-west England, where deposits are known in Devon and Cornwall. In the foreword to this volume I referred to the mystery of how my de-luxe copy of *Upper Coquetdale* found its way to Cornwall, but this pales into insignificance when compared to the mystery of how tin found its way, in substantial quantities, from Cornwall to Northumberland during the second millennium BC. We know that stone axes were somehow distributed over vast distances during the Neolithic, so exchange networks of some kind were clearly in operation well before the Bronze Age. Such networks must also have been in place to facilitate the distribution of flint to areas like Upper Coquetdale which had no natural flint deposits. Unfortunately, we have no real idea as to how such distribution networks actually worked. Regardless of the detail, however, the ultimate source of both bronze and tin must have been far away from Upper Coquetdale, and this distance, coupled perhaps with the physical danger of mining, may have added to the mystique of the metal ores and the objects into which these ores were fashioned. Alternatively, it is possible that some people in our region may have known or cared nothing about the winning of the ores, and may simply have acquired quantities of them on demand, perhaps as prepared ingots, from a middle man - rather as we might buy any number of goods from shops today without having a clue as to how they were originally or obtained or manufactured.

The production of bronze objects consists of two basic stages: the mining and preparation of the ore, and the casting of the finished object. We have seen that the former process probably occurred far away from our region, so will not consider it further in this discussion. The second stage, the casting of finished objects using clay or stone moulds, must have occurred locally, although there is no evidence of it from Upper Coquetdale. Some local settlements, perhaps of specially high status, may have had their own resident metalsmiths who may have worked exclusively for a local chief or other important individual. Other smiths may have been itinerant, travelling around from place to place collecting old tools and weapons for recycling, and providing new objects, or mending broken ones, on demand.

Opposite Page.
4.37 The Cragside sword (length 60cm), now in the Newcastle upon Tyne Museum of Antiquities.

Ethnographic evidence suggests that the metalsmiths may have been held in high esteem, and that their work would almost certainly have been regarded as a kind of alchemy: symbolically bound up with ritual and 'magic'. Various scholars have commented on the sexual imagery which may

4.36 The best preserved of the two Simonside swords, now in Alnwick Museum.

have been associated with the smelting of ores, with the bellows perhaps regarded as male and the furnace as female. The lives of individual bronze objects perhaps acted as metaphors for individual human lives, with stages of conception, birth, life, death and, importantly, regeneration: metal objects could be smelted down and recycled, people were perhaps also thought to be reborn in some form after having been cremated - the use of fire being critical to both smelting and cremation. People may have been familiar with the mechanics of human reproduction and of metallurgy, but the biology of the former and the chemistry of the latter could only have been 'understood' by reference to supernatural powers. As stressed in Chapter 3, prehistoric people would have regarded such supernatural powers as very much real: they were part of the everyday world, not abstract concepts to be thought about and worshipped only on Sundays.

We will now consider the few prehistoric bronze objects known from Upper Coquetdale. The best known of these are probably the Simonside swords (fig. 4.36). These now reside in the Duke of Northumberland's museum in Alnwick Castle, having been found in 1868 along with two lead objects thought to be sword pommels, three bronze rings of unknown purpose, and two other unidentified pieces of bronze. One sword is only fragmentary, but the other is complete, though broken. This fine specimen is a little over half a metre in length, and belongs to a type known to have been in use between 1000 and 800BC. It would originally have had a hilt of wood or bone, held in place by four rivets, three of which are still attached to the blade. Recent chemical analysis has demonstrated that the blade consists of a bronze alloy made up of 76% copper, 12.5% tin and 11% lead, with minute quantities of antimony, arsenic and silver. This composition is not unusual for a sword of this period: the lead being added to help to reduce the melting point of the alloy and to improve its fluidity, thus helping the casting process.

The story of the discovery of the Simonside swords is fascinating. They were noticed projecting from under a large rock by children playing in the region of the Cockpit Well and Cowet Well, beneath the north face of Simonside. The objects listed above were then recovered by Mr Ashton of Tosson Mill, who cleared the soil in the immediate vicinity of the large rock. It is impossible to be certain of the exact findspot today, but it must have been in the vicinity of a large rectilinear earthwork enclosure which might be of later Iron Age date. It is interesting that they were found close to the two wells, in an area that may have been boggy in earlier times due to the water flowing from what must originally have been natural springs. As we will soon see, many metal objects of similar date have been recovered from 'wet places' throughout Britain. In many such cases, the objects appear to have been deliberately broken, and are interpreted by archaeologists as 'ritual deposits'. Intriguingly, the complete Simonside sword appears to have been deliberately broken in two, in a way most unlikely to have occurred by accident, prior to its deposition: could it have been part of a ritual deposit in the shadow of the great sacred mountain?

A report in the *Proceedings of the Society of Antiquaries of Newcastle* for 1888 records the donation to the Society by Lord Armstrong of 'an ancient British leaf-shaped sword of bronze found at Cragside' (fig. 4.37). Two bronze rings, like those found with the Simonside swords, were also recovered with the Cragside find: these must have been associated in some way with the swords. Within the report, Dr. Hodgkin notes that this sword 'was found in the bed of the stream which flows through Cragside. I am very sorry to have to inform you that it is broken into two pieces.'

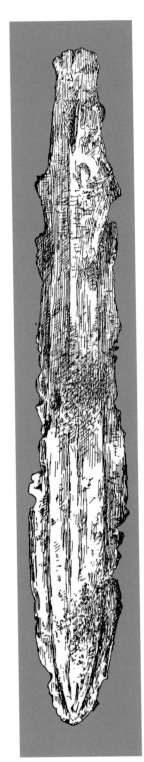

4.38 John Turnbull Dixon's drawing of the late Bronze Age knife from Cartington. (length 20cm) *Reproduced from Upper Coquetdale.*

Dr. Hodgkin would no doubt be interested to learn that such a breakage is now interpreted as a deliberate element of the process by which the sword was originally deposited. The Cragside sword, like the Simonside examples, is best interpreted as a ritual offering, though exactly why it ended up in this particular stream at Cragside must remain a mystery. Perhaps there are more in the locality awaiting discovery, with this example having been exposed by chance due to the erosive action of the stream.

Whether the Simonside or Cragside swords ever saw active service in battle is not known, but they must have been impressive objects when polished and perhaps functioned on an everyday basis as 'symbols of power'. We have offered a similar explanation for the architecture of hillforts: both swords and hillforts could have served 'military' purposes if required, but were perhaps only called into service very rarely, if ever. What we can be certain of is that the production of such implements was a specialist business, and they surely would never have been buried in the ground without what was perceived at the time to be very good reason.

A further object which we must consider here is a bronze knife from Cartington. Dixon tells us that this was found in a cist 'in a field between Whittle and Cartington Bank Head' in about 1890 (fig. 4.38). This is of a type known to archaeologists as a 'ribbed-tanged knife', after the distinctive raised ribs on the tang to which a handle of wood or bone would originally have been fixed. It was 'rediscovered' in London in 1981, bearing a label written in David Dippie Dixon's distinctive hand: 'found in 1890 by John Clark one mile west of Cartington Pyke Coquetdale.' This label makes no reference to a cist, and it is not at all clear why Dixon should ever have believed that it was found in one. It probably dates from between 900 and 700 BC, perhaps a thousand years after cist-burials had gone out of fashion. The Cartington knife is considered in detail in two *Northern Archaeology* papers by Adam Welfare and Colin Burgess, published in 1982, but there is nothing else that we can say for sure about the actual circumstances of its discovery. It may have been found in a wet place like the Simonside and Cartington swords, but was almost certainly not found within a cist. It is now safely housed within the Newcastle upon Tyne Museum of Antiquities.

We mentioned three late Bronze Age socketed axes from Warton at the beginning of this section. A fourth such axe was ploughed up at the base of Burgh Hill, Tosson, but Dixon records that this was already lost by 1903 and to the best of my knowledge its whereabouts remain unknown. It may yet turn up, perhaps on a local farmer's mantelpiece. These axes, along with the single earlier Bronze Age flanged axe, also from Tosson (fig. 3.53), complete the rather meagre corpus of known prehistoric bronze

4.39 The
Whittingham
(Thrunton) hoard.
The central sword is
c60cm in length.
Photo: Peter Forrester.

objects from Upper Coquetdale. It could be suggested that Bronze Age locals were particularly careful with their bronzes, ensuring that damaged examples were efficiently recycled and therefore that few entered the archaeological record. I confidently predict, however, that many more will turn up when we start looking for them, as suggested by recent events at Warton Farm.

We should briefly consider two further examples of late Bronze Age metalwork deposits from wet places just outside Coquetdale, one about 10km north of Rothbury, the other some 15km to the south. The first find was apparently made in about 1847 and is discussed in David Dippie Dixon's first great book, *Whittingham Vale*. He quotes from a report of a meeting of the Society of Antiquaries of London held on 30th January 1873:

> *Lord Ravensworth exhibited five weapons, consisting of two swords and three spearheads...The bronzes were found by workmen, when digging drains near Thrunton Farm, in the parish of Whittingham, Northumberland. The spot must formerly have been a quagmire, and is supplied with a copious spring of water. The arms were found sticking in the moss, with the points downwards, in a circle about two feet below the surface, perhaps left there by a party of soldiers who had halted at the spring, and been surprised.*

This is a fascinating explanation that may have seemed reasonable at the time, but I suspect that the 'surprised party of soldiers' never existed, and that this deposit is of a ritual nature and dates from about 900BC. The swords and spearheads, usually now referred to as the 'Whittingham hoard', are on display in the Newcastle upon Tyne Museum of Antiquities (fig. 4.39).

The other find to mention is the famous hoard from Wallington. This consists of 28 objects, including axes, swords and spearheads, all found during the draining of a swamp at Middleton Moss, in 1879 (fig. 4.40). The nineteenth-century recovery of part of a bronze cauldron while 'draining the bogs on Alnham Moor' (recorded in Dixon's *Whittingham Vale*) may also be related to the phenomenon of depositing valuable metal objects in wet places. Finds from elsewhere in Britain demonstrate that ritual offerings of metalwork were made in rivers, lakes and boggy places. It must be a possibility that bodies, whether cremated or not, were disposed of in the same way, perhaps being deposited at the same time as the metal objects. Such bodies would not necessarily leave any archaeological trace, and any slight sign of bodies that might have survived would almost certainly have been missed by workmen intent on the recovery of 'treasure'. I have little doubt that 'ritual' deposits of bronze tools and weapons like the Wallington hoard will eventually come to light in Upper Coquetdale. I am aware of several possible sites that might be worth investigating: hopefully, one day, we will be able to identify such a deposit and subject it to modern archaeological examination.

In marked contrast to the hundreds of burial cairns from the period covered in Chapter 3, there are only a couple of possible burials from the whole of Upper Coquetdale which might belong to the late Bronze Age or Iron Age. The first is a cremation beneath a small cairn within a cluster of 28 small burial monuments near the High Knowes palisades, above Alnham. George Jobey excavated three of these little structures (two cairns and a ditched enclosure) and a second ditched enclosure in another nearby cairnfield. Three of the excavated structures contained early Bronze Age burials, but the cremation in the fourth incorporated a 10cm long bronze pin that probably dates from the last couple of centuries BC. The second possible Iron Age burial is another cremation, this time inserted into an earlier cairn at Spital Hill, beneath Simonside. This has been classified as Iron Age on the basis of the unique pot deposited with it, but in fact this pot could be rather later, and the insertion of post-Roman burials in Bronze Age cairns is a widely recognised phenomenon throughout Northumberland. That leaves the

4.40 Some of the
bronze tools and
weapons from the
Wallington hoard.
Photo: Peter Forrester.

Alnham example as the only probable prehistoric burial from later than the mid-second millennium BC in the whole of Upper Coquetdale.

The addition of burials to pre-existing monuments is often thought to represent the desire of incoming people to associate their dead (and therefore themselves) with much older sites which may have been of mythical status. We suggested in Chapter 3 that Neolithic and early Bronze Age cairns may have originally been constructed to place ancestors in the landscape, and thus register a particular community's claim to the surrounding land for all time. Similarly, later burials in the same locations may have been intended to legitimise (probably fictitious) links between later communities and those original ancestors, thus staking a new claim to the same land. This may have happened at Alnham, conceivably by communities living within the nearby palisades or hillfort. However, there is currently no evidence for such practice elsewhere in Upper Coquetdale. It is possible that later burials were inserted into some of the early Bronze Age cairns excavated in the nineteenth century, as any such burials without accompanying grave goods may well have escaped detection. On balance, though, it would seem that virtually all late Bronze Age and Iron Age bodies were disposed of in a way that archaeology has yet to identify. We have suggested that people may have been cremated and their ashes scattered in wet places, but it may be that cremations were scattered on the fields that were now in regular use. There is no evidence for this, but early fields must have been of ritual significance as well as simply as places to grow food: casting the ashes of the dead onto the fields would leave no archaeological trace, but it wouldn't surprise me if, one day, some Bronze Age or Iron Age burials were to be found incorporated into ancient field boundaries.

The interest in wet places may have been related to the onset of wetter and cooler conditions which, as we have already noted, is recorded throughout Britain from about 1200BC. While it is difficult for us to try and understand the effects that the onset of wetter conditions would have had on communities which had existed for centuries in the uplands of Upper Coquetdale and elsewhere, it does make sense that wet places became the focus of religious activity at this time. Perhaps the gods were now worshipped in wet places, and such places throughout Britain began to receive offerings of valuable metal objects. Our habit of throwing coins into wishing wells and fountains probably retains a faint echo of this ancient practice. W. W. Tomlinson, in his splendid *Comprehensive Guide to the County of Northumberland* (first published in 1888 and subsequently reprinted many times) describes the 'Wishing Well' near Darden Lough 'into which the young people of the district used to drop a pin, breathing at the same time the desire of their hearts, little thinking, perhaps, that they were observing a custom derived from Pagan times, when offerings were made to the deities presiding over fountains and springs.' Still more recently, Harry Beamish, the local National Trust archaeologist, tells me that on draining the Lady's Well at Holystone (fig. 4.41) for repair works in the late 1990s he found a substantial assemblage of modern coins and other metal objects. Clearly, some people still feel the urge to cast metal objects into wet places more than 3,000 years after their Bronze Age ancestors began the trend.

Having established that wet places appear to have been of spiritual significance in the Iron Age, what else can we say about religious belief in later prehistoric Upper Coquetdale? In Chapters 2 and 3 we sought ideas from Australia and America as to how Stone Age and early Bronze Age people may have understood their world. For the period covered in this chapter, relevant information is available from sources a little closer to home.

Greek and Roman classical writers, such as Caesar (writing in the mid first century BC) discuss the Druids and various aspects of Celtic religion. A problem with such sources is that they tend to dwell on what were, to the classical mind, the more 'weird' aspects of Celtic religion. Hence we learn about human sacrifice and head-hunting. Of potentially greater value than the classical sources is the ancient Irish and Welsh literature which, although not written down until much later, is thought to refer back to Iron Age society. Given that both Ireland and Wales are predominantly upland areas, with economies based largely on stock rearing, there may well have been similarities between them and Upper Coquetdale in later prehistory. A combination of the literary sources and archaeology allows us to attempt a speculative account of the religious beliefs of Iron Age communities.

Very few specifically constructed shrines or temples are known from Iron Age Britain, and it seems that natural places provided foci for religious activity. Such places could have included sacred mountains, lakes, rivers, bogs, trees, or woodland clearings. We know that deities were linked with some such places: some, for example, were linked particularly with water veneration, while others were named after particular species of tree. Most such deities seem to have been peculiar to particular locations, there being no generally applicable pantheon of

Celtic gods. It is therefore not unreasonable to suppose that Upper Coquetdale had some special deities for which evidence is unlikely to be found elsewhere.

4.41 The Lady's Well, Holystone. Nothing of great antiquity survives for the visitor to inspect here, but the site was probably a sacred spring back in Iron Age times.

The classical sources refer to the Druids as being of paramount importance in Celtic ritual. Although the sources leave many questions unanswered, it does appear that the Druids were influential throughout pre-Roman Britain and Gaul. They were probably supported by tribal chiefs, though we will never know exactly how the relationship between chief and priest worked in practice. Who, for example, would make the final decision when chief and priest were in disagreement? Regardless of this, Caesar tells us that the Druids officiated at the worship of the gods, oversaw sacrifices, and made religious rulings on a variety of subjects.

Their power must have been bound up with their 'secret knowledge', built up over generations, and they were apparently prophets as well as priests. In my view, it may not be over fanciful to envisage Druids overseeing festivals, perhaps including sacrifices, on top of the old 'sacred mountain' of Simonside, or at any number of potentially significant places adjacent to the Coquet. One such place may have been the Drake Stone, just a couple of hundred metres east of Harbottle Lough (figs. 4.42, 4.43). In *Murray's Handbook to Durham and Northumberland*, published in 1873, it is recorded that:

Half a mile from Harbottle is the Drake Stone, a very interesting relic, being the Draag Stone of the Druids. By a small tarn near it is a druidical rock basin. The custom which still prevails in Harbottle, of passing sick children over the Drake Stone may be a relic of Druidical times, when they were probably passed through the fire on the same spot.

Today, we cannot be sure of the origins of such customs, but it is not impossible that they could stretch back to prehistoric times. While it may never be possible to recover archaeological evidence relating to such activity, a lack of hard evidence should not preclude sensible

4.42 Harbottle Lough, seen here from the Drake Stone, was described by David Dippie Dixon as 'a lonely eerie tarn in the hollow of the hills' with water that 'is always pure and very cold'. Although as yet uninvestigated by archaeologists, it is precisely the kind of place that would have attracted ritual offerings in late prehistoric times. *Photo: Simon Fraser. Illustration: Jim Proudfoot.*

4.43 The Drake Stone, perched spectacularly on top of Harbottle Crag, demonstrates the power of glacial erosion during the Ice Age. It may well have been of ritual significance throughout prehistoric times. *Photo: Simon Fraser.*

speculation. After all, religion would have been an essential element in the everyday lives of the later prehistoric people of Upper Coquetdale, no less real to them than the hillforts, field systems and artefacts which dominate today's archaeological record.

Both literature and archaeological evidence point to other elements of Celtic religion which seem to have been of considerable importance. The human head seems to have been venerated, perhaps as representing the soul, and heads were often carved in stone. Some animals (both wild and domestic) and birds were very important, and some deities could transform at will from human to animal form. The sun, moon and stars figured strongly in Celtic religion, as they must have done from the earliest times (indeed, much of Celtic religious belief must have its roots in the earlier belief systems such as those discussed in Chapters 2 and 3). The seasons provided the framework for a variety of annual festivals, many of which survive in amended form in today's calendar. Some deities were linked with the weather, with appropriate offerings no doubt being made in the event of extreme thunderstorms, blizzards or droughts. Given the agricultural basis of their society, fertility veneration probably underlay many aspects of Celtic peoples' religion, and some experts have suggested that an 'Earth Mother' goddess may have been of key importance. Death and the afterlife were important elements of Celtic belief, and Caesar records that their belief in the immortality of the soul encouraged bravery amongst Celtic warriors as it negated the fear of death. There were gods specifically associated with war and with death, and to meet death in battle was considered the most honourable way for a Celtic warrior to die. The number 'three' seems to have been of particular symbolic significance to Celtic people, something that may well still be reflected in today's apparently illogical concept of three as a 'lucky number'.

Clearly, Iron Age religion must have been a complex web of interconnecting elements, and no doubt different people believed different things just as people do today. We will never know the whole story, but it is interesting to note that some facets of Iron Age belief were clearly rooted in much earlier times, and that some still have influence, albeit perhaps subconsciously, on the behaviour of many people in the modern world.

In this account of Iron Age times there is one final subject that we must consider: that of ironworking. As with earlier periods, the Iron Age is conventionally considered to have begun with the introduction of new people and new technologies, including, in this case, the knowledge of iron working. Again, however, evidence for an influx of newcomers is lacking, and the adoption of new technologies and new ways of life by native communities seems the most likely explanation for most changes in the archaeological record during the Iron Age. The introduction of iron must have been of great significance to people in Upper Coquetdale, enabling the production of more efficient tools (especially agricultural implements) and weapons. To the best of my knowledge, however, not a single Iron Age iron object has been found in the valley. Why should this be? There are probably two main reasons. First, iron rusts in the ground, and iron objects (unlike those of bronze) soon turn to unrecognisable rusty lumps. Consequently, they can be indistinguishable in the soil from rusty bits of more recent farm implements, so are rarely picked up. A rusty 2,500 year old nail looks pretty much like a rusty 25 year old nail! Secondly, iron could be readily recycled, so perhaps relatively few objects were ever discarded. A further factor may be that iron objects were apparently not offered as 'gifts to the gods' in the same way as bronze ones. Thus we have no ritual hoards of iron axes or swords like those of bronze from Wallington and Whittingham.

My colleague, Iain Hedley, has a passion for industrial archaeology (and especially ironworking) and was recently employed by the Northumberland National Park Authority to run the *Discovering our Hillfort Heritage* project. He is therefore ideally placed to discuss Iron

Age ironworking. I hoped he might be able to throw some light on the subject, but what he actually confirmed was that very little is known about it. It seems a little ironic that we so readily use the term 'Iron Age' for late prehistoric times, yet know virtually nothing of the methods by which contemporary iron objects were produced.

Iain explains that there are two basic stages involved in ironworking. The first is smelting, whereby iron ore is heated in a furnace (at a much higher temperature than that required for bronze working) to form 'bloom', which is then hammered into iron bars. Iain believes that smelting may not have occurred in rural Northumberland until medieval times, despite the widespread local occurrence of iron ores. He thinks that local people may have imported bars, although there is a possibility that smelting did occur here and the careful analysis of some supposedly medieval iron smelting sites may yet provide late prehistoric dates.

The second stage in ironworking is smithing, whereby the results of the smelting process are transformed into finished objects through heating and hammering. This is the work of the blacksmith, who would have been kept busy maintaining and repairing iron tools as well as manufacturing new ones. There is some evidence for smithing in the form of small quantities of waste slag from a few Iron Age sites in Northumberland, including Harehaugh Camp. We do not know, however, whether the smiths were resident at such sites, or whether they were itinerant, travelling from settlement to settlement as required. Iain Hedley thinks it likely that Iron Age smiths were itinerant, although, of course, arrangements could change through time and it may be that some larger settlements did have resident smiths at some stages of the Iron Age, but not at others. Further information about Iron Age ironworking must be sought through carefully targeted excavation: for the time being we are bound to continue using the term 'Iron Age' to describe the final centuries of prehistory, while accepting that we have virtually no knowledge of local prehistoric ironworking.

Summary

The period covered in this chapter saw the development of permanently occupied farmsteads, even quite high up in the hills, with small-scale field systems. These early farmers practised mixed agriculture, and may at first have continued the age-old tradition of laying their dead to rest in burial cairns. After the onset of wetter conditions, during the centuries after 1200BC, people stopped using the old burial traditions, and religious interest seems to have become linked with the deposition of metal objects in wet places, perhaps eventually associated with 'Druids'. Some of the upland Bronze Age farmsteads were apparently abandoned in favour of defended 'palisades', which eventually gave way to hillforts, some of which had impressive ramparts (fig. 4.44).

The artefact record sees flint tools gradually giving way to bronze, and then to iron. Beautifully manufactured bronze weapons, including swords, coupled with the apparently defensive nature of the palisades and hillforts, have led archaeologists to speculate that the period was characterised by the development of a warrior aristocracy. This might be true, but the swords and hillforts may be indicative of demonstrations of perceived power rather than of regular warfare.

It is impossible to say for sure how violent society was throughout later prehistory. There may have been extended periods during which life was pretty much like the era of the border reivers in the sixteenth century AD, with more-or-less constant cattle raiding and feuds of varying intensity between different clans. Indeed, it is tempting to suggest quite close parallels between

4.44 Jim Proudfoot's reconstruction of life in the age of the hillforts, in about 200BC. Most Coquetdale forts may have had rather less elaborate defences than those shown here (which are based on a site further north in the Cheviots), but the general impression of the fort's internal features and surrounding landscape are certainly relevant to Iron Age Upper Coquetdale.

Iron Age society and that of the reivers, and Iron Age people no doubt had their equivalents of the great Border Ballads. Some hillforts may have functioned as prestige homes for local clan chiefs and their entourages, while others may have been little more than fortified farmsteads (perhaps equivalents of the bastle houses of the late sixteenth and early seventeenth centuries).

During the Bronze Age, the degree of human control over the landscape steadily increased, as more and more land was claimed for crops and pasture. However, although the land was increasingly 'tamed', the Iron Age interest in weapons and defended settlements suggests that the world was in some ways becoming a more dangerous place. When violence did occur between groups, then this would probably have been subject to a large degree of honour and traditional ritual. Combat would have been gruesomely hand-to-hand, but just as in later, Anglo-Saxon, times, to die in battle would have been a prestigious and honourable way for a warrior to leave this world. Conflicts may have been restricted to a 'warrior elite', just as modern wars (at least in the western world) are fought by professional soldiers. Late prehistoric fighting methods, however, bore little comparison with those of today: I sometimes wonder what an Iron Age warrior, steeped in the traditions of hand-to-hand combat, would have made of today's laser-guided missiles and nuclear bombs, whereby death is dealt to a distant 'enemy' through the touch of a button.

It used to be thought that the hillforts were abandoned by order of the Romans, but evidence from Scotland now suggests that at least some hillforts had aleady been abandoned by the last couple of centuries BC, and that people were living in small nucleated farmsteads of perhaps half a dozen roundhouses by the time of the Roman invasion. As with so many aspects of Coquetdale prehistory, more detailed survey and excavation of sites will be required if we are to resolve the chronology of, and reasons for, the abandonment of the mighty hillforts and the way of life that went with them.

Looking southwards over the Roman camps at Chew Green,
close to the source of the Coquet.
Photo: Tim Gates.

Chapter 5

The Roman Occupation and the End of Prehistory
(cAD79 - 410)

Introduction

Northumberland contains many spectacular remnants of the once mighty Roman Empire. Understandably, Romanists have dominated Northumberland archaeology, and massive resources are still poured into the study and management of Hadrian's Wall and associated military sites. Sadly, this has been to the detriment of the study of other periods, and to the serious study of everyday life in rural areas like Upper Coquetdale during Roman times. This obsession with Roman military archaeology is something of a throwback to the days of the British Empire: both Roman and British Empires were regarded as forces for good, bringing 'civilisation' to far off lands. More recently, people throughout the western world are developing an appreciation of what were previously defined as 'uncivilised' or 'primitive' societies, such as those of Native Americans and Australian Aborigines. Along with this appreciation comes a realisation of the appalling suffering inflicted on such peoples by western interests. In earlier chapters of this book we have borrowed ideas from such societies to help understand what life may have been like at various times in prehistoric Upper Coquetdale. It should be clear to anyone who has read those chapters that the Romans did not

5.1 First-century Roman cavalrymen, illustrated by Ronald Embleton. Initial encounters with the mighty Roman army may have been terrifying for local people, and the mere threat of military action may have been sufficient to subdue potentially anti-Roman factions within the native community. *Reproduced courtesy of Frank Graham.*

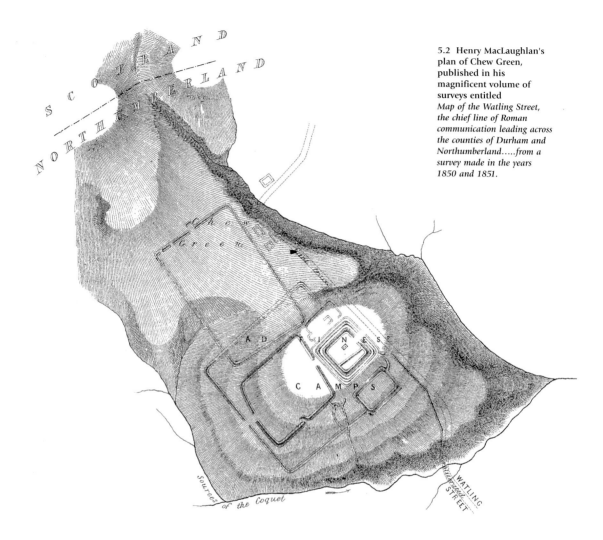

5.2 Henry MacLaughlan's plan of Chew Green, published in his magnificent volume of surveys entitled *Map of the Watling Street, the chief line of Roman communication leading across the counties of Durham and Northumberland.....from a survey made in the years 1850 and 1851.*

arrive in a barren land occupied by primitive savages, but in what was already a complex historic environment developed over millennia and ripe with significance to its people. Conventional views which contrast educated, civilised Romans with ignorant 'barbarians' are in themselves ignorant. The native way of life was very different to that of the Rome, but not necessarily any less complex or fulfilling.

In Britain, the Roman period lasted a little over 300 years, witnessed by only the final dozen of the four hundred or more generations of people covered in this book. In this chapter we will briefly consider the nature of Roman military activity, before examining native settlement patterns and everyday life under the influence of Rome. What I will try to stress throughout, however, is that these are not two separate subjects, and it is the changing nature of the relationship between traditional, native society and Roman influence which lends this period its particular fascination.

Roman military occupation

Although advance parties may have ventured into the area in earlier times, the full might of the Roman military machine was probably seen in Upper Coquetdale for the first time in the summer of AD 79 (fig. 5.1). It was during this year that the great Roman general, Agricola, headed north into Scotland with the clear intention of conquering the whole of Britain. His main route was along the great Roman road known to us today as Dere Street, constructed for the purpose from Corbridge up through Redesdale and across the head of Coquetdale before descending down into Scotland. The earliest Roman camp at Chew Green (figs. 5.2, 5.3) was probably constructed in, or very shortly after, AD79 to house troops passing along the new road. The nearby Brownhart Law signal station, from which fabulous views extend way into Scotland, was probably constructed at about the same time. A little further south, on the often bleak stretch of Dere Street between the Coquet and the Rede, at least eight marching camps were constructed. These did not contain permanent buildings, but were occupied temporarily by troops busy in the area (perhaps working on the construction or maintenance of Dere Street) or sometimes used simply for overnight stops. The soldiers would have slept in tents, which they packed up and took with them when they left.

In contrast to these marching camps, a great fort, which during the third century held a garrison of a thousand men together with 250 horses, was built at *Bremenium* (High Rochester) on the line of Dere Sreet. Another fort was built at Low Learchild on the Aln, on the line of the more easterly Roman road which left Dere Street north of Corbridge and headed over the lower ground towards Berwick. A further road was constructed between High Rochester and Low Learchild, and this bisected Coquetdale, crossing the river at Holystone (figs. 5.4, 5.5). One marching camp has been discovered along the line of this road, at North Yardhope about 3km

5.3 **Aerial view of the Chew Green Roman camps.** *Photo: Tim Gates.*

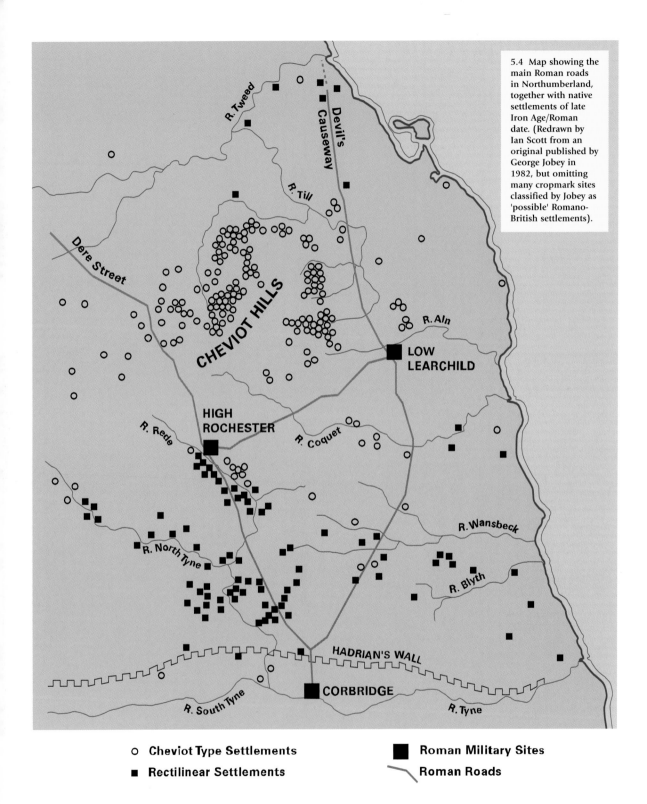

5.4 Map showing the main Roman roads in Northumberland, together with native settlements of late Iron Age/Roman date. (Redrawn by Ian Scott from an original published by George Jobey in 1982, but omitting many cropmark sites classified by Jobey as 'possible' Romano-British settlements).

○ Cheviot Type Settlements   ■ Roman Military Sites

■ Rectilinear Settlements   Roman Roads

5.5 *Left:* An excavated section across the Roman road at Holystone (reproduced from *A History of Northumberland* volume XV): A is the road's mid-rib, B & C are the kerbs.

Right: A section across the same road excavated in 1996 at Yatesfield Farm, Redesdale, 10km west of Holystone: note the well preserved kerb along the edge of the road surface.

5.6 Aerial view over North Yardhope Roman camp. The ramparts of the camp, rectangular in plan with curved corners, like a playing card, are clearly visible. The camp has been much damaged by drainage ditches which can be seen crossing the site. *Photo: Tim Gates.*

5.7 The network of
Roman roads enabled
the effective
movement of troops
and other traffic
throughout northern
England. Troops must
have passed regularly
along the road
through Holystone,
sometimes in large
numbers as portrayed
in this illustration of
troops on the move
by Ronald Embleton.
*Reproduced by courtesy
of Frank Graham.*

west of Holystone (fig. 5.6). Exactly when all these roads were constructed is unknown, but
they formed a network for the Roman control of Northumberland, enabling troops to
move rapidly throughout the region as required.

Despite defeating the Caledonian tribes at the great battle of Mons Graupius, somewhere in the
Scottish Highlands, Roman forces were recalled for duty elsewhere in the Empire and, despite
occasional further campaigns over the next three centuries (such as the brief episode
associated with the construction of the Antonine Wall, from Forth to Clyde, in the AD 160s),
the conquest of Scotland was never completed. Instead, under the reign of Hadrian in the 120s,
a wall was built from Tyne to Solway, and this is generally regarded as forming the northern
boundary of the Empire. Roman influence continued to extend well to the north of the Wall,
however, and troops must have passed through Holystone on a regular basis en route between
High Rochester and Low Learchild (fig. 5.7). Indeed, this road may well have been of
considerable significance in its own right, as it seems to have been located to separate the
upland of the Cheviots from the more low-lying land to the south. Perhaps the Romans were
seeking to demarcate and maintain a division between these two areas, which may well
approximate to the territories of two different tribes as will be discussed below. (My personal
view, for what it is worth, is that Hadrian's Wall never really marked the edge of the Roman
Empire. It was constructed by an Emperor who fancied himself as an architect, and I believe
that the sophistication of the Wall owes more to his architectural whim than to any great
military strategy. Roman influence certainly extended far to the north of the Wall, and

Coquetdale probably formed part of a great 'buffer state', effectively under Roman control if nominally independent, between the Wall and the potentially hostile highland tribes further north. However, it is only fair that I should point out that I am no Romanist, and many eminent scholars of Roman Britain would take issue with my dismissal of the military significance of their dear old Wall!)

Romans and natives

While much work has been done on Roman military remains, and quite a bit on native settlement patterns, it is the relationship between Roman and native that provides the greatest challenge to archaeologists studying this period. We will begin the consideration of this relationship with David Dippie Dixon's eloquent description of Chew Green, contained within Chapter I of *Upper Coquetdale*:

> *The situation of Chew Green and Gemel's-path amid those breezy uplands at Coquethead, lying in the very heart of the Cheviots, far removed from the route of the ordinary traveller, is extremely remote. Isolated from the outer world by many miles of 'mountain, moss, and moor,' its all-pervading stillness, broken only by the bleating of the hill-sheep and the plaintive cry of the curlew and the plover, conveys to the mind a feeling of impressive solitude. Yet there was a time when his lone spot resounded to the clang of weapons and the tramp of armed men; when the trained legions of the Romans marched along the newly-made Watling Street and garrisoned the camp below...where now the bent and purple heath hides the stain of ancient battle.*

In fact, there is absolutely no evidence that any battle was ever fought between Roman and native anywhere in or around Upper Coquetdale. The relative lack of Roman camps and forts throughout Coquetdale suggests that this region was never one which caused problems to the invaders, and there is good reason for believing that the region was never conquered by military force, but by negotiation. This was standard Roman practice: a negotiated settlement between a native ruler and Rome could be of major benefit to both, and was certainly preferable to the alternative of bloody conflict. A local leader who allowed Rome to pass unheeded through his (or her) territory would be guaranteed Roman protection against potential enemies elsewhere, and might also receive considerable reward in silver and gold, not to mention wine and other luxuries from the classical world. In short, the threat of violence coupled with the promise of treasure could be more effective for Rome than the simple use of violence alone. A local ruler's power and prestige could be greatly enhanced by aligning with the Romans, and the decision to side with Rome may not have been a difficult one to make when the alternative was inevitable annihilation by the Roman army (fig. 5.8). There was clearly scope for differences of opinion within native society. To an extent, the reaction of local people to the Roman military in late first-century Northumberland may have been similar to that of local populations to the presence of western forces in early 21st-century troublespots such as Iraq or Afghanistan. Some factions may have supported liaison with the occupying force, while others may have been bitterly opposed to it, perhaps mounting small-scale acts of sabotage in the attempt to disrupt Roman rule.

As already noted, the Roman occupation of northern England lasted a little over 300 years. Many changes would have occurred during this period, and these are of no less interest to the archaeologist than events at the beginning and end of the occupation. Perhaps the most interesting such changes relate to the perceived identities of local people. Whether or not local families saw the Romans initially as friends, most would soon have realised that cooperation

5.8 Ronald Embleton's emotive illustration of Roman forces sacking a native village. While events like this may have occurred on occasions in Upper Coquetdale, we currently have no evidence from the region for any conflict between Romans and natives. The threat of such action must, however, have been ever present.
Reproduced by courtesy of Frank Graham.

offered many potential benefits, while opposition must have appeared to most as ultimately futile. Perhaps the natives and the Romans became gradually more and more integrated as time went by, with some young men leaving their family farms for a life in the Imperial Army. Others may have moved and set up home in Roman towns such at Carlisle, Corbridge or Newcastle, or in the civilian settlements (known as 'vici') that grew up around many of the great Roman forts. This may have resulted in a gradual depopulation of some upland areas, although, as we are about to see, Coquetdale does not seem to have been particularly densely populated at any time during the Roman period. If we are to make progress in this field then we need to break down barriers between 'Roman' archaeology and 'native' archaeology, which are often studied as different subjects by different people. An integrated study of human activity in Upper Coquetdale during the first five centuries AD would undoubtedly provide some fascinating food for thought, and would certainly help to break down some traditional academic boundaries which currently do little to help our understanding of this fascinating period.

Patterns of native settlement

Given the lack of excavated evidence, it is impossible to be sure of the extent to which the distribution of so-called 'Romano-British' settlements actually reflects activity during Roman times as against the late Iron Age. Not long ago, it was assumed that hillfort defences were banned by the Romans, to be replaced by small, undefended settlements of stone-built roundhouses which can be seen overlying the abandoned ramparts of many hillforts: Lordenshaws is an excellent example (fig. 5.9). The large number of these settlements, both on hillfort sites and elsewhere, was thought to reflect the peaceful conditions of the Roman occupation (the so-called '*pax Romana*'), with previously hostile groups of cattle raiders now at peace with their neighbours and engaged in mixed agriculture under the watchful gaze of the Roman authorities. This was a sensible theory, as the Roman military authorities would obviously have preferred a landscape of undefended farmsteads to one littered with defended hillforts. Unfortunately, however, things are not so simple. What evidence we do have from Northumberland and surrounding areas suggests that most hillforts may have been abandoned several decades prior to the Roman conquest, and that many communities were already living in relatively undefended 'villages' of stone built round houses by the time that Romans appeared on the scene. Why this should have been the case is not known, and there is little point in discussing it in detail until we have better information about the chronology of the transition from hillforts to undefended settlements.

Although we cannot be sure about their origins, we can say something about the types of settlement in which local people lived during the Roman occupation. What we know about these sites is largely thanks to the work of George Jobey, who completed topographical surveys of many hillforts and Romano-British settlements throughout Northumberland, checking a few of these through small-scale excavations. These settlements fall into two basic types: 'rectilinear' settlements and 'Cheviot type' settlements. The former consist of stone-built roundhouses and stock yards within a more-or-less rectangular stone wall or earth-and-ditch perimeter. The latter consist of the same basic ingredients but are much more irregular in form, and often much larger in size. Two things will become immediately apparent from a brief glance at the distribution of these sites, as shown in fig. 5.4. Firstly, Upper Coquetdale appears to form a boundary zone between the distributions of the two types. Secondly, there is a remarkably low density of settlements within Upper Coquetdale when compared to regions to both north and south. Why should this be the case?

The settlement distribution shown in fig. 5.4 was compiled by George Jobey in 1982, since when several more sites have been discovered through aerial photography. The general pattern, however, remains valid: the striking thing about Upper Coquetdale being the relative lack of Roman period settlement of any kind. The valleys to the north contain numerous 'Cheviot type' settlements, while the Rede, North Tyne and Wansbeck valleys abound with 'rectilinear'

5.9 This air photograph of the Lordenshaws hillfort clearly shows that the south-west arc of the fort ramparts has been flattened: the flattened banks and infilled ditches here are overlain by the houses and paddocks of a Romano-British settlement which extends into the interior of the fort. (see also fig. 4.12d).

settlements. (On his original map, which forms the basis for fig. 5.4, Jobey included many 'possible' rectilinear settlements extending over lower-lying land from the Tweed to the Tyne. These have been omitted from fig. 5.4 in the interests of clarity, the key point to note about them being that their distribution does not overlap with the zone of Cheviot-type settlements extending from the Rede/Coquet to the northern Cheviots.) The relative distributions of these two types of settlement have yet to be satisfactorily explained. Some archaeologists believe that the rectilinear sites represent farmsteads 'planted' by the Roman authorities at approximately regular intervals throughout the landscape, in order to develop an easily regulated countryside and to encourage a regular supply of agricultural produce for the troops. While it is certainly fair to argue that Roman influence must have had much to do with the location of some of these settlements, such as those strung out along the line of Dere Street in Redesdale, it seems far fetched to suggest that they were all the result of Roman planning, especially as a couple of excavated examples in North Tynedale seem to have pre-Roman origins.

We must consider here some possible explanations for the apparent lack of Roman period settlements in Upper Coquetdale. Attempts to explain this as the result of naturally poor soils which may have been over exploited in earlier times, the narrow nature of the valley in its upper reaches, or the destruction of sites through later agricultural activity on the lower lying land all have some merit, but cannot really account satisfactorily for the observed distribution. I suggest that there are two major clues as to what might have been going on here during Roman times.

The first of these clues comes in the nature of native settlements in the vicinity of *Bremenium* Roman fort, as shown in fig. 5.4. The valley to the south-west of the Rede contains many rectilinear settlements, while that to the north-east has 'Cheviot-type' settlements. This surely suggests that this stretch of the Rede represented a boundary of some kind, perhaps a boundary between two different tribal groups attracted to this general area by the presence of the Roman fort and its substantial garrison. Some further support that we may be dealing with two separate groups may be claimed from the distribution of Iron Age hillforts: the area of Cheviot type settlements corresponds with the 'hillfort zone', while, as we saw in Chapter 4, there are few hillforts south of Coquetdale (although one good example exists above Otterburn, on the north-east bank of the Rede, not far from the cluster of Roman-British settlements above *Bremenium*). The fact that a recent Newcastle University/Northumberland National Park project has identified a large earthwork enclosure, possibly a hillfort, buried beneath *Bremenium* fort further complicates the distribution of Iron Age and Roman sites in this area. On balance, it would appear that the boundary zone suggested by the Roman-British settlements may well have considerable time-depth, extending back at least as far as the middle Iron Age. While problems still remain over the dating of sites, fig. 5.4 clearly suggests that the area between the Coquet and the Wansbeck was a transitional zone between two markedly different patterns of settlement during Roman times. Given that different settlement patterns could have existed within a single tribal territory, and that traditional tribal boundaries and settlement patterns may have become blurred under Roman influence, we cannot realistically expect to identify tribal boundaries with any degree of certainty from a simple distribution map such as this. However, if Coquetdale did lie within a border zone, then this might help to account for the relatively low density of Romano-British farmsteads in comparison to areas north and south.

A second clue to understanding the observed settlement pattern is provided by tantalising documentary records surviving from the Roman world. There are three relevant such sources. The first is Ptolemy's *'Geography'*, a list of landscape features and settlements, together with their approximate locations, and an indication of the territories of native tribal groups. This was compiled in the mid-second century, but clearly must have used earlier sources. Its interpretation poses many problems, and some places cannot be located with any degree of certainty. Nevertheless, it unambiguously locates *Bremenium* at today's High Rochester (this has been independently verified through the discovery of Roman inscriptions), and also identifies the River Aln. (It also records a place called *Alauna* which seems to me most likely to relate to Low Learchild, although Roman scholars seem reluctant to commit themselves on this.) The second source is known as the *Antonine Itinerary*, and dates originally from the early third century: it confirms the location of *Bremenium*, but is of little further relevance to the Coquetdale region. The third source is the *Ravenna Cosmography*, a list of places in the Roman World compiled at Ravenna (Italy) in the seventh century, apparently using source material of second-century date. This can also be difficult to interpret, but does also list *Bremenium* and *Alauna*. It also provides the earliest known reference to the Coquet, which it records as *Coccoveda*. This is a Celtic name relating to the Welsh '*cochwedd*', meaning 'red appearance'. We can therefore be reasonably certain people as far back as the Iron Age, and perhaps much earlier, referred to the Coquet as 'the Red River', presumably reflecting the quantity of red porphyritic pebbles which litter its bed. Tantalisingly, the *Ravenna Cosmography* also appears to record a place on the Coquet also named *Coccoveda*. This may be some as yet undiscovered settlement on the lower reaches of the river, but there must be a chance that it relates to Chew Green (the popular 'Latin' name for Chew Green, *Ad Fines*, is of no great antiquity.) Unfortunately, the matter is far from clear: some authorities believe that the second reference to *Coccoveda* is simply a clerical error, and that the name should apply only to the river.

This is all very interesting, but of what relevance is it to a possible tribal boundary along the Coquet in Roman times? Well, Ptolemy makes it clear that both *Bremenium* and *Alauna* lie within the territory of a tribe known as the *Votadini* (sometimes spelled *Otadini*), whose lands extended to the Forth in the north. The land to the south of the *Votadini*, including Durham and most of Yorkshire, was occupied by the *Brigantes*, apparently a confederacy of several partially independent tribal groups. Exactly where the boundary lay between the *Votadini* and the *Brigantes*, or, indeed, whether another tribe occupied an intermediate zone between the two, is not known. The above analysis of settlement patterns suggests that the southern boundary of *Votadini* territory may have lain somewhere in the zone between the Coquet, the Rede and the Wansbeck, perhaps incorporating the Simonside range, the cultural significance of which extended back to the very earliest times. Elsewhere, the boundary may have followed the line of the Grasslees and Elsdon Burns to join the Rede near Otterburn. This would place *Bremenium* within Votadinian territory, while also neatly accounting for the distribution of native settlements adjacent to *Bremenium* as seen in fig. 5.4. Further east, on the lowlands, the boundary may have been the Coquet or the Wansbeck.

Identifying boundaries from the distribution of archaeological sites can be fraught with difficulty, as boundaries can follow a variety of topographic features (eg. rivers, high hills, watersheds, bogs) and may exist as liminal zones rather than as clearly defined lines. These difficulties are further enhanced by the facts that we don't know which sites are contemporary with each other, that boundaries can fluctuate over time, and that a blurring of boundaries might be expected if the entire region was under Roman control. What we can be fairly certain of is that any boundaries present during the Roman period would have had some historic dimension, and that the land must still have been of some sacred significance, full of named places which were doubtless linked in communal memory with mythical events and individuals of earlier times. Under such circumstances, the suggestion that Simonside may have played a role in the demarcation of *Votadini* territory is perhaps not unreasonable.

I am convinced that there are patterns in the distribution of settlement in Upper Coquetdale that will, once we have undertaken a great deal of thinking and a little carefully targeted excavation, enable us to offer a convincing interpretation of life here, apparently on the border between two ancient tribal zones, in Iron Age and Romano-British times. Regardless of all this conjecture about boundaries, however, we must now consider a few of the settlements of presumed Romano-British date in Upper Coquetdale, and attempt a brief overview of life on a local farmstead using information gleaned from excavations elsewhere in Northumberland.

Everyday life during the Roman period

In discussing everyday life we must stress again the current impossibility of distinguishing between settlements of late pre-Roman and Roman times. There seems to have been much continuity across these periods, with people continuing to live in small villages of stone roundhouses and to practice mixed agriculture. It is tempting to suggest that local farmers would have sought to produce a surplus, either to pay taxes to the Romans or to exchange for luxury produce from the Roman world, but there is no clear evidence of this. The Bloody Moss pollen sequence suggests that there was no increase in cereal production during the Roman period over and above that which was normal throughout the later Iron Age. Exactly when the large tracts of cord rig such as those at Carshope and Ward Law (discussed in Chapter 4) were cultivated remains unproven, and we certainly cannot say for certain that these fields were used to grow grain during Roman times. However, the Bloody Moss sequence does suggest an expansion of pasture, so it may be that cattle were being reared in Upper Coquetdale to provide beef for the Roman military.

We can combine evidence from excavated Romano-British settlements elsewhere in Northumberland with the surface remains at local sites to build up a picture of everyday life in Upper Coquetdale during Roman times. For example, from the remains visible on the ground today, we can imagine a cluster of up to ten quite substantial stone-built roundhouses on the old hillfort at Lordenshaws. Each of these probably looked something like the reconstructed roundhouse which can be visited today at the Brigantium archaeological reconstuction park at Rochester in Redesdale (fig. 5.10). These houses would have provided comfortable homes for families, even during the worst winter weather. As with all the other prehistoric people described in this book, the inhabitants of the Lordenshaws Romano-British village would have lived lives full of complex symbolism. They doubtless had their own legends accounting for the old ruined hillfort which lay partly buried beneath their houses and fields. They kept cattle, sheep, goats and pigs, as well as dogs and horses. The diet was supplemented by a degree of hunting (eg of deer and waterfowl), fishing and gathering of wild produce. There is no visible evidence of cord rig fields at Lordenshaws: they probably did exist but the medieval and later ploughing which has clearly taken place here has removed any trace of them. The people would have grown their own vegetables and cereals, including types of barley and wheat which they ground using rotary querns to make flour. They would also have brewed (and drunk) their own beer. The manufacture and repair of iron tools and weapons may well have taken place on site, although whether such settlements had their own specialist smiths is not known. Some bronze working, for brooches, horse trappings and other trinkets, probably also took place here. Textiles would have been manufactured using wool from the domestic beasts, as evidenced by the spindle-whorls and weaving combs found on some excavations. Pottery would certainly have been made within the village, but nothing approaching the quality of the magnificent beakers and food vessels of earlier times. Instead the emphasis was on the production of practical, sometimes very large storage and cooking pots, generally without any form of decoration. Occasional Roman wares found their way to sites like Lordenshaws, as did the odd Roman coin and occasional luxury goods such as wine. Local communities did not have a monetary economy, so all exchanges would have been via some form of barter, perhaps including the trading of livestock, metalwork or even people.

Similar settlements, of which some remains can still be seen today, were built on the old hillfort sites at Old Rothbury, West Hills (Rothbury) and Alnham Castle Hill. Detailed survey will in due course probably uncover evidence for such sites at other hillforts. During his excavation of one of the High Knowes palisaded sites in the 1960s (see Chapter 4), George Jobey discovered an overlying stone-built house of presumed Roman date. This house had a central hearth, and outside it was a stone-walled courtyard.

5.10 This replica Romano-British stone-built roundhouse can be visited at the Brigantium Archaeological Reconstruction Centre, Rochester. Its dimensions are based on an excavated example at Woolaw in Redesdale. Many such houses must have stood in Upper Coquetdale during Roman times.

The excavations recovered numerous sherds of coarse, hand-made pottery, but unfortunately little information was forthcoming about the occupants of the site. It was presumably a small farmstead, perhaps occupied by a single family, and the presence of only a single house suggests that the settlement may not have thrived for very long. Exactly why this exposed site should have been chosen for the farmstead in preference to many more sheltered locations that were presumably available is something of a mystery, but signs of the old ruined palisade, perhaps abandoned centuries earlier, must, for some reason, have influenced the decision.

The reoccupation of so many earlier settlement sites during Roman times requires explanation. These sites include Iron Age hillforts that may have been abandoned for only a few generations, if at all, and Bronze Age settlement sites (such as Debdon Whitefield, where stone built roundhouses occur in the same area as a cairnfield of Bronze Age date) that may have lain abandoned for a thousand years or more. Perhaps some of these earlier sites still provided good settlement opportunities in Roman times, so that reoccupation was essentially coincidental. Another explanation could be that remains of earlier field systems could be renovated and reused: a field wall could be built more easily using stone quarried from an earlier tumbled wall than by quarrying all the stone afresh at an alternative location. Thirdly, the reoccupation of a site bearing clear indications of earlier settlement may have been of symbolic significance, though we cannot be sure exactly why. Whatever the explanation, the resulting multi-period sites and landscapes can be impossible to comprehend fully from surface evidence alone. Indeed, the surface evidence can be very confusing and even misleading. Only careful excavation can demonstrate the time-depth at such sites, thus enabling the development of a variety of possible interpretations of the observed sequences.

Perhaps surprisingly, there are few settlements of probable Roman date on sites away from the hillforts, suggesting that fewer new settlements were founded here than in other parts of

5.11 The carving at the little shrine to Cocidius at Yardhope.
Photo: Beryl Charlton.

Northumberland. A few possible contemporary settlements have been recorded away from hillfort sites, such as the group of five stone roundhouses above the Barrow Burn (1km west of Harbottle Lough), the ten stone-built houses at Debdon Whitefield (one of which was excavated in 1907, revealing antlers, animal bones and charcoal) and the Uplaw settlements on Clennell Street (discussed in the previous chapter). It is also probable that other sites may have been destroyed through later development, which has been more extensive in parts of Upper Coquetdale than in some of the more remote Cheviot valleys. After all, if a site was suitable for a farm in Roman times then it may still be suitable for a farm today: I would hazard a guess that many present day farmsteads occupy the sites of later prehistoric or Roman settlements. Alternatively, if, as suggested above, this really was a boundary zone, then perhaps fewer settlements were founded here than towards the heartlands of tribal territories to both north and south.

Finally in this brief consideration of everyday life in Romano-British Upper Coquetdale, what can we say of the religious practices of the people? Unfortunately, on the basis of the available evidence, the answer has to be very little. Roman soldiers brought their own religions with them, and there is plenty of evidence of these from various sites along Hadrian's Wall and elsewhere. The extent to which any of these were actually practiced in Upper Coquetdale is not known, but there was certainly a degree of interaction between the religious beliefs of the Romans and those of the native people. Native religion would, I think, have been firmly rooted in the local environment: particular sacred sites would represent particular myths and legends, and thus be intimately associated with specific deities. However, evidence from several Roman inscribed altars from Northumberland proves that some local deities became linked with Roman gods. In our region, the most fascinating evidence for this comes in the form of the shrine to Cocidius (fig. 5.11), overlooking the Roman road through the valley of the Holystone Burn, near Yardhope on the Otterburn Training Area. This little shrine, only discovered in 1980, consists of a natural niche in the rock with the figure of the god carved onto the rock face just outside its entrance. The site was excavated by Beryl Charlton and Margaret Mitcheson soon after its discovery, but no clear evidence as to its date or use was recovered. Despite this lack of evidence, the excavation report was still deemed sufficiently important to be published within the internationally famous journal *Britannia*.

In their report, the excavators speculate that the shrine's carving may have been executed by Roman soldiers based at the nearby marching camp of Yardhope, or perhaps at *Bremenium*, and that the site may already have been a sacred spot in pre-Roman times. Cocidius, the 'red god', has been recognised from several carvings and inscriptions along Hadrian's Wall (the similarity between his name and that of the Coquet - *Coccoveda* - is probably coincidental, but may not have gone entirely without comment amongst local people). He has been linked with Mars and Silvanus, the Roman gods of war and hunting, and seems to have been of special importance in the Roman frontier zone. We can speculate at length about the possible significance of this little shrine to Roman soldiers and local farming families, but, as Charlton and Mitcheson state in their excavation report, 'only the god on the rock knows the truth and he remains watchful, but silent'.

It is just possible that Christianity may have taken its first tentative steps into the region during Roman times, but if so then its presence was short-lived. In general, religious belief amongst the farmers of Upper Coquetdale during the Roman era probably differed little from that of their Iron Age ancestors. The same places probably retained sacred significance: to my mind these would have included the summit of Simonside, along with a number of springs and other wet places such as Harbottle Lough (fig. 5.12) and the Lady's Well at Holystone. The importance of the Lady's Well is perhaps reflected in the fact that the Roman road from *Bremenium* to *Alauna* was aligned to pass right by it. It may have functioned in a similar way to Coventina's Well at Carrowbrough on Hadrian's Wall, where votive offerings including at least 22 stone altars and an estimated 15,000 coins were found in the nineteenth century. Any ancient structures at the Lady's Well would have been much disturbed when the present structure was built in Victorian times, and, to my knowledge, no Iron Age or Roman artefacts have ever been found here. Nevertheless, I remain quietly confident that one day something will turn up to demonstrate the importance of this place to local people in late prehistoric times. It may even have attracted an occasional votive offering from the Roman forces based at *Bremenium*, some of whom may have stopped to pay their respects to the local gods while out and about demonstrating their power over the local people.

After the Romans

The pay chests for what was left of the Roman army ceased to arrive in the early fifth century, and it is generally assumed that the region descended into chaos with local war-bands, some incorporating the last vestiges of the Roman garrisons, vying for supremacy over each other. Some of the old hillforts may have been reoccupied, and in some cases their defences rebuilt, by these war-bands. The lack of contemporary written sources could reasonably result in this period also being classed as 'prehistory', and thus included in this book, but we must draw the line somewhere. Eventually, in the sixth century, the *Votadini* reappear in literary sources as the *Gododdin*, based in Edinburgh and south-east Scotland, and Coquetdale presumably fell within the territory of the local British kingdom of Bernicia, governed from Bamburgh. By the mid-sixth century Bernicia was an Anglian Kingdom, and by the early seventh century it had been united with Deira, to the south, to form the great Anglian kingdom of Northumbria. At some point during all this, the local people left the hills and began to live in lowland villages of rectangular, timber-built houses. In the sixth and seventh centuries, Rothbury was probably such a village. But this is another story, which we must save for another time.

5.12 We suggested in chapter 5 that Harbottle Lough was probably of sacred significance and may have attracted ritual offerings: there is no reason to believe that it would not have retained such significance throughout, and perhaps beyond, Roman times.

The Upper Coquetdale Community Archaeology Project (UCCAP) provides opportunities for local people to undertake their own archaeological projects.

Chapter 6

The Future of Prehistory in Upper Coquetdale

The pleasures of prehistory

The prehistoric past has much to offer the future. I believe that an appreciation of the distant past, the ways in which our ancestors may have understood their world, is genuinely life-enhancing, and can contribute positively to our individual and collective futures. While this does not mean that everyone should be forced to study archaeology, the teaching of more archaeology in schools would certainly be no bad thing and many more opportunities should be made available for people to learn about the distant past than is currently the case. I remember a conservation project that the National Park Authority organised for pupils of Rothbury First School back in the early 1990s (fig. 6.1). The children came up to Lordenshaws

6.1 Rothbury schoolchildren help with erosion repair at Lordenshaws hillfort in 1993.

hillfort for a day and dismantled a walkers' cairn (which walkers were continually enlarging by the addition of stones illegally removed from the fort ramparts), before placing the stones in eroded sections of the ramparts and returfing the damaged areas. I remember commenting at the time that this was much cheaper way of getting the job done than paying contractors to do the work! It was also, of course, a great opportunity for the children, and their teachers, to learn something about local archaeology. I find it depressing that so little is done about archaeology in schools when it is such an important and exciting subject, and I hope that it will be possible to arrange several similar practical exercises in Upper Coquetdale in future. I rarely get the chance to work directly with schoolchildren (other than my own, who inevitably think archaeology can 'sometimes be a bit boring') but whenever I do it seems that most of them fancy a go at being an archaeologist when they grow up. Of course, hardly any of them will become archaeologists, but neither will they become film stars, astronauts or train drivers! The important thing is that they have an awareness of archaeology which they can build on in later years should they wish to do so.

Simonside - The Sacred Mountain?
31 December 1999

6.2 The souvenir card printed for the Simonside 'Millennium Event', featuring artwork by Tony Hopkins.

Getting the message across to children early in their lives is important, but, in my experience, most adults are also keen to learn about the distant past when the opportunity is provided. This has become clear to me at numerous events in Upper Coquetdale and elsewhere. The most spectacular of these was undoubtedly the Millennium Event on Simonside which involved about eighty people on New Years' Eve 1999 (fig. 6.2). This was based on a walk around Simonside, visiting several archaeological sites including some of the early Bronze Age burial cairns excavated by David Dippie Dixon. It also involved much more: the excellent storyteller, Pascale Konyn, told fascinating tales relating to the prehistoric past at particular sites; traditional music, played on Northumbrian pipes, was provided by Andrew Miller and Jim Grant; and a spectacular firework display lit up the summit of Simonside as night fell on the old millennium. Unfortunately, the stated aim of 'watching the final sunset of the millennium from the top of the sacred mountain' was defeated by cloud and mist, but luckily this was not sufficiently dense to cloud our view of the fireworks. Getting everyone safely down the hill in the dark in pouring rain was not without incident, but everyone enjoyed the day while also gaining a greater appreciation of the prehistory of Simonside. I hope that it will be possible to hold more of these events in future as local interest in the subject continues to grow.

Another local Millennium event, in which I was honoured to be invited to participate, was the unveiling of the Brinkburn and Hesleyhurst 'Millennium Stone'. Due to various delays this wasn't finally unveiled until 1st September, 2002. It is a large boulder, carved with the names of all the residents of the two parishes, which stands in the community field with a splendid view across the valley towards Simonside (fig. 6.3). I was asked to address the event on the subject of ancient stone carving, and once again I was delighted to sense the great public interest in local prehistory. I remember reading a passage from Dixon's *Upper Coquetdale*, and during discussions afterwards I could have taken several dozen advance orders for this book had I thought of doing so! I hope that all the people I spoke to on that occasion manage eventually to get hold of a copy, and that it goes some way towards satisfying the demand for knowledge about prehistoric rock art and other aspects of local prehistory. The thinking behind the Brinkburn and Hesleyhurst Millennium Stone probably bears little relation to the ancient reasoning behind the production of nearby cup-and-ring marks, but the desire to leave a more-or-less permanent message carved in stone ties the two, perhaps separated by 5000 years, neatly together. There is a fine view of Simonside to be had from the Millennium Stone, but in this particular case I do not seek to read any special religious significance into this, though I do know that local people greatly appreciate the stone's stunning landscape setting.

I believe that an interest in the distant past is innate in most of us. That is why the parts of my job dealing with public interpretation are so easy - most of the time I am telling people about things they are already eager to know more about. But prehistory is not only interesting, it is also important. This is because it teaches us about other ways of living, other ways of thinking. It can be difficult, even today, trying to work out what someone else really thinks or believes about something, so to try and do this for people in the distant past might be regarded as

pointless. But it isn't. In this book I have suggested ways in which our distant ancestors may have viewed their world. I have done this partly by reference to Native Americans and Australian Aborigines, who live complex spiritual lives uncluttered by much of the nonsense of the modern western world. To stand on top of Simonside today and wonder whether people thousands of years ago regarded the place as a sacred mountain is certainly not a waste of time. In fact quite the opposite - it can in itself be a spiritually rewarding experience. To stare at a pile of stones in the knowledge that it was once a burial place for local people, and to think for a moment about the events that must have taken place here thousands of years ago, can also help to make us more aware of our place in our world.

6.3 Local people at the Brinkburn and Hesleyhurst 'Millennium Stone' on 1st September 2002.

I like to think that David Dippie Dixon and I have many interests and values in common, but there is one fundamental way in which we differ. So far as I can gather, he seems to have been a committed Christian. I am not. I need to see beyond any conventional religion to seek something deeper and more meaningful. I believe that spiritual fulfilment should be sought ultimately from within ourselves, with inspiration gathered from all manner of opportunities provided by our environment. The spirituality of native peoples such as those of the Americas and Australia, and what we know of Celtic spirituality, both come closer to satisfying me than any conventional religion in the modern world. I think much of the attraction of these belief systems comes from the fact they are rooted in real places, in 'special' places set within the everyday landscape, rather than in an entirely abstract concept of an all-powerful 'God' who is 'out there somewhere'.

A Christian church can be built anywhere, and immediately becomes a focus for worship. In contrast, a truly sacred place, with its unique characteristics and ancient ancestral connections, is something that cannot be 'created', although its significance certainly can change through time. That is not to say that prehistoric people did not build temples - they certainly did. But these were intimately linked to the wider landscape, and probably also to the heavens, whereas a Christian church is often entirely detached from the history and meaning of the surrounding landscape. Prehistoric people, of course, did not have the option of Christianity, but they got along quite nicely without it, and I doubt very much whether it would have appealed to them had it been available. In more recent times, 'the curse of Christianity', under the admittedly well intentioned guise of bringing 'civilisation' to 'uneducated natives', has had much to do with the destruction of many traditional belief systems throughout the world. Whether or not the people in those societies are now happier, or spiritually more content, than they were in earlier times must be open to much doubt.

I do not wish to labour the point, but I do believe, despite everything that has happened over the past two millennia, and the current dominance of Christianity over the western world, that we all still have it in us to reach back and sense the spirituality of our prehistoric ancestors. Even in the modern 'scientific' world, there are many things that defy explanation. Some people chose not to think about them. Others accept explanations offered by conventional religion or philosophy. It is, of course, up to each and every individual to deal with such matters in their own way. I choose to seek inspiration from my prehistoric ancestors, and I would certainly recommend such an approach to anyone who cared to ask. In the search for spiritual fulfilment, five minutes on top of Simonside at any time of day or night (whatever the weather!) will always satisfy me more than an hour in a church on a Sunday morning.

Of course, the prehistoric past was no 'Garden of Eden'. Life was hard and often cruel, as well as short. If offered the choice, I would certainly not opt to give up my modern, cosy life to live back in prehistory (in any case, I am a little over forty years of age, so as a prehistoric person would probably already be dead!). An understanding of the problems faced by our prehistoric ancestors in their everyday lives should lead to an even deeper appreciation of their complex spirituality. Without any of the shallow and often pointless distractions of modern life, these people lived meaningful lives in their world. Progress is inevitable, as it always has been, but it should be tempered with an appreciation of the past. On a practical level, this is why it is important to make provision for archaeological research when planning new developments in the landscape. Such work is not undertaken simply in order to dig for treasure, but because of its potential to contribute to our understanding of our archaeological heritage, and an appreciation of the distant past has much to offer each and every one of us, in all sorts of different ways.

Towards the future

We discussed the collection of prehistoric flintwork from ploughed fields at Low Farnham in Chapter 3. On page 120 of *Upper Coquetdale*, David Dippie Dixon tells us that:

> *While Canon Greenwell was engaged in his work on Holystone Common, he observed an intelligent-looking boy standing by, eagerly watching the proceedings. The Canon spoke kindly to the lad, and finding that he was greatly interested in what he had seen, explained to him about the cairn and its contents, the modes of burial, and other information relating to the burial customs of the early inhabitants of the valley. At the same time he also told him to pick up every piece of flint he might happen to see in the fields when ploughing or harrowing. The result of this friendly chat between the man of science and the ingenious county lad is the fine collection of flint implements that have been gathered in the fields at Low Farnham by Mr. John Nicholson, of the Sheepbanks, for he it was who attracted the attention of Canon Greenwell on Holystone Common some forty years ago.*

I was fascinated to read this and to learn that John Nicholson was following the advice of the great Canon Greenwell when picking up all those flints. Today, there is much scope for local people to build on John Nicholson's important contribution, and it is important that opportunities are provided for people in the valley to get involved in such work. After my lecture to the Rothbury and Coquetdale History Society, in December 2003, to celebrate the centenary of the publication of David Dippie Dixon's *Upper Coquetdale*, I made two promises. The first was that I would develop the lecture into a publication, which I am now relieved to have done. The second was that I would help to set up a programme of fieldwork for local people to carry out themselves. Many people think that archaeology can only be done by professionals after years of studying at University, but this is certainly not the case. As the above case of John Nicholson, and the more recent contributions of people like Stan Beckensall and John Davies demonstrate, much useful work can be done by people with no archaeological qualifications. There is an enormous amount of such work waiting to be done in Upper

6.4 Elanor Johnson working with local volunteers at the first UCCAP community excavation, summer 2005.

Coquetdale, including fieldwalking, site survey and possibly also some small-scale excavation. There is also an infinite amount of thinking that needs to be done to try and make sense of all the data we have at our disposal, and anyone can have a go at this!

Over recent years, the Northumberland National Park Authority has taken the lead in setting up a number of fascinating projects, undertaken in partnership with various professional archaeologists. Several are discussed in this book, including pollen analysis at Bloody Moss and Caudhole Sike, the Otterburn Training Area aerial survey, survey and excavation at Harehaugh Camp, and survey work at Lordenshaws. It has been a privilege to be involved with these projects and I have gained much pleasure through discussing them with local people, but the agenda has now changed. Sadly (for legal reasons I am unable to discuss any details), my employment with the National Park Authority came to an end as this book went to press, so my ability to influence future archaeological projects in Upper Coquetdale will be much reduced. However, this need not matter, as a new initiative, which will hopefully generate much exciting new work, is already underway. This is the Upper Coquetdale Community Archaeology Project (UCCAP), which encourages local communities to undertake their own archaeological research, thus fulfilling the second of my above-mentioned promises. Initially a three year project, UCCAP has been developed by the Rothbury and Coquetdale History Society in association with the National Park Authority, and has enjoyed support from numerous partners including Northumberland County Council, the National Trust, the Ministry of Defence, Forest Enterprise, Rothbury Middle School and the Thropton and Netherton Women's Institutes. The project has been most fortunate to secure the services of Elanor Johnson as project officer (fig. 6.4). Elanor, a graduate of Newcastle University, took up post in May 2005 and has seen the project go from strength to strength. About 150 local people attended a launch meeting at the Jubilee Hall in Rothbury in June 2005, since when more than 100 people have taken part in UCCAP fieldwork including the first annual project excavation (figs. 6.5, 6.6), fieldwalking (figs. 6.7, 6.8) and surveying. In addition, several events including evening classes in pottery and stone tools, and an extremely popular 'Archaeology Day' at Barrowburn (fig. 6.9), have all proved very successful. Many more events are planned for the next couple of years,

6.5 Two views of excavation in progress at the Harehaugh 'long cairn'.

including 'Artefact Roadshows' to which farmers will be invited to bring along finds made on their land for identification (fig. 6.10) and 'Business Workshops' at which local business people will be encouraged to use the historic environment to help market their businesses. The project will also encourage local artists and craftspeople to seek inspiration in the distant past (fig. 6.11). Regularly updated information about UCCAP is provided on the National Park website, which also includes details of how to join the project. The ultimate aim is for the people of upper Coquetdale to 'own' the archaeology of their valley, and, in consultation with local professional archaeologists, to make their own informed decisions about how to manage it.

With such ownership comes great responsibility, such as the need to strike a sensible balance between the desire for short-term discoveries and the need for long-term conservation initiatives, or the need to open and interpret sites for the public while also seeking to ensure

6.6 Peter Carne, excavation director, leads an on-site discussion at the Harehaugh 'long cairn'. Such discussions, in which all volunteers were encouraged to participate, were held regularly during the excavation, enabling everyone to contribute to the ongoing interpretation of the site.

6.7 Fieldwalking at Elilaw, autumn 2005.

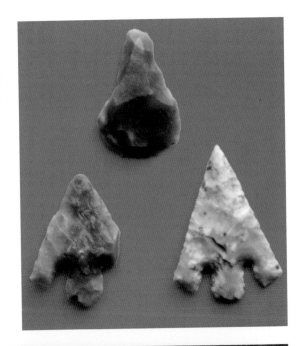

6.8 Two arrowheads and a scraper, all probably about 4,000 years old, found during fieldwalking at Low Farnham in autumn 2005.

that archaeological remains are not damaged by visitors. Such balances are not easy to achieve. I often get frustrated listening to conservation bodies arguing for the allocation of substantial resources for the indefinite preservation of everything for some unknown future occasion when new techniques of investigation will be available. The logical end result of such an approach is that no excavation would ever take place anywhere, as all sites would have to be saved for the future unless they were significantly threatened in some way and could not be saved. I accept that conservation is very important, and spend much of my own time engaged in conservation work. But much of our current policy is based on initiatives developed in southern England, where many more excavations have been completed in the past and relatively few sites

6.9 Members of the public were encouraged to make their own 'prehistoric' pots, which were then fired at a 'Fire and Stone' event at Barrowburn in December 2005. The event also included demonstrations of flint knapping.

6.10 John Bradbury pictured with two Bronze Age axes at the spot where he found them in Clover Field, Warton Farm, with a snow covered Simonside in the background.

John was the local shepherd and was simply walking across the field in summer 1988 when he noticed the axes lying on the surface. Why they should ever have been discarded here, on a low knoll with no obvious sign of Bronze Age activity, is a mystery. Many more such finds must have been made by eagle-eyed farmers over the years, and even more still lie in the ground awaiting discovery! The Upper Coquetdale Community Archaeology Project encourages farmers to bring along such objects for identification, and will help local people to make new discoveries for themselves.

survive uninvestigated. In areas like Upper Coquetdale we have much catching up to do, and we must have the confidence to undertake a number of small-scale, carefully targeted excavations to improve our general knowledge. Such work is also of conservation value, as it enables the development of meaningful conservation policies taking into account the nature of buried deposits within specific sites. It also raises awareness of, and concern for, local archaeology among local people, including farmers and landowners who will consequently seek to avoid damaging sites and landscapes of potential archaeological importance. The ideal scenario is to have professional archaeologists (including academics from Durham, Newcastle and Edinburgh Universities) and local people working together to secure an exciting future for the archaeology of Upper Coquetdale. It must be local people, however, who take the lead role.

The next 100 years

When considering the future of archaeological research in Upper Coquetdale, there is so much to do that it can seem impossible to know where to start (and remember that this book is only about prehistory - there are another 1600 years of archaeology between the end of Chapter 5 and the present day!). Fortunately, help is at hand in the form of professionally written research agendas which at the time of writing are nearing completion. A research agenda highlights gaps in our knowledge and, taking into account the nature of the archaeological resource and its potential for answering particular questions, suggests a number of foci for future projects. There will be one such agenda for the Northumberland National Park, and another covering the whole of north-east England. It should be possible to adapt the relevant sections of these to provide a focussed agenda for research into prehistoric Upper Coquetdale, thus helping with the acquisition of funds for projects. A good idea might be to draw up a research agenda for the region, with the stated objective of reviewing and updating it once a decade. No doubt, some decades will see relatively little progress, but, with a little luck and lots of hard work, others will witness considerable advances in our understanding. After ten such decades, a research agenda for prehistoric Upper Coquetdale in the early 22nd century should be very different from one drawn up today. By then, we should be asking new questions and seeking to answer these using new techniques of investigation and new modes of thinking. While I doubt that anyone will have 'solved' the conundrum of our cup-and-ring marks, I'm sure that lots of very clever people will have had a great deal of fun trying, and will certainly have developed some ingenious new suggestions.

6.11 Local potter Graham Taylor, of Crown Studio, Elsdon, holding a pottery vessel inspired by the ancient standing stones of Northumberland.

David Dippie Dixon's *Upper Coquetdale* has given much pleasure to many people over the past 100 years, and if this volume contributes in any way to the pleasure to be gained from living in, or visiting, this beautiful place (fig. 6.12) over the next 100 years than it will have served its purpose. I hope that lots of local people will enjoy reading it, and that some will wish to find out more through further reading, visiting sites, and joining local societies. Of these, I hope that many will wish to take part directly in local research projects. Perhaps, at some point within the next 100 years, it will be possible to set up a Museum of Upper Coquetdale, to put on permanent display some of the wonderful finds such as those currently cluttering up the British Museum stores. This would provide a focus for further research, and could also house the multitude of exciting new finds that I confidently predict will be made in the valley over the next century and beyond. Ideally, such an institution should be located in Rothbury, although an alternative could be to set it up at Cragside under the stewardship of the National Trust. Either way, it, along with an associated programme of ongoing archaeological research, would represent a fitting tribute to the life and work of David Dippie Dixon.

6.12 A silent witness to 10,000 years of prehistory, Simonside continues to stand guard over today's beautiful Coquetdale landscape.
Photo: Simon Fraser.

The Author

Paul Frodsham studied Archaeology, Anthropology and Geography at the University of Durham, graduating in 1985. He worked as an archaeologist in Cumbria, London and Berkshire, before being appointed as the Northumberland National Park Authority's first archaeologist in 1992. Since arriving in Northumberland he has been responsible for numerous projects, many of which are described in his book *Archaeology in Northumberland National Park* published in 2004 by the Council for British Archaeology. He has published many academic papers and popular articles on a variety of archaeological subjects, has appeared in several local and national television programmes, and has led numerous popular events and guided walks throughout Northumberland and elsewhere. Paul left the National Park Authority in 2006 to set up his own consultancy specialising in heritage interpretation. In addition to archaeology and the Northumberland landscape, he lists his main passions as his daughters Katie and Claire, his library (which includes an ever-growing collection of antiquarian books about Northumberland), his garden, and the study of Philosophy.

Getting Involved

The Upper Coquetdale Community Archaeology Project (UCCAP)

UCCAP's stated mission is 'to give local archaeology back to local people'. It was set up by the National Park Authority and the Rothbury and Coquetdale History Society to provide training in archaeology for local people. It achieves this through an annual excavation and numerous events and classes. The project currently has funding until summer 2008 but will hopefully continue much longer. Membership of UCCAP is open to everyone. Details can be found on the National Park website: www.northumberland-national-park.org.uk

Sites to Visit

Many fascinating archaeological sites are accessible to the public throughout Upper Coquetdale. These include mysterious Neolithic rock carvings, Bronze Age burial mounds, impressive Iron Age hillforts, and the extraordinary Roman camps at Chew Green. Access arrangements can change, so details are not provided here. For up to date information about local sites open to the public please contact or visit the National Park Authority's Visitor Centre at Church House, Rothbury (01669 620887).

References

Listed here are all references specifically cited in the text, together with other publications consulted during the writing of the book which may be of interest to readers seeking more detailed information about particular topics.

For information about specific sites discussed in the book, readers are encouraged to consult the *Northumberland Historic Environment Record* (maintained by the Northumberland County Archaeologist based at County Hall, Morpeth) or the *Keys to the Past* website **(www.keystothepast.info).**

Anon. 1891. *Archaic Rock Inscriptions; An Account of the Cup & Ring Markings on the Sculptured Stones of the Old and New Worlds.* London: A. Reader.

Archaeological Practice Ltd. 2004. *Harehaugh Hillfort Archaeological Project.* Unpublished report for Northumberland National Park Authority.

Arkle, T. 1879. The Simonside Find. *History of the Berwickshire Naturalists' Club* **8** (1876-1878), 176-7.

Barber, M. 2003. *Bronze and the Bronze Age. Metalwork and Society in Britain c.2500-800BC.* Stroud: Tempus.

Bate, D.M.A. 1912. On a Northumberland Barrow and its Contents. *Proceedings of the Society of Antiquaries of Scotland* **X**, 15-26.

Beckensall, S. 1983. *Northumberland's Prehistoric Rock Carvings. A Mystery Explained.* Rothbury: Pendulum.

Beckensall, S. 2001. *Prehistoric Rock Art in Northumberland.* Stroud: Tempus.

Beckensall, S. 2001. *Northumberland. The Power of Place.* Stroud: Tempus.

Beckensall, S. 2003. *Prehistoric Northumberland.* Stroud: Tempus.

Beckensall, S. & Frodsham, P. 1998. Questions of Chronology: the Case for Bronze Age Rock Art in Northern England. *Northern Archaeology* **15/16**, 51-69.

Bradley, R. 1997. *Rock Art and the Prehistory of Atlantic Europe: Signing the Land.* London: Routledge.

Brewis, P. & Dixon, D.D. 1915. Pre-Roman Remains in Upper Coquetdale. *Proceedings of the Society of Antiquaries of Newcastle-upon-Tyne* (3rd series) **VII** (No. 4), 37-52.

Bruce, J.C. 1880. *A Descriptive Catalogue of Antiquities, Chiefly British, at Alnwick Castle.* Newcastle upon Tyne: Albert Reid.

Burgess, C. 1968. *Bronze Age Metalwork in Northern England c.1000 to 700BC.* Newcastle upon Tyne: Oriel Press.

Burgess, C. 1980. Excavations at Houseledge, Black Law, Northumberland, 1979, and their implications for earlier Bronze Age settlement in the Cheviots. *Northern Archaeology* **1** (part 1), 5-12.

Burgess, C. 1982. The Cartington Knife and the Double-Edged Knives of the Late Bronze Age. *Northern Archaeology* **3**, 32-45.

Burgess, C. 1984. The Prehistoric Settlement of Northumberland: A Speculative Survey. In R. Miket & C. Burgess (eds), *Between and Beyond The Walls: Essays on the Prehistory and History of North Britain in Honour of George Jobey.* Edinburgh: John Donald. 126-175.

Burgess, C., Ovens, M. & Uribe de Kellett, A. 1981. The Ground and Polished Stone Implements of North-East England: A Preliminary Statement. *Northern Archaeology* **2** (part 1), 6-12.

Butler, C. 2005. *Prehistoric Flintwork.* Stroud: Tempus.

Charlton, B. 1996. *Fifty Centuries of Peace and War. An Archaeological Survey of the Otterburn Training Area.* Otterburn: Ministry of Defence.

Charlton, D.B. & Mitcheson, M, 1983. Yardhope: A Shrine to Cocidius? *Britannia* **14**, 143-155.

Cowan, J.D. 1932. The Dixon Collection. *Proceedings of the Society of Antiquaries of Newcastle-upon-Tyne* (4th series) **V** (No. 4), 233-236.

Cowan, J.D. 1966. Two amber beads from Simonside. *Archaeologia Aeliana* (4th series) **XLIV**, 217-218.

Cummins, W.A. & Harding, A.F. 1988. The petrological identification of stone implements from north-east England. In T.H.McK. Clough & W.A. Cummins (eds) *Stone Axe Studies volume 2.* York: Council for British Archaeology Research Report No. 67, 78-84.

Cunliffe, B. 1992. *The Celtic World.* London: Constable.

Davies, J. 1983. The Mesolithic Sites of Northumberland. *Northern Archaeology* **4** (part 2), 18-24.

Devereux, P. 2000. *The Sacred Place. The Ancient Origin of Holy and Mystical Sites.* London: Cassell.

Dixon, D.D. 1885. Ancient British Flint Implements found at Low Farnham, Coquetdale. *History of the Berwickshire Naturalists' Club* **10** (1882-1884), 347-349.

Dixon D.D. 1885. British Urn found at Screnwood, near Alnham, Northumberland, with remarks on other Antiquities in that neighbourhood. *History of the Berwickshire Naturalists' Club* **10** (1882-1884), 544-546.

Dixon, D.D. 1892. Notes on the Discovery of British Burials on the Simonside Hills, Parish of Rothbury, in Upper Coquetdale, Northumberland. *Archaeologia Aeliana* (2nd series) **XV**, 23-32.

Dixon, D.D. 1895. *Whittingham Vale, Northumberland. Its History, Traditions and Folklore.* Newcastle upon Tyne: Robert Redpath.

Dixon, D.D. 1903. *Upper Coquetdale, Northumberland. Its history, traditions, folklore and scenery.* Newcastle upon Tyne: Robert Redpath.

Dixon, D.D. 1912. *A Private Family History.* Unpublished manuscript.

Dixon, D.D. 1913. The Cartington oak coffin. *Proceedings of the Society of Antiquaries of Newcastle-upon-Tyne* (3rd series) **VI** (No. 7), 81-84.

Dodds, M.H. (ed) 1940. *A History of Northumberland* Volume XV. Newcastle upon Tyne: Andrew Reid.

Doubleday, T. (ed) 1852. *The Coquet-Dale Fishing Songs.* Edinburgh: Blackwood.

Ekwall, E. 1960. *The Oxford Dictionary of English Place Names.* Oxford: Oxford University Press.

Embleton, R. & Graham, F. 1984. *Hadrian's Wall in the Days of the Romans.* Newcastle upon Tyne: Frank Graham.

Evans, J. 1872. *The Ancient Stone Implements, Weapons, and Ornaments, of Great Britain.* London: Longmans, Green, Reader, and Dyer.

Evans, J. 1881. *Ancient Bronze Implements, Weapons, and Ornaments of Great Britain and Ireland.* London: Longmans, Green & Co.

Evans, J.G. 1975. *The Environment of Early Man in the British Isles.* London: Paul Elek.

Feest, C.F. (ed) 2000. *The Cultures of Native North Americans.* Cologne: Konemann.

Ford, B., Deakin, P. & Walker, M. 2002. The Tri-radial Cairns of Northumberland. *Current Archaeology* **182**, 82-85.

Frodsham, P. 1996. Spirals in Time: Morwick Mill and the Spiral Motif in the British Neolithic. In P. Frodsham (ed) *Neolithic Studies in No-Man's Land. Papers on the Neolithic of Northern England from the Trent to the Tweed.* Northern Archaeology **13/14** (special edition). 101-138.

Frodsham, P. 2000. Worlds without ends: towards a new prehistory for central Britain. In J. Harding & R. Johnstone (eds) *Northern Pasts: Interpretations of the Later Prehistory of Northern England and Southern Scotland.* (British Archaeological Reports, British Series 302). Oxford: Archaeopress. 15-31.

Frodsham, P. 2002. Lord of the Cups and Rings: the Beckensall Trilogy. *Northern Archaeology* **19**, 39-47.

Frodsham, P. 2004. *Archaeology in Northumberland National Park.* York: Council for British Archaeology.

Frodsham, P. 2004. 'So much history in this landscape. So much confusion, so much doubt'. In P. Frodsham (ed) *Interpreting the Ambiguous: Archaeology and interpretation in early 21st century Britain.* (British Archaeological Reports, British Series 362). Oxford: Archaeopress.

Frodsham, P. (in press). The Phallic Explanation. A late nineteenth-century solution to the cup-and-ring conundrum. In C. Burgess, P. Topping & F. Lynch (eds) *Beyond Stonehenge. Essays in Honour of Colin Burgess.* Oxford: Oxbow.

Frodsham, P. & Hedley, I. 2005. *People of the Breamish Valley.* Hexham: Northumberland National Park Authority.

Gates, T. 1983. Unenclosed settlements in Northumberland. In J. Chapman & H. Mytum (eds) *Settlement in North Britain,* 1000BC-AD1000. (British Archaeological Reports, British Series 118). Oxford: BAR. 103-148.

Gates, T. 1997. *Air Photography and the Archaeology of the Otterburn Training Area.* Unpublished report for Northumberland National Park Authority.

Gibson, A. 1978. *Bronze Age Pottery in the North-East of England.* (British Archaeological Reports, British Series 56). Oxford: BAR.

Gibson, A. 2002. *Prehistoric Pottery in Britain and Ireland.* Stroud: Tempus.

Grant, C. 1967. *Rock Art of the American Indian.* New York: Promontory Press.

Grant, C. 1983. *The Rock Art of the North American Indians.* Cambridge: Cambridge University Press.

Greenwell, W. 1877. *British Barrows. A Record of the Examination of Sepulchral Monuments in Various Parts of England.* Oxford: Clarendon.

Hare, A.J.C. 1873. *A Handbook for Travellers in Durham and Northumberland.* (Revised edition). London: John Murray.

Hedley, R.C. 1892. Burgh Hill Camp. *Archaeologia Aeliana* (2nd series) **XV**, 33-36.

Hodgkin, Dr. 1888. Note on the Cragside sword. *Proceedings of the Society of Antiquaries of Newcastle-upon-Tyne* (2nd series) **III** (No. 40), 408.

Jobey G. 1964. Enclosed stone-built settlements in Northumberland. *Archaeologia Aeliana* (4th series) **XLII**, 41-64.

Jobey G. 1965. Hillforts and settlements in Northumberland. *Archaeologia Aeliana* (4th series) **XLIII**, 21-64.

Jobey, G. 1974. *A Field-Guide to Prehistoric Northumberland. Part 2.* Newcastle upon Tyne: Frank Graham.

Jobey, G. 1982. Between Tyne and Forth: Some Problems. In P. Clack & S. Haselgrove (eds) *Rural Settlement in The Roman North.* Durham: University of Durham. 7-18.

Jobey G. 1983. Excavation of an unenclosed settlement on Standrop Rigg, Northumberland, and some problems related to similar settlements between Tyne and Forth. *Archaeologia Aeliana* (5th series) **XI**, 1-21.

Jobey, G. & Tait, J. 1966. Excavations on palisaded settlements and cairnfields at Alnham, Northumberland. *Archaeologia Aeliana* (4th series) **XLIV**, 5-48.

Kinnes I.A. & Longworth, H. 1985. *Catalogue of the Excavated Prehistoric and Romano-British Material in the Greenwell Collection.* London: British Museum Publications.

Lancaster University Archaeology Unit & Archaeological Services, University of Durham. 2000. *Simonside Landscape Survey.* Unpublished report for Northumberland National Park Authority.

Mackenzie, E. 1825. *An Historical, Topographical, and Descriptive View of the County of Northumberland.* Volumes I & II. (Second edition). Newcastle upon Tyne: Mackenzie & Dent.

MacLauchlan, H. 1852. *The Watling Street. The chief line of Roman communication leading across the Counties of Durham and Northumberland, from the River Swale to the Scotch border.* (2 volumes: Atlas and Memoirs). London: privately printed.

MacLauchlan, H. 1864. *Eastern branch of the Watling Street, in the County of Northumberland, from Bewclay near Portgate on the Roman Wall to Berwick-upon-Tweed; together with a branch extending from High Rochester to Whittingham.* (2 volumes: Atlas and Memoirs). London: privately printed.

MacLauchlan, H. 1867. *Notes not included in the memoirs already published on Roman roads in Northumberland.* London: privately printed.

Manning, A.D. 1996. *Palaeoenvironmental Investigations at Caudhole Moss near Lordenshaws in the Simonside Hills.* Unpublished report for Northumberland National Park Authority.

Martin, J.W. 1999. *The Land Looks After Us. A History of Native American Religion.* Oxford: Oxford University Press.

Masters, L. 1884. The Neolithic Long Cairns of Cumbria and Northumberland. In R. Miket & C. Burgess (eds) *Between and Beyond The Walls: Essays on the Prehistory and History of North Britain in Honour of George Jobey.* Edinburgh: John Donald. 52-73.

Mawer, A. 1920. *The Place Names of Northumberland and Durham.* Cambridge: Cambridge University Press.

Miket, R. 1974. Excavation at Kirkhill, West Hepple, 1972. *Archaeologia Aeliana* (5th series) **II**, 153-187.

Moores, A.J. & Passmore, D. 1999. *Holocene Vegetation Histories and Human Activity in Upland Coquetdale; Pollen Records from Bloody Moss, Otterburn Training Area and Caudhole Moss, Simonside Hills.* Unpublished report for Northumberland National Park Authority.

Morris, R.W.B. 1979. *The Prehistoric Rock Art of Galloway and the Isle of Man.* Poole: Blandford Press.

Newbigin, E.R. 1930. A Memoir of the late David Dippie Dixon, FSA. *Archaeologia Aeliana* (4th series) **VII**, 115-118.

Newbigin, E.R 1932. Incised rocks near Lordenshaws Camp. *History of the Berwickshire Naturalists' Club* **27** (1929-1931), 327-329.

Newbigin, E.R. 1932. Deep trackways on Simonside Hills. *History of the Berwickshire Naturalists' Club* **27** (1929-1931), 330-333.

Newbigin E.R. 1932. Notes on a series of unrecorded incised rocks at Lordenshaws. *Archaeologia Aeliana* (4th series) **IX**, 50-67.

Piggott, S. 1958. Native Economies and the Roman Occupation of North Britain. In I. A. Richmond (ed) *Roman and Native in North Britain.* Edinburgh: Nelson.

Rivet, A.L.F. & Smith, C. 1979. *The Place-Names of Roman Britain.* London: Batsford.

Robson, D.A. 1965. A Guide to the Geology of Northumberland and The Borders. *Transactions of the Natural History Society of Northumberland, Durham and Newcastle upon Tyne,* **XVI** no. 1 (new series).

Robson, D.A. 1976. A Guide to the Geology of the Cheviot Hills. *Transactions of the Natural History Society of Northumbria* **43** No. 1.

Salwey, J. 1913. *Guide to Rothbury, Northumberland.* Alnwick: The Voluntary Committee of the Urban Council.

Simmons, I. & Tooley, M. 1981. *The Environment in British Prehistory.* London: Duckworth.

Smith, C. 1992. *Late Stone Age Hunters of the British Isles.* London: Routledge.

Tait, J. 1965. *Beakers from Northumberland.* Newcastle upon Tyne: Oriel Press.

Tate, G. 1865. *The Ancient British Sculptured Rocks of Northumberland.* Alnwick: Henry Hunter Blair.

Taylor, C.F. (ed) 1995. *The Native Americans. The Indigenous People of North America.* London: Salamander.

Tomlinson, W.W. 1888. *Comprehensive Guide to Northumberland.* Newcastle upon Tyne: William Robinson.

Topping, P. 1989. Early Cultivation in Northumberland and the Borders. *Proceedings of the Prehistoric Society* **55**, 161-179.

Topping, P. 1993. Lordenshaws Hillfort and Its Environs. A Survey by the Royal Commission on the Historical Monuments of England. *Archaeologia Aeliana* (5th series) **XXI**, 15-27.

Waddington, C. 1999. *A Landscape Archaeological Study of the Mesolithic-Neolithic in the Milfield Basin, Northumberland.* (British Archaeological Reports, British Series 291). Oxford: Archaeopress.

Waddington, C. 2003. A Mesolithic Settlement Site at Howick, Northumberland: a Preliminary Report. *Archaeologia Aeliana* (5th series) **XXXII**, 1-12.

Waddington, C., Blood, K. & Crow, J. 1998. Survey and Excavation at Harehaugh Hillfort and Possible Neolithic Enclosure. *Northern Archaeology* **15/16**, 87-108.

Waddington, C. & Passmore, D. 2004. *Ancient Northumberland.* Milfield: Countrystore.

Wake, T. 1939. Excavations at Witchy Neuk, Hepple. *Archaeologia Aeliana* (4th series) **XVI**, 129-139.

Welfare, A. 1980. The Miniature Cinerary Urn from Scrainwood, Alnham, Northumberland. *Northern Archaeology* **1** (part 2), 12-23.

Welfare, A. 1982. The Bronze Knife from Cartington, Rothbury, Northumberland. *Northern Archaeology* **3**, 19-31.

Welfare, A. 1982. Flanged and Socketed Axes, Rothbury. A Note upon a Short Flanged Axe from the Neighbourhood of Rothbury, Northumberland, and upon a Socketed Axe of Type Yorkshire from Warton, Thropton, Northumberland. *Northern Archaeology* **3**, 53-58.

Young, M.J. 1988. *Signs from the Ancestors: Zuni Cultural Symbolism and Perceptions of Rock Art.* Albuquerque: University of New Mexico Press.

Young, R. (ed). 2000. *Mesolithic Lifeways: Current Research from Britain and Ireland.* Leicester Archaeology Monographs No. 7. Leicester: University of Leicester.

Zimmerman, L.J. 2003. *American Indians: The First Nations. Native North American Life, Myth and Art.* London: Duncan Baird.

Index of Sites and Finds